An
Old-Fashioned Senator

—

Orville H. Platt

KENNIKAT PRESS SCHOLARLY REPRINTS

Dr. Ralph Adams Brown, Senior Editor

Series in

**AMERICAN HISTORY AND CULTURE
IN THE NINETEENTH CENTURY**

Under the General Editorial Supervision of
Dr. Martin L. Fausold
Professor of History, State University of New York

Orville H. Platt

An
Old-Fashioned Senator

Orville H. Platt

Of Connecticut

The Story of a Life Unselfishly Devoted to the
Public Service

By

Louis A. Coolidge

Volume I

KENNIKAT PRESS
Port Washington, N. Y./London

109445

AN OLD-FASHIONED SENATOR

First published in 1910
Reissued in 1971 by Kennikat Press
Library of Congress Catalog Card No: 74-137907
ISBN 0-8046-1475-X

Manufactured by Taylor Publishing Company   Dallas, Texas

KENNIKAT SERIES ON AMERICAN HISTORY AND
CULTURE IN THE NINETEENTH CENTURY

INTRODUCTORY NOTE

A MONG all the public men whom the writer of this
sketch has known in the course of an experience
in Washington embracing twenty years, Senator Platt
seems to have approached most nearly the perfect
measure of disinterested service. That he should have
been above any temptation to profit materially from
his official place implies no special virtue, for that is
fortunately a common attribute of Senators of the
United States; but he possessed the rarer quality of
disregard for contemporary applause or posthumous
fame. He was ready to do each day's pressing duty
conscientiously and unselfishly without regard to its
effect upon his political fortune or personal prestige,
and having the faculty of effective co-operation in
an exceptional degree, he held the unbounded confidence of his associates. The impression created by
watching his public conduct from year to year has been
strengthened since this book was undertaken by a study
of his private life from boyhood and by a perusal of the
fragmentary correspondence which, through no design
of his, survives him. His record from youth to age
was one of uncalculating consistency—of harmonious
intellectual and spiritual development.

In the decision of vital questions of legislation he
was for years an important and frequently a controlling factor. During an eventful time he exercised a
more pervasive influence than any other Senator, yet

v

so unobtrusively that it was almost the close of his career before his work received adequate recognition except from those who could appraise it near at hand. The Platt Amendment first brought him the distinction he deserved, but that document was only the triumphant application of principles which he had long maintained. His place in American history will be larger as the years go by.

In trying to delineate a character unusual in public life, it has been found expedient to review briefly the significant legislation of a quarter of a century to the shaping of which Senator Platt's practical wisdom, unfailing courage, and acknowledged loftiness of purpose were indispensable.

L. A. C.

Boston, February 22, 1910.

CONTENTS

Contents

Contents

Orville H. Platt

Orville H. Platt

CHAPTER I

JUDEA

Birth and Ancestry—The Litchfield Hills—Early Days in Judea—
Abolition and Religious Dissent—The Underground Railroad—
Boyhood on the Farm.

ORVILLE HITCHCOCK PLATT was born in the
little town of Washington, Litchfield County,
Connecticut, July 19, 1827. His father was Daniel
Gould Platt; his mother, Almyra Hitchcock Platt. He
was fortunate in his inheritance, in the time and place
of his birth, and in the surroundings of his early years.
Through both father and mother he was descended
from long lines of New England farmers, who, generation after generation, had stood for something in the
communities in which they lived. From father to
son they held office in the church and in the town.
They were landowners, deacons, tithing-men, and
captains of militia. One ancestor was imprisoned by
Governor Andros in 1681 for daring to attend a meeting
of delegates "to devise means to obtain a redress of
grievances under his arbitrary rule." Another was
among those who marched to Fishkill in the Burgoyne

campaign of October, 1777, to reinforce General Putnam.   Orville Platt's grandfather, John, was also a
soldier in the Revolution and belonged to the band of
"Prison Ship Martyrs."   His own father was deputy
sheriff and judge of probate, a school-teacher at times,
as well as a tiller of the soil.   It was a sturdy, loyal,
patriotic, efficient New England stock.[1]

For a boy to have been born in Litchfield County in

[1] THE PLATT *Genealogy:* The Platt family was established in
New Haven County, in 1638, when (I) RICHARD PLATT, an Eng-
lishman, and his wife Mary, with their four children, landed at New
Haven.   He was one of the sixty-one who formed a church society,
August 22, 1639, and proceeded at once to settle at Milford.   Of
his eight children, the third, (and second son,) (II) ISAAC, was enrolled in 1666 among the fifty-seven landowners of Huntington,
Long Island, where he had probably lived some years. He was
recorded there in 1687.   In Milford, he married Phoebe Smith,
March 12, 1640, and, more than twenty years later, he married at
Huntington, Elizabeth, daughter of Jonas Wood.   He was captain
of militia, and held every office of consequence in the town, where
he died July 31, 1691.

He had six children; the eldest son and second child, (III)
JONAS, born August 16, 1667, married Sarah Scudder, and had
four sons: (IV) OBADIAH, the eldest of these, purchased lands in
Fairfield in 1724.   He married Mary Smith, August 10, 1722, and
had eight children.   The wife and mother died November 16, 1771,
at Ridgefield.   (V) JONAS, their second son and third child, born
October 9, 1727, settled at Redding, where he was married, October
17, 1747, to Elizabeth, daughter of Ephraim Sanford of that place.
Both were admitted church members at Redding, July 5, 1749.
They had ten children, of whom the eldest, (VI) JOHN, was baptized
February 5, 1752, at Redding.   Both father and son served as
soldiers in the Revolutionary Army, and the former was made
prisoner in the Danbury raid in April, 1777, but appeared among
those who marched to Fishkill in the following October, to reinforce
General Putnam.   The son was taken prisoner at Fort Lee, Novem-
ber 16, 1776.   He married Elizabeth Parmelee July 7, 1775, and
settled after the war in the town of Washington, Connecticut.
Their children were: John, born February 21, 1776; David, born
August 31, 1778; Ruth Ann, March 31, 1782; Betsy, May 8, 1790;
Daniel Gould, July 25, 1797.

the early days of the last century was to have been placed in the pathway of opportunity. Nature has been gracious to the region round about. Lying at the southernmost spur of the Berkshires, villages perched on the brows of many hills look out over the winding valleys of the Housatonic and Shepaug. The town of Litchfield is one of the historic places of America, rich in memories of famous men and happenings. It was the seat of the earliest law school in America, and the home either temporary or permanent of many who were eminent at the bar or in the pulpit. Lyman Beecher preached there for years; Henry Ward Beecher and Harriet Beecher Stowe were born there. It was the home of Oliver Wolcott and the birthplace of Ethan Allen. It had been the home of Colonel Talmadge, an aide on General Washington's staff. Aaron Burr lived there for a year as a young man. Horace Bushnell, whose name is honored throughout the world, was born in Litchfield and spent his youth at New Preston, near-by. Many others might be named whose fame lends interest and character to the charming town. In the early years of the last century, the

---

(VII) DANIEL GOULD PLATT, married Almyra Hitchcock, January 3, 1817, and they had children: Orville, born March 11, 1822, who died in 1826; Orville Hitchcock, born July 19, 1827, in Washington; and Simeon D., born February 12, 1832. The father died October 26, 1871.

1638.
 RICHARD PLATT, New Haven, Connecticut.
 ISAAC, Huntington, Long Island.
 JONAS,
 OBADIAH, Fairfield and Redding.
 JONAS, Redding.
 JOHN, Redding and Washington.
 DANIEL GOULD, Washington, Connecticut.
 ORVILLE HITCHCOCK, Washington.

place was at its best, and Orville Platt, born and bred twelve miles to the south in the equally beautiful village of Washington, could hardly have avoided absorbing some of the inspiration of the environment. Within a radius of fifteen miles of his birthplace, were two other towns of Litchfield County rich in associations. At New Milford to the south, Roger Sherman lived for twenty years. At Torrington, an equal distance to the north, John Brown was born.

The town of Washington in its own right could claim distinction. It was organized during the throes of the struggle for independence by uniting two ancient Ecclesiastical Societies, and it is said to have been the first community in America to adopt the name of the Father of his Country. The older of these societies, comprising the village of Judea, lay on a level plateau overlooking the valley through which the Shepaug goes tumbling down to meet the Housatonic. Four miles away, on the other side of a high hill, were the villages of Marbledale and New Preston, which comprised the other Ecclesiastical Society. It was in the village of Judea that Orville H. Platt was born,—a community puritan and conservative to the roots. New Preston, on the other hand, had always been known as the home of religious and political dissent. It was the youthful Platt's good fortune to develop into manhood at a time when that part of New England, like many others, was in the midst of a moral revolution. The year in which he was born, 1827, was the year in which William Lloyd Garrison became the editor of the *National Philanthropist*. Four years later, Garrison established *The Liberator*. The ancient community of Washington offered fertile soil in which to sow the Abolition seed, and Daniel Gould Platt was one of those who received the seed gladly. In 1837, shortly after the martyrdom of Lovejoy, an Abolition convention met at Hartford, and Daniel Platt attended it with his wife. There were four others in attendance from Judea—Mr. and Mrs. John Gunn, and Mr. and Mrs. Lewis A. Canfield—representatives of a family which was to count for much in Orville Platt's life. From that time, for many years, this faithful group were the centre of a storm of persecution by which less heroic souls would have been overwhelmed. The pastor of the Judea church was Reverend Gordon Hayes, an able and bigoted theologian. Abolitionism he regarded as a heresy and he set about to stamp it out. He devoted sermon after sermon to attacks upon the strange doctrine, denouncing it in the name of patriotism and religion. He found sanction for slavery in the Bible, and he was as honest as he was earnest in his attacks upon those who sought to bring it to an end. The Abolitionists were equally intense. They held meetings in which their speakers cried out against slavery as a sin and forswore communion with slaveholders as collusion with sin. Finally an extraordinary episode brought on the crisis with a rush. Miss Abby Kelly in 1839 was known far and wide as an Abolition speaker. In August of that year she was preaching the New Evangel throughout western Connecticut, and Daniel Platt and Lewis Canfield with their wives drove to a neighboring town and brought her to Washington, where she remained for a fortnight, appearing at numerous Abolition meetings. For women to speak in public was in those days an almost unheard of thing, and for one to enter actively into the discussion of political affairs was revolutionary and abhorrent. Parson Hayes and his conservative congregation were

shaken with wrath.   The impudent challenge of the
Abolitionists was met with promptness and decision.
Under the date of August 8, 1839, there appears in the
records of the Judea church the following entry:

At a meeting of the church convened in consequence of a
notice of a meeting of the Anti-Slavery Society at which
it was said a female would lecture:
Resolved,   That we are opposed to the introduction of
female public lecturers into this society by members of
this church, and to females giving such lectures in it.

This action was followed promptly by Mr. Hayes in
a sermon from the following plain-spoken text:

Notwithstanding I have a few things against thee, because thou sufferest that woman Jezebel, which calleth her-
self a prophetess, to teach and to seduce my servants to
commit fornication, and to eat things sacrificed unto idols.
And I gave her space to repent of her fornication; and
she repented not.
Behold, I will cast her into a bed, and them that commit
adultery with her into great tribulation, except they repent of their deeds.—Rev. ii., 20–22.

The sermon fitted the text.   The reverend preacher,
looking over to where Miss Abby Kelly sat in the congregation, referred to female lecturers travelling alone
by night and by day, and plainly intimated that the
lady's character was no better than it ought to be.   As
the benediction was pronounced, John Gunn called
down from the gallery that the minister's insinuations
were false.   As the preacher was leaving the church,
Miss Abby Kelly walked directly up to him and said:
"Gordon Hayes, you have said things most injurious
to my character.   I hope God will forgive you."
After such an episode, the warring factions could not

listen to the word of God from the same pulpit. The Abolitionists withdrew and organized a church of their own. Their secession was followed promptly by excommunication. They had no recognized place of meeting, but gathered in different villages all over the county, often compelled to resort to barns and groves. Among these covenanters were Daniel Gould Platt and Almyra Hitchcock Platt. Their oldest boy, Orville, was then at the impressionable age of twelve years.

A little later, the Reverend Gordon Hayes himself became discredited by the vigor of a sermon denouncing calisthenics, promiscuous dancing, and tableaux as the service of Satan and the sure concomitants of vice. He was dismissed from the church, and with his departure the differences gradually were healed. The Abolitionists who had been excommunicated were privately invited to re-unite with the church. They declined, but the bitterness of the conflict was at an end.[1]

[1] Of this time, nearly fifty years later, Mr. Platt wrote:

"It was the time of the fierce Anti-Slavery excitement—one of those periods in the history of communities when the hearts of men are stirred to attack great and hideous wrongs, and to do battle for the right with a zeal and courage which cannot be hindered or abated until the right triumphs—a time when not only fetters on human limbs but fetters on human thought were to be broken.

"A great reform had begun. A few men had seen the wickedness of slavery and had fathered the movement for its Abolition. Human rights in the eyes of these men had become sacred, and they had determined that they should be recognized and respected. Slavery was strongly intrenched and defended. Its power was everywhere felt; its influence penetrated the state, the church, society. It was a fearful sin and crime against God and against man, and eyes to see its wickedness and courage to attack it were given to only a few rare souls. They made the fight manfully and nobly, but they were met and opposed by almost the entire

From father and mother of deep religious convictions, militant Abolitionists who were ready to suffer excommunication from the church for an ideal, Orville Platt inherited a conscience, righteous courage, and lofty principles.   Every particle of information that comes

people.   An Abolitionist was but one against a hundred or a thousand.   The assailants of slavery were proscribed, shunned, mobbed, and treated as social outcasts.   Neither they nor their children were welcomed in the house of one who was not an Abolitionist.   The social proscription of those days can scarcely be understood or imagined.   Probably the world has never seen a loftier courage or more heroic living than was manifested by the men who saw their duty to the slave, and through the slave to humanity.   The slave was a *man*, and as such, men were ready to suffer all things in his behalf, to die if necessary.

" Like all reformers, the Abolitionist was aggressive.   Slavery was the crime of crimes, and it was, in his conviction, the solemn duty of all men to attack it,   Whoever defended or apologized for it was as wicked as the slaveholders.   The Whig party was deemed to be governed by the slaveholders, so the Abolitionists withdrew from it and made war upon it.   The Constitution was claimed to guarantee the right of property in slaves, and the Abolitionists repudiated and denounced the Constitution.   But the battle raged fiercest in the church.   Slavery was defended from the Bible; church organizations refused, upon the demand of the Abolitionists, to pass resolutions against the institution, or to say that slaveholding was incompatible with church membership or Christian character; while ministers preached in favor of slavery and against the Abolitionists.

" The little town of Washington was in a fever of excitement. The minister from the pulpit thundered anathemas against the Abolitionists, while they, in their turn, denounced the church, and those of its members who apologized for slavery and the slaveholder, as equal in guilt with him.   The minister proclaimed the authority of the church to bind its members; the Abolitionists, in turn, defied the church.   The doctrines of the church came to stand for religion, and the Abolitionists attacked not only the church but its creed.   The church retorted with the cry of infidelity, excommunicated the unruly and insubordinate members, and was, for the time being, victorious.   It will be readily seen that such a conflict went to the roots of religious faith and doctrine. Men became freethinkers, in the sense that they thought freely

down to us concerning this remarkable couple tends to increase our respect for them. For years they carried on their fight against slavery, buoyed up by the inspiration of the little band of Abolition co-workers. Many years after their death, an old friend in a reminiscent letter dated July 6, 1901, wrote to Senator Platt of a visit to Judea in 1847:

I was at home in your father's house. He is one amongst the early Abolitionists who is silhouetted on my memory most vividly, and of all the Anti-Slavery women, your mother is so distinctly in the foreground, the others of our State seem accessories. I cannot define the elements of her personality and character, but they stand out in my memory with such clearness that half a century has not dimmed the features.

Your father was a full-grown man in stature, as well as in conscience and intellect; your mother, a heroic soul, one among ten thousand. I see her now as she was in 1842–8 to the hunted Abolitionist, "the shadow of a great rock in a weary land."[1]

---

and fearlessly. Sometimes, doubtless, they were wrong, but always in earnest and outspoken. Creeds could not bind the consciences of such men. They found a law higher than creeds; they inquired only what was duty to God and man, and did their duty as they saw it."

[1] A school-fellow has said of Orville Platt's father and mother: "Daniel Platt was a man of fine face and figure, intelligent, kindly, and courteous. He took a prominent part in town politics and religious meetings, and was a forcible, modest, and convincing speaker. Orville's mother was a stately, handsome woman, quiet in manner, prudent in speech, but positive in her convictions. She seldom mingled in social gatherings, but found her greatest pleasure in the simple home life, attending to her domestic duties, reading the Scriptures and standard works, and teaching her boys by precept and example the virtues of goodness, charity, sobriety, and whatever else contributed to the development of sturdy self-reliance and manly manhood. In all the essentials of wise character building she was never lacking. The impress she left on

Daniel Platt's home was a station on the underground railway. Many a trembling black refugee came there by night to be forwarded by him on the road to Canada. The usual route was by way of New Milford, to Washington, whence they were taken by night to General Uriel Tuttle's in Torrington or Dr. Vaill's on the Wolcottville road. Orville, a boy in his teens, used to accompany his father frequently on these trips. The slaves stayed, as a rule, but a short time at the Platt farm, though some remained for several weeks until it was learned, through the channels of communication among Abolitionists, that their whereabouts was suspected; then they were sent on.

Aside from such incidents typical of an heroic time, the lad's life was that of the ordinary farmer's boy of the day. His parents had neither poverty nor riches. The farm his father tilled was rented on shares. The home, a typical farmhouse of the time, still stands. One who remembers the early days says:

Orville's mind was wholesome and lasting. She was ever a living memory in his heart, and he never spoke of her except in terms of reverent affection. She was an excellent housewife, baked her own bread, made her own butter, and kept the wearing apparel of father and sons, as well as her own, in excellent condition. Farmers' wives had to work in those days, and Mrs. Platt never shirked her share. Her kitchen, dining- and sitting-rooms (the parlor was a later innovation), were always cleanly and inviting."

Almyra Hitchcock was one of a numerous family, several of whom emigrated to the Western Reserve in Ohio, where their descendants still live. A brother was Samuel J. Hitchcock, born at Bethlehem, Connecticut, and graduated at Yale in 1809. He was a tutor at Yale from 1811 to 1815, and was subsequently, until his death, instructor of law. He received the degree of LL.D. in 1842. Died in 1845. He was mayor of the city of New Haven, judge of the Court of Common Pleas, and commissioner of bankruptcy during the continuance of the national bankruptcy law. Another brother, Benjamin, was an editor of the New Haven *Journal and Courier.*

The home was a two-storied white structure about a mile from town, facing southerly, a pleasant yard in front enclosing shrubbery and the inevitable lilac bushes, the earliest harbingers of a New England spring. It was situated on a high plateau sloping to the roadway and thence to a ravine, through which ran a brook that crossed the road farther down, affording a favorite drinking place for horses. On the east was the garden patch, and north, the farm, small-sized and stony. The roadway passing by the house made a circuit towards the north through chestnut woods, then turning to the right came to the house of Elnathan Mitchell, a brother of the famous scientist, Professor Mitchell of North Carolina.

During the busy haying season, as a rule, twelve or thirteen men would be employed, and the mother always took care of them unaided by any maid. In the morning, when all were gathered for family worship, the father would read the Scripture and the mother would explain it. Young Platt worked with his father until he was eighteen years of age. Sometimes he worked for other farmers for wages. Daniel Nettleton, who used to be employed on the Platt farm during haying, says of him:

Orville was a fine mower, cutting faster and closer, and carrying a much wider swath than any of the men. It was the custom in those days to start a large number of men mowing, one just behind another, and Orville was always put ahead, leading the field from the start and right through.

As a boy [Mr. Platt wrote once to a friend], I used to make maple syrup on my father's farm, after the rude methods of those days, carrying sap buckets on a neck yoke sometimes a quarter to a third of a mile, boiling it away to syrup or sugaring-off point in an old potash kettle in an outhouse at home—so I think I know when it is good.[1]

As a boy just bursting into young manhood Orville Platt is remembered as "fine-looking, tall, and handsome, with beautiful dark brown hair and eyes." One who afterwards came to know him intimately says:

All my life I have carried in my mind the picture of Orville Platt and his younger brother, Simeon, as they used to come into the gallery of the old Judea church. Orville was the tallest and handsomest young man I have ever seen.

[1] Many years later in the United States Senate, Mr. Platt referred to conditions in his native State during his boyhood as follows: "I am not a very old man, but recollection carries me back fifty years, when there was no railroad, no coal used, no steam power used; no woollen factories except of the rudest sort; no telegraph in Connecticut. Possibly there were one hundred tons of coal consumed in the State annually. It is possible that there was the rude beginning of manufacturing establishments in which steam was the motive power; but practically there were none of these improvements in Connecticut. The people were rural and agricultural; a few shops, water furnishing the motive power, were scattered up and down the streams of the State, but almost the entire population were engaged in agriculture. It was a time when the handbrake and the hetchel prepared the flax which was raised within her borders, when hand-spinning and the hand-loom prepared it for use. My mind goes back and takes in the days of my early boyhood, when wool was carded by hand, when it was spun and woven by the mothers and the daughters, when it was then taken to the fulling-mill and when the tailoress came and in the household cut and made the cloth into garments for the use of the family. It was the day of the village shoemaker, the day of the grist-mill, the day of the stage-coach, the day of the pillion. There were no carpets; no piano; few books; hand-sewing only; hand-knitting; the tallow candle; the unwarmed, unlighted church; the schoolhouse with its hard, rough benches; and the slow post-route, the mail once a week; a weekly paper only. It was a week's journey from Connecticut to Washington; six weeks' journey from Connecticut to Ohio. Five thousand dollars in those days was a competence and $10,000 was a fortune."

CHAPTER II

TEACHER AND PUPIL

The "Master of the Gunnery"—A Pupil's Tribute—School Days—
Ostracism for Anti-Slavery Views—Teaching School in Judea—
A Year at Towanda—Admission to the Bar—Marriage—Re-
moval to Meriden—A Lover of the Woods—Judea Revisited—
The Adirondacks.

FREDERICK W. GUNN, the "Master of the Gunnery," well beloved by generations of schoolboys
and revered by the elders, merits a place in this book for
the noble influence he exerted on Orville Platt's life.
Although ten years the senior of the younger man, he
was friend and comrade as well as teacher. No story
of Washington and Litchfield County would approach
completeness which failed to say something of this
extraordinary man. He was a younger brother of that
John Gunn who was associated with Daniel Platt in
Abolition activities and he was destined to be as stout
an adversary of slavery as any of his elders. No
more tender tribute to a friend was ever penned than
the sketch which Senator Platt contributed to a memorial of Mr. Gunn printed in 1887. It reveals much
of the inner life of both men and is significant of the
influences that went to shape the character and career
of the younger.

"He was more to me than a teacher," writes the pupil
grown old; "my love for him was the love one has for
father, brother, and friend."

13

Frederick W. Gunn was born in 1816 about a mile from Washington Green. He was the youngest of eight children, all of whom became identified with the Anti-Slavery cause. The eldest, John, "a man singularly gentle, open-hearted, simple, and honest, but made of the stuff we worship in heroes and martyrs," was conspicuous in the leadership of the little Abolition band and was identified closely with Daniel and Almyra Platt. It has been said of him that "although by nature one of the most modest and quiet of men, and shrinking from public gaze, he surprised both friends and foes by becoming one of the boldest, sternest, and most aggressive champions of the slave."

Frederick, the "Master of the Gunnery," entered Yale College in the Class of 1837. Among his classmates were Chief-Justice M. R. Waite, William M. Evarts, Edwards Pierrepont, and Benjamin Silliman.

His scholarship was good but not conspicuous [says his pupil biographer in words that might well have been self-descriptive]. He was not a bookworm; not a plodder. The time and energy which, perhaps, otherwise applied, might have won him the first honors, were largely used in the study of literature and poetry. . . . Transferred to the city he lost none of his love for country surroundings. He excelled in the study of botany. He loved the freedom of the open fields—the solitude of the seashore. In those days as all through his later years, he was fond of hunting and fishing. He enjoyed such pastimes with the relish of the true hunter and angler, whose real pleasure is found, not in killing game and catching fish, but in the exhilaration which comes to one who roams alone the woods and fields, in the quiet peace of mind experienced when he wanders by the brookside, and watches the flow of the rippling water. . . . His ideal was manliness. His development of that ideal was along the line of physical, intellectual, and sentimental growth. He cultivated muscle, health, imagination, taste, intellect! . . . His idea of education, acted upon in his own college experience as well as when he came to be a teacher, was the perfecting of a noble manhood—the creating of a noble life.

After leaving college, he began teaching at the Academy in New Preston, and, in 1839, he opened his school in the Academy at Judea. It was here that Orville H. Platt, who had begun his education in the Old Red Schoolhouse on the Green, first fell under his inspiring influence. Mr. Gunn's success at New Preston had given him prestige, and at the beginning his school was filled beyond its capacity. But a great change was at hand:

His development had thus far been in the direction of mental and sentimental growth [says his biographer]. His brain had become keen and analytical; he was logical, and a dangerous antagonist in debate. He had cultivated a pure and elevated taste, and an admiration for the noble and heroic, but his moral nature as yet had had little to test it. Naturally of upright life, he had had little occasion to think of abstract principles or to study abstract questions of duty. But a crisis was coming. Manliness, truth, principle, were words which were to have new meanings for him. Right was to become to him the touchstone of life. To follow duty wherever and however it seemed to lead was to be for him a new experience, and duty and right were to lead him into the face of trials, of difficulties, of opposition, of persecution, through detraction and abuse, such as we, with the lapse of these intervening years, can scarcely realize.[1]

[1] "It is not easy to sketch the life of a friend whose memory we cherish as a rich legacy. For as we knew him through the medium of our love, as we perceived his admirable qualities through the lens of a silent sympathy, it is very natural that we should shrink

It was near the beginning of the fierce Anti-Slavery agitation. Frederick Gunn, convinced by the arguments of his brother John that slavery was wrong, became a leader on the Anti-Slavery side. His fearlessness, his severity of attack, his ability of statement, and his force of argument marked him out for special

---

from disclosing to others the estimate of his character we have thus acquired. We do not like to analyze his character; we prefer rather to regard it as a unit. It seems unnatural to weigh and compare its differing constituents, to question and decide which particular trait most endeared our friend to us, or made him most helpful to others; above all, the consciousness that we can never so describe him that he will appear to others as he did to us, and the certainty that our portrait will be sadly imperfect, make us feel at the outset that we may regret having attempted the work. And so I hesitate, almost fear, to attempt the story of Mr. Gunn's early life and struggles. He was more to me than a teacher; my love for him was the love one has for father, brother, and friend. To those who knew him as I knew him, all I can write will seem unappreciative. To those who knew him but casually, it may, in some measure, set forth and account for his rare development of manhood and manly goodness. . . .

"Mr. Gunn was a rarely developed man, possessing largely all those generous qualities and characteristics which inspire confidence and love in others. Keen and vigorous of intellect, he was tender and true of heart. He was proud, not haughty. His pride was that of conscious nobility, and rectitude. He loved God, loved man, loved truth; and he served God, served man, served truth. He hated evil, wrong, falseness, meanness, and he made war on them always. He was unflinching in his devotion to principle—uncompromising in his conflict with the wrong. He was pure and virtuous in life, reverent toward goodness and purity, but contemptuous toward bigotry and shams. He had the courage of his convictions, and practised rigidly what he believed. He was generous in his sympathies, warm in his friendships, ardent in his love. There was no malice in his nature. Open and frank in his intercourse, helpful in conduct, his example and teaching were an inspiration. His great aim was to live a noble life himself, and aid others to live such a life. His ideal standard of living was more divine than human, and his struggle was to attain his ideal. He may have been faulty; who is perfect? He may have been harsh in his judgments at times; but it was not because his nature was harsh. He was

condemnation. He was not a church member, his manner was not reverential, he had little regard for the outward formalities of the church, and therefore was the more easily branded an "infidel." The issue between him and the minister was well defined and undisguised. The minister proclaimed him a heretic. He proclaimed the minister a bigot and attacked what the minister preached as religion with all the weapons at his command. Argument, invective, ridicule, satire he used unsparingly. The church members and the whole community other than the Abolitionists sided with the minister. Mr. Gunn was stigmatized as an Abolitionist and an infidel—words of intense reproach, the import of which we now but feebly realize.

The story of how the "Master of the Gunnery," after persecution and exile, established and maintained in Washington a school for boys which shed a beneficent influence of incalculable extent and power so that when he died in 1881 he was followed to the grave by such grief and blessings as followed Dr. Arnold of Rugby, belongs to other pages than these. Only that is written of him here which helps to interpret the wholesome and inspiring surroundings of Orville H. Platt's early life; and who can estimate the noble influence upon the mind of a clean and whole-hearted boy, with a natural love for woods, streams, and fields, exerted by close

---

gentle and tender as a woman; but in the championship of the weak he struck harder than he thought. He was unambitious, careless of worldly honors, indifferent to wealth or fame. Had he chosen he could have easily filled a larger place in the world's notice. He neither achieved nor sought success as the world measures success; but he realized the great aim of his life in that he lived and died a true man, and impressed on many lives the seal of a sterling manhood."—From Mr. Platt's "Memorial" in *The Master of the Gunnery*.

association with this open-minded, nature-loving, man-loving instructor of youth.

Orville Platt first became a pupil of Mr. Gunn's in 1840 when he was thirteen years old; and during the next eight years he enjoyed the closest relations with his teacher. First he attended the Academy, near the Meeting-House, on the Green, and when one by one the church members and followers of Parson Hayes withdrew their children from the school, the son of Daniel Platt, the Abolitionist, remained.

At school, his favorite study was mathematics; but he was fond of ancient and modern history and of geography, and studied Latin, but not Greek. He is said by a school-fellow to have been "correct in his phrasing, accurate in pronunciation, and choice in his English." He never violated the school rules, and he was of a serious nature, bent on making the most of his opportunities. He joined in outdoor sports. At baseball he was a good runner and catcher, but "when it came to hitting the ball, he lunged at it with terrific force." In football he is described as a "towering, dominating figure. Sometimes he could be tripped or outgeneralled; but once under way, the ball in advance, he followed it up with tempestuous force." He could beat all the other boys at a standing jump and had a record of twelve feet to his credit. He is remembered as having always been fair and square in the school-boy games. "If he accidentally stepped on or rolled over anybody he was as sorry as his limping or disabled competitor could be."

Through allegiance to an ideal, Mr. Gunn's first school in Judea was ruined. At the end of four years the number of his pupils was reduced to nine—all children of Abolitionists. Mr. Gunn was forbidden the use of the Academy building, and moved his little school to the house of his sister, Mrs. Canfield, on the site of which the Gunnery now stands. In 1845, some friends in New Preston, who remembered his success there as a teacher and who sympathized with him in his persecution, determined to "show Judea that Mr. Gunn could teach school in New Preston even if he *was* an Abolitionist." They invited him to return and he did so. His enemies in Judea tried every device to prevent parents from sending their children to a school taught by a "heretic and an infidel," and some were dissuaded; but many Abolitionists from surrounding towns sent their sons and daughters to New Preston and this made the school a success.

Orville Platt attended the school for three winters, living for two winters with Mr. Gunn. The third winter he himself taught at the schoolhouse on Christian Street, aptly named, according to tradition, because at one time every house on the street was owned by a professed Christian. For this he received eleven dollars a month and "boarded around" after the manner of the district school teacher of the day—making his headquarters at the house of the chairman of the district committee who employed him, and who took him in when the family to which he happened to be assigned for a week were so poor he did not care to board with them.

In 1847, Mr. Gunn abandoned New Preston, at the urgency of friends who had settled in Towanda, Pennsylvania. Towanda was the home of David Wilmot, the author of the Wilmot Proviso. The Abolition sentiment was strong and to be an Abolitionist did not subject one to reproach. He became principal of a large school there; but before leaving New Preston he persuaded young Platt to accompany him as assistant. Mr. Platt, then twenty years old, spent one winter at Towanda. It was an eventful winter for him, for it brought him in contact with the young woman who was to become his wife, and with whom he was destined to spend forty-three years of his life—Miss Annie Bull, the only daughter of one of the leading families of Towanda with whom Mr. Platt made his home. They were married May 15, 1850. They had two sons, one of whom died in infancy. The other, James P. Platt, is now a judge on the Federal bench.

In the spring of 1848, Mr. Platt returned to Judea, and began the study of the law. He had the privilege of reading under Gideon H. Hollister of Litchfield, one of the recognized legal authorities of the day. It was no child's play; for he was obliged to read Blackstone and the other standard works at home and then drive or walk over to Litchfield, twelve miles away, to recite to Mr. Hollister, whom he surprised one day by repeating from memory the long opening chapter of Blackstone without a break.

During the winter of 1848, he taught in the Academy on the Green and he seems to have eked out his salary as teacher by private instruction. The returns were not dazzling, if we may judge from the following receipted bill which has come down to us:

Truman Woodruff, to O. H. Platt, Dr.,

To tuition of John, 11 weeks..............$2.96
Incidental expenses...................   .37$\frac{1}{2}$

3.33\frac{1}{2}$

Rec'd payment, March 2d, 1849.

O. H. PLATT.

However, he was able to lay by a little money, and we find him in the spring abandoning this means of livelihood and taking up his residence in Litchfield where he entered Mr. Hollister's office. In the spring of 1850 he was admitted to the Litchfield County Bar and immediately went back to Towanda to be married. For a time after his marriage it was a question whether he would make his permanent home in Towanda or not. For six months he was in the office of Ulysses S. Mercur, afterwards Chief-Justice of the Supreme Court of Pennsylvania, and, at the end of that period, he was admitted to practice in the Pennsylvania courts. The home call was too strong, however, and shortly after his admission to the Pennsylvania Bar he concluded to return to Connecticut. He lived with his father, while looking about the State to determine where he should settle as a lawyer.

Bearing letters of recommendation from Senator Truman Smith and others, to Judge Eleazar K. Foster and James Donaghe, then Collector of Customs at New Haven, he sought their advice, and followed it by locating at Meriden, a rising industrial town, twenty miles north of New Haven. On December 1, 1850, he went to Meriden and engaged an office which had to be fitted up for him. While waiting for the office to be completed he returned to Judea, spending the winter with his father. He went to Meriden finally in the spring of 1851, to begin the active practice of the law.[1]

[1] In the summer of 1902, in order that his granddaughter might know something of his early life, Mr. Platt dictated the following, at Mrs. Platt's request: "I was born July 19, 1827, in the house which stood on the left-hand side of the road leading from Blackville to Davies Hollow, some fifty rods beyond the old Samuel Baldwin place. Only the cellar remains, and that is filled with small trees which have grown since the house was torn down. The

So he left the haunts of his boyhood to enter the activities of the world; but the time never came that his heart did not turn toward the familiar places in Judea. After all, that was his home; he loved to dwell upon its beauties and charm, and many a time his wandering

---

property is now owned by Charles C. Ford, and with his permission I have transplanted a young ash, which is growing finely on my lawn at Kirby Corner. The barn formerly connected with the house is still standing. The road on which the homestead stood was known as 'Sabbaday Lane,' possibly, because it led to the First Episcopal Church in Washington, which stood in Davies Hollow near the little old burying-ground.

"My father was Daniel G. Platt, and my mother was Almyra Hitchcock Platt, whose family lived in Bethlehem. When I was born my father was a farmer and taught school in winter. I remember he took me with him as a child, one day, to the schoolhouse which stood on the Canfield place nearly opposite the entrance to Arthur Woodruff's lot. This building was removed to the site now occupied by the town hall on the Green, and was fitted up and became what was known as the 'Old Red School House.'

"When I was perhaps two years old, my father moved to what is now the Aspinwall place, the property then being owned by the daughters of Matthew Mitchell, who was, I think, a brother of Elnathan Mitchell. They lived in South Britain, and my father rented the farm from them on shares. It extended on the north to the road leading to Blackville, known as 'Goose Hill,' embracing all the land south of a line drawn from there to the road running north from Powell G. Seeley's, being bounded on the north by Nelson and Charles Ford's land. It also embraced the lots south of the Aspinwall place (called in my boyhood the 'Punishment Lots'), as well as the land owned now by Charles Daignan, on which is situated the reservoir from which water is brought to the Green.

"I have sometimes wondered whether the 'hills standing round about it' made our forefathers name our part of the town Judea— it looks down on the beautiful valley of the Shepaug, and the whole country is full of running brooks. The first time I went fishing, I was about four years old—my tackle was a common string, with a bent up pin for hook, and I landed one small shiner, as Miss Julia Canfield sat beside me on the bank.

"I lived at the Aspinwall place, working on the farm (after I was old enough) until the year 1847, and first attended school in the Old Red School House on the Green, but cannot tell whether my

feet strayed back to the Litchfield hills, where every
house and every field had its reminiscence.   Above all
things he liked to roam the woods, and he was never
so happy as when tramping his favorite trails and
whipping his favorite streams.   He was one of the most

first teacher was Antoinette Judson, or Sophia Turner, who became
Mrs. Preston Hollister.   I know it was taught by a Mr. Northrup
also, who came from New Milford.   Later, I went to the Academy
which stood on the rock north of the town hall, taught by a Mr.
Jennings and subsequently by Mr. Gunn.   The Academy, under
Mr. Gunn's tuition, dwindled in attendance on account of the
Abolition troubles, until finally he did not attempt to teach in
the Academy building, but had a school in Mr. Lewis Canfield's
house, where the Gunnery now stands, living there with his sister,
Mrs. Canfield.   The schoolroom was small, and was entered from
the hall by the front door as it now exists.   I think there were
only eleven pupils.   I do not recall all of them—they were mostly
sons and daughters of pronounced Abolitionists.

"After a while Mr. Gunn abandoned the project of a school in his
sister's house, and taught, for possibly three winters, the Academy
in New Preston which I attended, living with him at Mrs. Cogswell's
for two winters, the third, teaching at the schoolhouse on Christian
Street, at eleven dollars per month, boarding around.   Abiel
Lemon, who employed me, was chairman of the district committee,
and his house was headquarters, *i. e.*, when the people were so
poor I did not wish to board with them, he took me in.

"The next fall, 1847, I went with Mr. Gunn to Towanda, Pennsylvania, as his assistant in a large school of which he had become
principal.   Returning in the spring I commenced the study of
law with Gideon H. Hollister of Litchfield, going up there to recite
to Mr. Hollister.

"In the winter of 1848, I taught in the Academy on the Green,
Mr. Gunn still being in Towanda.   The following spring I went to
Litchfield permanently, entering Mr. Hollister's office, which was a
brick building on the east side of South Street; Judge Seymour had
an office in the same building.

"I was admitted to the Litchfield County Bar in the early spring
of 1850, and immediately went back to Towanda, where I was
married on May 15th of that year.

"I was six months in the office of Ulysses S. Mercur, who was
subsequently Chief-Justice of the Supreme Court of Pennsylvania.

"It was a question whether I would settle there or not.   At the

skilful fishermen anywhere to be found. He knew the
haunts and habits of all fish; knew just how to lure them,
what bait to use in varying circumstances.   Yet it
made little difference to him whether he was lucky in
his sport or not. He went fishing for the sake of going,
for the pleasure of being in the woods, of building a
fire outdoors to cook his primitive meal of bacon and
toasted bread and coffee; of loafing under the trees and
by the brooks. He was versed in the lore of the woods.
He loved to stroll through them slowly, picking the
leaves and blossoms here and there, examining them
and classifying them in his mind. He knew every
tree, every shrub, and every flower, the note of every
bird, the ways of every wild thing, animate or not. A
little later in life the call of the forest carried him
farther away from civilization to the Adirondacks and
to fishing grounds in Canada. In the Adirondacks,
near Long Lake, he built him a shanty which he called
a camp, under the shadow of Mt. Seward, a seven-mile
row to the post-office, and an all-day ride by buckboard
to the nearest railroad. To this spot, for many years
up to the last summer of his life, he hurried just as soon
as he could get away from the grinding work of legislation. There he lived as close to nature as he could
get. Five years of his life, he said once near the end
of it, he had spent outdoors in the woods. In these
surroundings he passed happy days. The guides all
loved him as one of their own. No matter how ill or

---

end of six months I was admitted to practice in the courts of that
State, and then concluded to return to Connecticut, bringing my
wife with me. My father in the meantime had moved from the
Aspinwall place to the house which he had built upon a small farm
on the Litchfield road, next beyond what is now known as the
'Mason place,' and I went there and began to look about that I
might decide where to settle as a lawyer in Connecticut.''

useless he might feel on leaving the Capital, no sooner would he approach the familiar scenes than his spirits would begin to revive; and when he reached the camp and the familiar shanty he seemed to shed like an uncomfortable coat the melancholy with which at such seasons he was too frequently oppressed. With Charlie Long, Steve Lamos, or Charlie Sabbatis, the guides, he would fall at once unconsciously into the vernacular, asking for all the trifling history of the little community in the woods and swapping stories and experiences with as keen a zest as though that were the only existence he ever knew. He would hardly unpack his baggage before he was swinging through the forest with sweeping strides as happy and hopeful as a boy. No matter how much under the weather he might have been there was no further need for doctors or attendants. He was back with nature once more, communing on terms of equality with the denizens of the wild.

Mr. Platt was twice married. The wife of his youth was for many years an invalid, requiring his constant watchfulness and care, and to the last she was sustained and comforted by a considerate, sympathetic devotion such as is rarely seen. When she died in November, 1893, he felt as though the bottom had dropped out of his world.

Forty-three years of married life have passed into memory [he wrote nearly a year later to a boyhood friend]. It has been, still is, hard to accustom myself to the change, hard to catch on again, or to feel that anything is left for me but waiting for my time to come. I try to meet things as a courageous man should, but I cannot get above the feeling that I must plod on alone henceforth.

The next years of his life were the most gloomy that

he had ever known, and nothing but the necessity for
constant attention to his duties in the Senate carried
him through. Then came a change which broadened
the current of the stream. When he was studying law
in Litchfield, one of his friends and counsellors was
Truman Smith, for many years in Congress, and United
States Senator from 1849 to 1854. A daughter, Jeannie
P. Smith, had known him then and looked up to him
from a distance as a young man grown. They lost sight
of each other, one wedded, going to Meriden, the other
to Washington D. C., and afterwards to Stamford. She
became the wife and then the widow of George A. Hoyt,
a successful man of business and affairs. Later they
were brought together again. For several years they
had neighboring camps in the Adirondacks, and the two
families became devoted friends. She was a woman
of travel, and culture, and familiar with public affairs,
and it was not strange that they should be drawn to
one another. On April 29, 1897, they were married and
the new alliance, coming at the dawn of a period when
great and absorbing issues were to compel his attention,
was of a value to the Senator which it is not easy now
to calculate. To the end he rested unquestioningly
and with a feeling of relief upon her cheerful counsel and
assistance. One service she rendered for which those
who cared for him must ever be grateful. She built
him a house at Kirby Corner near one of his favorite
spots in Judea. The two entered into the joy of planning and furnishing it with as much delight as though
they were to have unending years of pleasure there.
At Kirby Corner in the last stage he passed days of rare
contentment and there he welcomed the end.

CHAPTER III

MERIDEN

Meriden and the First Church—Twenty-eight Years a Practising
Lawyer—A Political Organizer—Judge of Probate—Chairman
of American and Republican State Committees—Secretary
of State—A Member of the General Assembly—Speaker of
the House—"Picture Platt"—State's Attorney—The Bible
Class—Masonry—The Metabetchouan Fishing and Game Club
—Interest in Business Development—Financial Reverses.

WHEN the young lawyer arrived in Meriden in the
spring of 1851, he found a thriving town of
3,000 people. He lived there twenty-eight years, before he was sent to the Senate; and up to the day of his
death, it was his legal residence and voting place,
although his winters were passed in Washington and
his summers either in the Adirondack woods or in the
quiet seclusion of Judea.

Wherever he might go, his interest in the progress of
Meriden went with him. There was the home he had
earned by years of practice at the law; there was the
church of which he early became a member; there were
the friends of his young manhood who had helped him
to his first political success. He saw the village
multiply in population and industry almost beyond
the recognition of his early days, and the time never
came when he did not look forward with pleasure to
the home-coming at the close of each session of
Congress.

His law office at first was on Colony Street, in a brick building owned by Almon Andrews, since destroyed by fire and rebuilt and now owned by the Grand Army of the Republic.

When I first went to Meriden [Mr. Platt said three years before his death] I boarded with Doctor Hough, whose house stood upon the ground now occupied by the First National Bank; afterwards, I boarded with Mr. Morgan, and later went to housekeeping. The first law business I did was to draw five warranty deeds for Mr. Andrews, of whom I rented my office, for which I received one dollar and twenty-five cents.

He thus began humbly like any other briefless young lawyer entering as a stranger into the life of a small though busy community. For the first year or so cases were few and unremunerative. He had so much time on his hands that he was always available for the recreations of the village, and ready to accept an invitation to a game of checkers or chess. Many a day he would shut up his office and go fishing. Some of his old associates say he would do this even though he happened to be in the midst of a case; but a better version seems to be that he did not have enough cases to interfere with his fishing.[1]

---

[1] In the early years of his life in Meriden, Mr. Platt with a number of other young professional and business men of the county organized a baseball club which used to play on the old hospital grounds at New Haven. It is said to have been the first attempt in the State of Connecticut to play the national game under systematic rules. The club was divided into two nines which played against each other two or three times a week, and in the list of the players appear names which later became well known. One was N. D. Sperry, Secretary of the Republican National Committee at the time of Lincoln's first election, a financial backer of Ericsson in the building of the *Monitor*, and for many years a member of Congress. Another was Alfred H. Terry, afterwards Major-General

But it did not take long to establish friendly relations with the substantial citizens of the village, and within two years of his arrival he stood so well that he was elected Judge of Probate, a position which he occupied from 1853 to 1856. Whatever may have been his early

---

Terry, the hero of Fort Fisher, and a famous Indian fighter. Fifty years later on the occasion of a reception tendered Mr. Sperry at New Haven, Mr. Platt wrote from his country home:

"WASHINGTON, CONNECTICUT,
September 29, 1903.

"DEAR MR. SPERRY:

"I am invited to come down and attend the reception to be given you on the fifteenth of October and have been wondering what I can say about you. It occurs to me that I would like to tell the story of our baseball game, and I wish that you would write me the names of as many of those who took part as you can recollect. I am unable to recall all of them for certain, but will give you those I can.

"There must have been two nines—eighteen in all:

Yourself,	Myself,
General Terry,	Harry Lewis,
Mont Woodward,	J. B. Candee,
William E. Downs,	Arthur D. Osborne,
Dave Peck,	Clark from Hamden,
Dwight (was it not?),	Tall man, captain of Blues or Greys, whose name escapes me.

"Possibly Kellogg was there; I rather think he was; perhaps Wooster, Theodore Buell, and Major Bissell were, and I think John Woodruff was.

"Was Root, of the clock shop, one of them, and John C. Hollister another?

"If I am right about these, we have the eighteen, but as I cannot be positive, I wish that you would put on your thinking cap and complete the two nines. The game was played on the lot where the New Haven hospital now stands, was it not?

"Do you remember who were pitchers and who were catchers, or anything else about it which would be interesting to such a gathering?"

Mr. Sperry helped to complete the nines for him as follows:

"The tall man you mention must have been Captain Charles

disposition there is no doubt about the strictness with which he attended to business from the time he first entered public office; and the habits of those days remained with him to the end,—habits of patient, scrupulous, almost plodding industry. He began immediately to take an active part in politics. An Abolition Whig and Free-Soiler—his first vote had been cast for Van Buren in 1848—he undertook the work of extending the Abolition sentiment in the community. The lessons instilled in him in boyhood by the little band of friends of freedom in Judea were not forgotten. His arrival in Meriden almost coincided with the inception of the Kansas-Nebraska struggle, which colored national politics for the next decade, and it was inevitable that one so trained and so endowed should participate to the best of his endeavor in the political activities of his limited environment.[1]

T. Candee, the father of Everett Candee of the Street Railway Company. On the whole as I think the matter over perhaps Kellogg was a member. Wooster was not. Theodore Buell was not. Major Bissell was not. John Woodruff used to be with us once in a while and perhaps Root, of the clock shop, but they were not regular members. John C. Hollister was a member."

[1] The responsibilities of active political organization, which were undertaken elsewhere by the Free-Soil party, were assumed in Connecticut largely by the American party, which in the early days embodied the living Anti-Slavery spirit of the State. Mr. Platt accordingly became identified with the American movement, together with N. D. Sperry and a few other earnest young men who afterwards figured prominently in Republican politics. He became Chairman of the State Committee of the American party prior to 1856 and retained the chairmanship in 1856, working in harmony with the Republican State Committee when the State chose Fremont electors. A little later he became Chairman of the Republican State Committee and he was Secretary of State during the administration of Governor Holley in 1857-8, having previously served as clerk of the State Senate in 1855-6.

To Philip E. Howard of Philadelphia, who inquired about the

From that time until his election to the Senate, he was one of the most effective party workers in the State, and one of the best political organizers. He had a rare faculty of quiet control, and then, as later, his word went far. The story of his slow but steady growth in political favor during the twenty-eight years of his stay in Meriden, of the gradual expansion of his reputation and acquaintance to county and state limits, found its parallel on a national scale between the time of his election to the Senate and the enactment of the Platt amendment. From first to last, without self-advertising or spectacular devices, his development

---

connection of Henry Clay Trumbull with Connecticut politics before the war, Mr. Platt wrote on September 1, 1904: "I remember the fact of Mr. Trumbull's activity in those times; remember to have heard him make political speeches, and some of the anecdotes with which they were interspersed, but my personal intercourse and friendship for him dates from rather a later period. I was originally a 'Know-Nothing' and belonged to what was called the 'American party,' so that at the organization of the Republican party the work was taken up by others. We supported Fremont with all our might in 1856. I had been Chairman of the American, or American-Union party, as we called ourselves prior to 1856, and perhaps in 1856 we had a double organization — I cannot remember—that is, two committees—and it is possible that I still retained the chairmanship of the American party in 1856, working in harmony with the State Committee of the Republican party, then just organized. We carried Connecticut in 1856 for Fremont, and I know that Mr. Trumbull was very active at that time. I cannot make it seem true that he was ever a member of a State committee of which I was chairman. After 1858 I was Chairman of the Republican State Committee for two or three years. Unfortunately, I have no memoranda or data from which I could refresh my recollection. My memory is of that peculiar kind that when a particular piece of work is accomplished, I put it one side and forget all about it until something occurs which makes it necessary for me to recall it. Others seem to have memory which retains the details of everything in which they have been engaged, or with which they have been connected."

was constantly upward and outward. Judge of Probate for Meriden; Clerk of State Senate; Chairman of American and Republican State committees; Secretary of State; member of Senate; member of State House of Representatives; Speaker of House of Representatives; State's Attorney for New Haven; United States Senator—the precise dates do not so much matter.

It was during his term as State Senator in 1861–2 that an incident occurred which brought him for the moment into a prominence which may not have been altogether agreeable. There was in Connecticut a pervasive Copperhead sentiment at the beginning of the War, just as there had been a pro-slavery sentiment there during the Kansas-Nebraska struggle, when one Connecticut Senator, Isaac Toucey, voted with the Democrats of the South against Salmon P. Chase's amendment to Douglas's Squatter Sovereignty bill: "Under which, the people of the Territory, through their appropriate representatives, may, if they see fit, prohibit the existence of slavery therein." Some of the leading Democrats of the State loudly vociferated their lack of sympathy with the steps taken to save the Union. William W. Eaton announced that, if any Massachusetts troops crossed Connecticut, they would have to do it over his dead body. One of the most prominent of the Copperheads was a former Governor of the State, Thomas H. Seymour. So far had the declarations of these men spread, that friends of the Union began to question whether a false impression would not go out to the country of the feeling of the State. Mr. Platt was one of the younger Senators, fired with the zeal of early convictions brought to white heat in the furnace of war. He felt that something should be done to emphasize the loyalty of Connecticut, and—whether after consultation with others is not known—he introduced a resolution reciting the circumstances and providing that the portraits of Governor Seymour and Governor Toucey, which hung in the chamber with those of other Governors, should be turned to the wall. The resolution was adopted; some one dubbed the author of it "Picture Platt," and thus he was called for many years by the opposition press in the State. The incident he rarely referred to in after years, and the details of it seem to have passed out of his mind; but he felt that his action was fully justified.[1]

One of his earliest steps after establishing his home in Meriden, was to unite with the First Congregational Church. He continued this association until his death, although in the later years his connection was, necessarily, not active. He was a deacon of the church until he left for Washington, D. C. For a long time he conducted a Bible class, which was regarded as one of the institutions of the place, and to which many of the principal men and women of the town belonged. His teachings were marked by earnestness and common-sense, and some of his pupils say his exposition of the Scriptures often seemed inspired. He had no use for cant. His son recalls that once when he was home from college he dropped into his father's office, and they started for a walk. As they passed the church, evangelistic services were going on, and the father said, "Let's go in." The evangelist was exhorting with

[1] "I think it was Thomas H. Seymour whose portrait was removed from the Senate chamber on my motion—that is my recollection of it,—and that years afterwards, when the War was over, it was brought back. The Democrats have never forgiven me for it and never will, and yet I think it was an entirely justifiable action."— Letter of O. H. Platt to A. H. Byington, January 29, 1903.

great fervor, calling down the terrors of eternal punishment; after he had been laying on the scourge for some time, he came down among the congregation, and started straight down the aisle to where the elder Platt was sitting at the head of a pew, with his legs crossed as usual. Throwing his arm over Mr. Platt's shoulder he asked, "My brother, are you a Christian?" The future Senator looked up slowly, without uncrossing his legs, and barely unclosing his lips—"If what you have been telling us is true about what is necessary to be a Christian and what is not," he said deliberately, "I don't think I am!"

Some of his most agreeable associations with Meriden grew out of his interest in Masonry. He was an early member of Meridian Lodge, No. 77, which dated from about the time of his arrival in the town, and later joined in the institution of St. Elmo Commandery, No. 9, K. T. Most of his closest friendships had their beginning there, and throughout his life he always made a point of being in Meriden if possible at the ceremonies on Good-Friday when his old companions got together. He delivered addresses on the fiftieth anniversary of Meridian Lodge and the twenty-fifth anniversary of St. Elmo Commandery, which bear the marks of careful preparation, and disclose a deep affection for the order to which he belonged.

Another connection dating from early days in Meriden was his membership in the Metabetchouan Fishing and Game Club, which had a fishing preserve in Canada comprising two hundred square miles of territory. He originally leased the preserve, as he used to explain, "in the days when I was young and foolish." He soon found that he could not get there often and that it was more than he could afford to keep up. So some of his friends took it off his hands, and formed a club, building a clubhouse in the unbroken forest, with camps on the lakes and rivers. Next to the Litchfield hills and the Adirondacks, he liked to go there, though it rarely happened that he could get so far away.

He was deeply concerned in the business development of his town. He was forever urging the advantage of establishing new industries, and this interest of his resulted not long before his election to the Senate in the one great financial setback of his life. A number of his local friends undertook to establish a cutlery concern and he became the counselling spirit in the enterprise, although he had little pecuniary interest in it. He worked hard to get it started, and the promoters came to him to go on their notes. He accommodated them without thinking how much paper he was putting his name to and got in beyond his depth. The concern failed and he found himself involved for nearly $25,000. He turned over all his own property and part of his wife's property to the creditors of the failed concern. While he was in the worst of his trouble he received from his brother Simeon, who was a farmer in Litchfield County, a good-sized check with the laconic memorandum: "Orville, use this." He returned the check with an equally laconic note: "Much obliged, Simeon, but I got myself into this mess, and I shall get out of it." But he never did quite get out of it. He went ahead strictly paying every dollar, giving his notes where he could not pay in cash, and taking them up as he found himself able to do so, but he carried the burden up to the day of his death, and some of the notes were cancelled only when it came to the settlement of his estate.

He was not a jury lawyer. He confined himself

almost entirely to patent, corporation, and real-estate law. Until 1875, he was alone in his office. Then he took into partnership his son James, recently graduated, and for many years the old sign, "O. H. & J. P. PLATT," remained on the office door. At the time of his election to the Senate, his practice was the most extensive in Meriden, and almost all the important manufacturing concerns in the town were among his clients. Every one had confidence in him. Every one was familiar with his tall figure sauntering up the street and felt free to go to him for help or sympathy. He was commonly known as "O. H." and few took the pains to call him by any other name.

The years of his stay in Meriden were not eventful, but they served to give him an acquaintance throughout the State which proved of value when he came before the Legislature for election to the Senate. He was called a good campaign speaker, and was in demand for political occasions in his own town and in others, so that people got in the habit of associating his name with Republican affairs. It was known among his friends that he had only one ambition. His service as Secretary of State in 1858, Speaker of the House of Representatives in 1867, and State's Attorney for New Haven between 1877 and 1879, came along in the ordinary course of politics. He could have been chosen Governor and might easily have been elected to Congress, but he did not care for either place. There was only one political office he wanted and that was the United States Senatorship. He thought that with his temperament and training he could do better work in the Senate than anywhere else, if he should ever have the opportunity. His chance came at last in the fall of 1878. For several years Connecticut had been in the control of

the Democratic party. W. W. Eaton, the "peace
Democrat" of Civil War days, and William H. Barnum,
afterwards Chairman of the Democratic National Committee, represented the State in the Senate, having
taken the places made vacant by the death of Senators
Buckingham and Ferry in 1875. Barnum's term was
to expire on March 4, 1879, and the election of a
Republican Legislature in 1878 opened the way for a
Republican successor.

CHAPTER IV

THE MIDNIGHT CAUCUS

A Skilfully Conducted Canvass—The Midnight Caucus—Election
to the Senate—Newspaper Criticism—Reception at Meriden.

THERE is no more interesting chapter in the political
history of Connecticut than the story of the
campaign for the Senatorship which culminated in the
famous midnight caucus of January 16–17, 1879, and
the selection of Mr. Platt as the Republican nominee.
In general estimation, Gen. Joseph R. Hawley was
easily the leading candidate, and outside the State it
seems to have been assumed that he would be successful.
He had acquired a wide reputation for independence and
courage, was the one distinctly national character in
the State, and was understood in some way to represent
popular sentiment as against the scheming of professional politicians. He had a splendid record for bravery
in the Civil War, to which he was recognized as one
of the State's most notable contributions. He had
been Governor of the State, Permanent Chairman of the
Republican National Convention in 1868, a Presidential
Elector in the same year, President of the Centennial
Commission at Philadelphia in 1876. At the election
of 1878, he had been chosen a member of the House of
Representatives for the second time, after an interval
of several years, having served one term in 1871 and
1872, and having twice suffered defeat. He was the

editor of the Hartford *Courant*, a strongly appealing personality both in the State and out.

Marshall Jewell likewise had a reputation extending beyond the limits of the State, of which he had been Governor for three terms. As Minister to Russia, and Postmaster-General under President Grant, as a conspicuous figure in Republican national conventions, as a member of the Republican National Committee, of which he became Chairman in the following year, he had many friends and adherents. He was strong especially among the active political workers, and, being regarded as their candidate, suffered accordingly.

Henry B. Harrison was one of the best-known lawyers in the State, frequently mentioned for important office, and was recognized as a high-minded man, from whom much was to be expected. Into this group of eminent men, the modest Meriden lawyer ventured to intrude himself as a competitor for the highest honor in the gift of the State. He had seemingly few qualities to commend him to the Legislature in preference to any one of the others. He was known, it is true, as a competent lawyer, as a political worker and organizer of proved astuteness, as an efficient public servant in the various positions in which he had served, and as a citizen of sterling worth; but it may be doubted, when his candidacy was announced, whether there were many who imagined he would be a serious factor, much less that he could secure the prize. He had one advantage which those who interested themselves in his candidacy regarded as a political asset. He had no enemies and nowhere in the State was there a politician of consequence who did not have a kindly feeling for him. Though he was the first choice of few, he was acceptable as a second choice to many.

Moreover, his friends figured that either of the two leading candidates, Hawley and Jewell, both living in Hartford, would prefer to see the Senatorship go to some one outside of Hartford if unable to get it himself.   There was to be another vacancy at the end of two years, when the term of Senator Eaton expired, and the election of a Hartford man to the existing vacancy would be a serious handicap to any Hartford candidate in 1881.   The nucleus of Mr. Platt's support was in his own town of Meriden, with its three representatives in the Legislature, H. Wales Lines in the Senate, and Samuel Dodd and James P. Platt in the House.   A campaign committee was organized, consisting of H. Wales Lines, Charles L. Rockwell, Judge Levi E. Coe, John W. Coe, and William F. Graham. Friends of the candidate were assigned each to canvass a county in the State, while a score or more other Meriden men volunteered to help by visiting other towns and interviewing members-elect to the General Assembly.   It was the plan of the little band of campaigners not to antagonize any of the other candidates, to stimulate and extend the friendly feeling already existing toward Mr. Platt in all parts of the State, to make him the second choice of as many members-elect as possible, so that when the time came for either Hawley or Jewell supporters to look for another candidate, they would naturally turn to Platt.   Thus his canvass progressed unobtrusively, but with gradually accumulating interest, until a few days before the time for the Republican caucus.   By that time the committee had some twenty-five votes on which they thought they could count—at least for sympathetic support, and friends of other candidates began to figure on the Platt following as something to be seriously considered. At the beginning of the canvass, Mr. Platt had instructed his managers that they should make no trades, bargains, or combines of any kind with any one. Those instructions were faithfully carried out. A few days before the caucus, however, some of Mr. Platt's friends became anxious. There were rumors of bargains and agreements. One proposition was made, that the Platt support should go to one of the other candidates on condition that Mr. Platt should be chosen Senator two years later; in the meantime, the son James Platt to be appointed judge on the State bench, which was his ambition. All these suggestions were rejected, but word was carried to the candidate of what was going on, with a suggestion that he ought to be in Hartford. A few hours before the caucus, Mr. Lines, the Chairman of the Platt Campaign Committee, received the following dispatch at Hartford:

NEW HAVEN, CONNECTICUT,
January 14th.

To Honorable H. WALES LINES,
Senator Sixth District.

My duties here make it impossible for me to give direction or even thought to the senatorial matter. I leave it entirely with you and the Meriden representatives, with these suggestions: Make no combinations or bargains, and entertain no proposals for anything. Let no friend of mine disparage any other candidate. Put the argument solely on what you may think of me, my ability to represent the State, and the best interests of the Republican party.

O. H. PLATT.

The message was hardly needed, for it was in line with what Mr. Platt's managers had understood his wishes to be. It was not made public until some time after

the caucus, and then it helped to contribute to the
satisfaction with which the people of the State were
learning to contemplate the outcome of the contest.

The caucus began at eight o'clock and remained
continually in session until 2:27 the next morning.
Interest was intense. Former speaker Bugbee of
Killingly was made chairman because his preference
was unknown. Hawley's friends were anxious for
nominating speeches; but supporters of the other
candidates at a meeting before the caucus decided
that no speeches should be made, and their wishes
prevailed. On the first ballot, which is designated
in the newspaper reports as "informal" but which
is said by some who were there not to have dif-
fered in character from the others, Hawley had 49
votes; Jewell 35; Platt 24; Harrison 14; W. T. Minor
of Stamford 14; P. T. Barnum 10. Platt's strong
showing on this ballot was a surprise to all except
his friends. It was known that there were three, and
probably five who would stand by him until his election
or defeat. Three of these came from Meriden. There
is some question as to the identity of the others; but
honors lie with two of the following names: Senator
Lyman W. Coe and Representative Bradley R.
Agard of Torrington, and Representative Henry Gay
of Winchester. Some who were primarily for Platt
favored Hawley as second choice and when they saw
the Jewell vote increasing on subsequent ballots they
became alarmed lest Jewell should be nominated and
transferred their votes to Hawley. So it came about
that as ballot after ballot was taken, the Platt showing
fell steadily till, on the eighth formal ballot, it reached
the dauntless five, and there for three ballots it stuck,
while the Harrison strength slowly grew, and Hawley's

on the ninth and tenth ballots bounded to seventy-one, within five votes of the nominating point.

On the tenth formal ballot, Hawley had 71 votes, Jewell 51, Harrison 23, and Platt 5. On the eleventh ballot, Hawley had 64, Jewell 53, Harrison 21, and Platt 10. From that time the Platt strength showed a gradual increase, Harrison's fell away, the Jewell votes disintegrated ballot after ballot, and the Hawley support fluctuated. It was evident that the Jewell managers, at the head of whom was William H. Hayward of Colchester, were trying to effect combinations first with the Harrison, and then with the Platt contingents, so as to prevent the success of Hawley, who was approaching dangerously close to the nomination. The game was skilfully played. Enough votes were thrown to one candidate and another to sustain the contest, but the transfer of strength was so gradual as not to precipitate a rush to Hawley. At midnight, the nineteenth ballot stood: Hawley 60; Jewell 42; Platt 25; Harrison 16; S. W. Kellogg 5; Barnum 2. So it went on for eleven more ballots, when, for the first time, Platt forged ahead to second place: Hawley 63; Platt 39; Jewell 37; Harrison 10. The thirty-third ballot gave Hawley 66; Platt 61; Jewell 18; Harrison 7. On the thirty-fourth ballot, Platt leaped to first place, with 74 votes; Hawley 72; Jewell 3; Harrison 2. He gained one vote from Hawley on the thirty-fifth ballot, so that he was within one vote of the nomination, and on the thirty-sixth ballot the longed for vote came.[1] Just where it came from has ever since been a source of friendly dispute among the politicians of the State. There are living to-day at least a dozen men, each of whom can relate with circumstantial detail how it

[1] The full record of the balloting in the midnight caucus follows:

happened—how he delivered that missing vote. It is no part of this history to settle the dispute, although one incident may be recorded. That Marcus E. Baldwin of Woodbridge was one of those who cast his vote for Platt for the first time on the decisive ballot, appears from the proceedings of the meeting at Meriden held the night after Mr. Platt's election by the Legislature, when Mr. Baldwin was introduced facetiously, by Senator Lines, as "one of the men who, when he came

INFORMAL BALLOT

Joseph R. Hawley,	Hartford,	49
Marshall Jewell,	Hartford,	35
Orville H. Platt,	Meriden,	24
Henry B. Harrison,	New Haven,	14
William T. Minor,	Stamford,	14
P. T. Barnum,	Bridgeport,	10
Charles B. Andrews,	Litchfield,	1
Benjamin Douglas,	Middletown,	1
		148

FORMAL BALLOTS

	1st	2d	3d	4th	5th	6th
Hawley..........	55	59	62	63	61	67
Jewell...........	39	43	43	46	49	47
Platt............	25	20	19	22	15	13
Harrison.........	13	14	18	17	25	21
Barnum.........	9	7	4	1		
Minor...........	7	5	4			

	7th	8th	9th	10th	11th	12th
Hawley..........	65	67	71	71	64	65
Jewell...........	50	50	46	51	53	52
Platt............	9	5	5	5	10	16
Harrison.........	24	28	28	23	21	16

	13th	14th	15th	16th	17th	18th
Hawley..........	61	64	59	59	59	58
Jewell...........	48	46	41	39	36	33
Platt............	23	26	29	25	28	29
Harrison.........	18	14	20	18	18	16
Chas. B. Andrews.			1	5	3	1
S. W. Kellogg...				2	4	4
Barnum.........				1	1	6
Minor..........						1

to Mr. Platt, never left him until he was elected." Mr. Baldwin had been a Harrison man from the beginning, although he was an intimate associate of many of Mr. Platt's friends. The representatives from New Haven County were in the habit of running up to Hartford every day on the same train, and there was much good-natured chaffing back and forth. Baldwin was especially vehement in support of Harrison, declaring that he should vote for Harrison " first, last, and all the

FORMAL BALLOTS

	19th	20th	21st	22d	23d
Hawley..........	60	60	58	61	60
Jewell...........	42	45	47	47	46
Platt.....	25	26	28	28	24
Harrison.........	16	14	17	14	12
Kellogg..........	5	4	1		
Barnum..........	2				
Lyman D. Brewster.....		2			
W. T. Minor.....		1	1		

(11.45 P.M.)

	24th	25th	26th	27th	28th
Hawley..........	67	65	62	62	57
Jewell..........	47	43	41	41	40
Platt...........	25	29	31	31	33
Harrison........	11	12	17	16	12

	29th	30th	31st	32d	33d
Hawley..........	63	63	64	64	66
Jewell...........	40	37	34	26	18
Platt...........	36	39	43	51	61
Harrison........	12	9	8	9	7

	34th	35th	36th		
Hawley..........	72	71	72		
Jewell..........	3	3	1		
Platt...........	74	75	76		
Harrison........	2	2			

Two ballots were declared void, as more votes were cast than there were present in the caucus.

time." Finally James P. Platt said to him: "I'm a pretty good Platt man, but I'll tell you what I'll do. If the time ever comes when my vote will nominate Harrison, you can have it. But you must agree that if the time ever comes when your vote will nominate Platt, you will give it." "Agreed," said Baldwin, and neither thought of the incident again till just before the decisive ballot. James Platt had noticed the two persistent votes for Harrison, and it flashed across his mind where one of them came from; he went over to Baldwin, and asked him if he remembered the conversation on the train going up from Meriden. "I do," replied Baldwin. "Well," said young Platt, "this is the time and this is the place." Baldwin cast his vote for Platt. At 2.30 A.M., the result of the thirty-sixth formal ballot was announced: Platt 76; Hawley 72; Jewell 1, and Platt was nominated. On January 21st, the election took place in joint assembly of the Legislature. It resulted: Platt 139; Barnum 94; scattering 1; not voting 10.

The nomination when it came was a surprise to the successful candidate. He spent the eventful night in Meriden, remaining in the telegraph office until midnight, and during the early evening he received frequent despatches from Hartford. When his vote fell off to five, he gave it up and went to bed and to sleep. After the caucus adjourned, the Meriden campaigners caught the first train for home and drove up from the station to the house in the early morning. They all ran upstairs, where they found Platt asleep. They woke him up, John Coe shouting, "Get up there, you old United States Senator!" but they could not get Platt to believe it until he had heard the whole story of the caucus to the end.

It would be agreeable to set down here that the action

of the midnight caucus was received with approbation everywhere. The truth is, however, that for a time there was a feeling of disappointment, which found expression, thinly veiled, in many of the newspapers within the State and openly in most of those without. Popular fancy seems to have fixed itself upon General Hawley, which was not at all to be wondered at, and failing him, there were several names which would have appealed to it before the one which for the first time now challenged its attention. General Hawley came forward handsomely in the shadow of personal disappointment, in a short editorial paragraph which appeared in the Hartford *Courant* of the following morning, and which must have been written within the hour of the announcement of his defeat. It is possible that what he wrote served as an introduction of Mr. Platt to many of the people of Connecticut, as it did to all beyond the borders of the State. General Hawley could not refrain from alluding gently to "the influences that caused the various changes in the balloting," but he added:

Mr. Platt is fifty-one years old, a native of Washington, Litchfield County, an able lawyer, at present Attorney for the State in New Haven County. His first prominent appearance in public life was as Secretary of State in 1857–8, during Governor Holley's administration. In 1861–2 he was a Senator from the sixth district; in 1864 and 1869 he was in the House, the latter year being elected Speaker.

He is a gentleman of most honorable character, sound judgment, well-balanced mind, familiarity with political affairs, and much sagacity in conducting them. He is sound in principle, an Anti-Slavery man and Republican from his boyhood, a good hard-money man and sure to have convictions and follow them. This much his chief competitor takes pleasure in writing hastily at the late hour which announces his nomination.

Other newspapers printed slighting comments which their authors lived to regret, and there were fugitive suggestions in Democratic journals that the Democrats in the Legislature should combine with a minority of Republicans to elect Hawley, who of course would not have tolerated such a thing. Two years later, in 1881, he was unanimously nominated by the Republican caucus, was elected Senator, and served by Platt's side for nearly twenty-five years.

Among Mr. Platt's neighbors, and among those who knew him, the feeling toward him was cordial and appreciative. The New Haven *Union* said:

O. H. Platt holds high rank in the estimation of the people of Meriden, among whom he has lived and worked these twenty-seven years, and bears a public and private character beyond reproach. He is a deacon in the First Congregational Church with which he has been connected since the Reverend W. H. H. Murray[1] preached there, and he is forward in all Christian work in his adopted town. A man of few words, of fewer promises, and stern unyielding will, he rarely fails a friend in need or turns back from the path he has marked out for himself. He is pre-eminently noted for two things: unselfishness, in political as well as social life, and true earnestness. As a friend remarked: "He has not a selfish bone in his body. The best years of his life he has devoted to others, and that is one reason he is to-day a poor man."

The friends and neighbors in Meriden deferred their greeting until after the formal action of the Legis-

---

[1] Mr. Murray did not preach in Meriden until 1864, some years after Mr. Platt became a member of the Church. He had earlier preached in the Church at Judea for a little while.

lature had set the seal of certainty upon the choice of the caucus. On the night following the election, there was a reception at the Meriden house, with illuminations and a midnight supper. There had been no formal preparations, but the crowds were dense, and for two hours men of every calling assured the newly elected Senator of their good-will. In the midst of the reception "Neighbor Platt" was led to the platform where he spoke a few characteristically simple words:

I thank you, my friends, for this kind reception. This is neither the time nor the place to make a speech, and yet I think I would be lacking in the common feeling of humanity if I did not express to you in some way the thanks I feel for the respect you have ever shown me. It touches me, coming as it does from you men who have known me longest and best—the men I have lived with these twenty-eight years. I have lived a somewhat transparent life. You know what I have done and what I have failed to do. It is that that makes this demonstration the more acceptable and touching to me. I think no man could have lived in a place so long and been more sensible of the kindly feeling entertained toward him than I. I want to thank all my friends, but especially my Meriden friends. They were not politicians, but were full of love and devotion, and labored for my welfare without hope of reward; and such kindly feeling and disposition touches me to the heart. Their faith makes me rejoice more at their gratification than my success. As I meet you here and have met you elsewhere, so shall I be pleased to meet you at all times. I shall be glad to meet you at any time or place—glad to meet the kind friends whose memory I shall always cherish. Just now everything is new and seems unreal. I can scarcely appreciate the future. How I shall bear myself, how I shall walk in the new path in which I am set, time will show. I do know that I shall try to do right as I see the right and I have faith to believe that this will bring me through to the end without discredit to you, to myself, or to the State. My friends, this is no place for an announcement of my political views. I have in the course of my life dealt and received many hard political blows, but I have always tried to act right and shall so continue. I thank you again for your kindness, and I trust that all your expectations with reference to me will not be disappointed. Good-night.[1]

[1] At the supper which followed the reception, there were many complimentary speeches from members of the General Assembly and friends. A dispatch was read from Mr. Platt's old teacher, F. W. Gunn, as follows:

"WASHINGTON, CONNECTICUT,
January 22d.

"To MAYOR LINES:
"Washington, the place of his birth and growth to manhood, joins with Meriden, the home of his mature life and active labor, in congratulations upon the election of Honorable O. H. Platt as a Senator of the United States—'An honest man's the noblest work of God.'"

After this, Mr. Platt was called to his feet again. The rest of the proceedings may be described in the words of the Meriden *Daily Republican* the following day:

"Mr. Platt rose and made one of those earnest, thoughtful, ringing speeches that took his own townsmen, who heard him, back to the grand speeches he made in Town Hall in the presidential and other campaigns, when the services of our best and most powerful men were required on the political platform. He began by referring to the senatorial contest just closed, and how deeply he felt the responsibilities of the new duties to which he was called. In endeavoring to discharge them, he would be guided solely by what he had always considered a safe rule to follow, and had made the rule of his life—doing what he believed to be right. To say that he was gratified at being surrounded by so many of his immediate neighbors and good personal friends did not express how he felt, and if any one thing more than another gave him special gratification, it was to know that his old friends of years ago, in the home of his boyhood, Litchfield County, were rejoicing at his election. Another source of gratification to him was that his four competitors were gentlemen whom he was proud to call his friends, and he knew of no four gentlemen whom he would more freely call on for a personal favor, than on Joe Hawley, H. B. Harrison,

Marshall Jewell, and Governor Minor.   And he was glad to observe that Connecticut had such noble men to select a Senator from, for had either been elected, the State would have been honored, and the principles of the Republican party faithfully vindicated. Mr. Platt then went on to say that he rejoiced that no friend of his, in the most heated hour of the campaign, had dropped an unkind or offensive word toward any of these gentlemen.   Had they done so, it would have been painful to him.   He felt that had either been elected instead of himself, they might have brought more ability to the discharge of the duties of the position, but none of them could exhibit a greater desire to do right.   It was the desire to do right that signalized the victory and achievements of the Republican party, and, knowing of that desire, he was proud to have been identified with that party of progress since its birth.   It was the determination to do right that lifted politics from the mire, and nerved conscientious men to become politicians.

"Mr. Platt then reviewed the Republican party and the previous parties of which it is an outgrowth, covering a period of thirty years, every year of which was devoted by the Republican party and its predecessors with similar principles to contending for the rights of man.   He liked the Republican party because it made these rights of man its cardinal principle, and because it did so, he was a Republican, and he could sincerely say that in all his active participation in Republican campaigns, he never thought of self, never sought nor cared for political place, his ambition being to lift the Republican party to a plane where the rights and equality of man would be recognized all over the land, and that a free ballot would be cast, whether in South Carolina or Connecticut.   'This must be and shall be accomplished,' said Mr. Platt.   'With that principle to contend for, the party contending for it cannot fail.' Mr. Platt then deprecated in strong words the use of money in elections.   It provoked him, he said, when he heard it said that campaigns could not be carried on without a lavish or corrupt expenditure of money.   The falsity of the assertion has been demonstrated, and he was thankful that it had been demonstrated by the Republican party.   Mr. Platt, after dwelling on this point at some length, referred to the currency question, remarking that like all other issues of the day it had only two sides, right and wrong, and he firmly believed that the man who was right was he who advocated a currency that would have a standard value all over the world, without being subjected to daily fluctuations.   He stood there, and he believed the great mass of the Republican party stood there.   Mr. Platt closed by recognizing the distinguished honor and privilege of representing Connecticut in the councils

109445

of the nation. He loved Connecticut because it was his native State and he had grown with its growth. He had proudly watched its progress, not only in the pursuits of the sturdy farmer, but in its manufacturing interests, which had increased little by little, until every railroad and stream was dotted with a manufactory, a tribute to the thrift of the commonwealth—a commonwealth that had in it many of the sons and daughters of the passengers of the *Mayflower*, whose puritanical blood was a certain protection against all vague 'isms' and socialistic and communistic ideas and heresies that were seeking a place in New England. In Connecticut they would make no headway. Mr. Platt resumed his seat amid a storm of applause.

"At the close of Mr. Platt's remarks, Mr. Worthington took the floor voluntarily and said the election of Mr. Platt was a cause for more than usual gratification, because it was accomplished without expenditure of a cent for liquor of any kind, or for any other corrupt purpose. It proved that Mr. Platt was true to the principle of total abstinence, and he would therefore propose, in cold water, the health of Honorable Orville H. Platt. The whole company rose, and with glasses raised, duly responded, after which the company separated."

The following day the new Senator went to Hartford to meet the members of the Legislature. The Meriden *Republican* gave a naïvely interesting picture of the event:

"For the first time since its completion, Senator Platt was in the State Capitol to-day. He went up from here on the nine o'clock train and took his accustomed seat in the smoking-car. It soon became generally known on the train that the new Senator was on board. Many came from other cars and carelessly passed by to get a good, square look at the man of whom they had heard so much the past few days.

"Arriving at Hartford, Senator Platt strolled leisurely over the Capitol, accompanied by Senator Lines and Representative Platt, son of the Senator. At the Capitol the Senator was conducted to the governor's room, where Governor Andrews gave him a cordial greeting. The new Capitol was then looked over, and Senator Platt commented on the beauty of the work and paid many compliments to the fidelity of the Capitol Commissioners. Soon after the House convened, the news was circulated that Senator Platt was in the building and a general desire to see him was expressed. Speaker Wright sent a friend of Senator Platt to him to know if he would not present himself in the House, if sent for, after official recognition of his presence in the Capitol was announced. Senator Platt sent back word that he preferred to have no formality, but that he would drop into the House just before adjournment and see how many faces he knew there and how many knew him. On Speaker Wright being informed of Mr. Platt's wishes, Mr. P. T. Barnum, who was conversing with the Speaker at the time, said that would never do.

" 'The new Senator must show himself and give us all a good look at the man we voted for.' A few minutes later, as the House was about to adjourn, Senator Platt entered, accompanied by his son, and both sat at the latter's desk, and Speaker Wright at once went to Mr. Platt. Then P. T. Barnum arose from his desk and said: 'Mr. Speaker: This House has always been running me and remarking upon their desire to see my show. But I think we have with us what will please them more than anything I could present. I understand our distinguished Senator-elect, Orville H. Platt, is in this House, and I move you, sir, that he be invited to the Speaker's desk, that we all have the pleasure of looking on his genial face.' Speaker Wright conducted Senator Platt to the desk and declared a recess of five minutes. Senator Platt, on rising, was received with deafening applause, again and again repeated. He said:

" 'You can scarcely expect me to say hardly more than to tender to you my acknowledgment for what you have done in selecting me to represent the State of Connecticut, in the Senate of the United States. Others might have been chosen who would represent you more ably, but no man, I am sure, can bring to the service a more ardent love for the State than I. I think I know something of the people of this State, of its industries and wants, and certainly I shall try to faithfully represent its people, its industries, and its wants. I have seen its manufacturing interests grow from the smallest beginnings, until now manufacturing interests dot every railroad and stream in the State. I have seen its wealth trebled, and its population vastly increase. I think I know something of its people, and as much as I admire the people of other States I do think that there is more of the loyal spirit and character which distinguished those who came over on the *Mayflower* than can be found in any other State, in its institutions and its people; and God helping me, I never shall be recreant to the trust you have committed to me.'

"Senator Platt was loudly applauded at the close and soon left the House. He visited the Senate Chamber and engaged in social conversation with the Senators who invited him to their private room off the Senate, where a pleasant hour was spent. The Senator during the afternoon called on several personal friends in Hartford, each of whom most cordially congratulated him and declared themselves not only satisfied, but well pleased with his election. The visit was a very pleasant one to the Senator-elect."

CHAPTER V

First Experiences at Washington—The Forty-Sixth Congress—
Eulogy of Rush Clark.

THE newly created Senator was given little time to
prepare himself for the opportunity thrust into
his hand. His election had taken place in the closing
days of the last session of the Forty-fifth Congress, when
the situation growing out of differences between President Hayes and the Democratic leaders at the capital
resulted in a filibuster which prevented the passage of
two great supply bills, the Army Appropriation bill and
the Legislative, Executive, and Judicial.   President
Hayes, accordingly, was compelled on the 4th of
March to issue a call for a special session of the Forty-
sixth Congress, to meet on March 18, 1879. Mr.
Platt was hurried into his new duties at Washington.
He bade good-bye to the old scenes at Meriden with a
feeling of regret, looking toward the future without
elation, yet without self-distrust.   His old friend John
Coe drove him to the station the day he left Meriden to
go to Washington. Little was said by either until
just as they were about to part, when Mr. Platt
remarked slowly:

"John, I'm going to the United States Senate;
you won't hear much of a fellow named Platt for some

years. I'm going to listen and learn, and I won't begin to talk until I stand for something."

Mr. Platt took his seat on the first day of the session. Among those who appeared at the presiding officer's desk with him to take the oath of office were William B. Allison of Iowa, Matt. H. Carpenter of Wisconsin, Roscoe Conkling of New York, John J. Ingalls of Kansas, John A. Logan of Illinois, Justin S. Morrill of Vermont, George H. Pendleton of Ohio, Daniel W. Voorhees of Indiana, John P. Jones of Nevada, Wade Hampton of South Carolina, Zebulon B. Vance of North Carolina, and George G. Vest of Missouri. Of these, all except Vance, Pendleton, Hampton, and Vest had seen previous service. Other members of the Senate with whom Mr. Platt found himself associated were John T. Morgan of Alabama, A. H. Garland of Arkansas, Newton Booth of California, Henry M. Teller of Colorado, Thomas F. Bayard and Eli Saulsbury of Delaware, Benjamin H. Hill of Georgia, David Davis of Illinois, Joseph E. McDonald of Indiana, Samuel J. Kirkwood of Iowa, Preston B. Plumb of Kansas, James B. Beck of Kentucky, William Pitt Kellogg of Louisiana, James G. Blaine and Hannibal Hamlin of Maine, Henry L. Dawes and George F. Hoar of Massachusetts, Zachariah Chandler and Thomas W. Ferry of Michigan, William Windom of Minnesota, Blanche K. Bruce and L. Q. C. Lamar of Mississippi, Francis M. Cockrell of Missouri, Allen G. Thurman of Ohio, Henry B. Anthony and Ambrose E. Burnside of Rhode Island. With some of these men, Allison, Morrill, Vest, Teller, Hoar, and Cockrell, he had associations almost throughout his political career.

With the scrupulous regard for seniority and precedent which characterizes the procedure of the Senate, he was placed at the tail-end of three committees—none of the first importance—Pensions, Patents, and the Select Committee to investigate and report the best means of preventing the introduction and spread of epidemic diseases. All committees were in control of the Democratic majority, so that there was little which the least important member of the minority could be expected to accomplish.[1]

It is not to be wondered at that little was heard from the country lawyer, unexpectedly elevated to the United States Senate, taking his seat within two months of his election. In this first session, lasting from March 18th, to July 1st, and monopolized by a bitter partisan discussion of the use of Federal troops at the polls, it is recorded that he introduced two bills for the relief of constituents and that he spoke six times. His entire activities during the session are covered in thirty-four lines of the Congressional Record. His first forensic appearance in the Senate occurred in the course of a

[1] The composition of these committees was as follows:

PENSIONS: Withers (chairman), McPherson, Groome, Call, Farley, Ingalls, Bruce, Kellogg, Platt.

PATENTS: Kernan (chairman), Coke, Slater, Call, Booth, Hoar, Platt.

EPIDEMIC DISEASES: Harris (chairman), Lamar, Garland, Jonas, Paddock, Sharon, Platt.

Late in the session Mr. Hoar withdrew from the Select Committee to inquire into alleged frauds in the late elections, of which he was the last member, and Mr. Platt took his place. His seniors on this committee were Wallace (chairman), Bailey, Garland, McDonald, Kernan, Teller, Cameron of Wisconsin, and Kirkwood.

At a late stage of the session a committee was appointed to consider a bill introduced by Senator Pendleton to provide that the principal officers of each of the executive departments might occupy seats on the floor of the Senate and House of Representatives, and Mr. Platt was placed at the end of this committee, which had the following membership: Pendleton, Voorhees, Bayard, Butler, Farley, Conkling, Allison, Blaine, Ingalls, Platt.

speech by his colleague, Mr. Eaton, on the Legislative, Executive, and Judicial Appropriation bill. It is given as a matter of history:

MR. EATON: I want to say here, and my colleague will agree with me, that in nearly every town in Connecticut no matter which party is in power, not in all towns, but in most, a fair share of the jurors is given to the weaker party. It is so in my own town always. So it is with justices of the peace.

MR. PLATT: Will my colleague permit me to interrupt him?

MR. EATON: Certainly.

MR. PLATT: That ought to be the case, but there are far too many towns in the State where it is not the case.

MR. EATON: I know it is the case to a certain extent.

Not a sensational or dramatic entrance upon a public career! The assurance given John Coe on the drive to the station at Meriden was in a fair way to verification.

During his second session he was not much more active. He is credited with making "remarks" on thirty different occasions. Most of them were casual and related either to the business of the Committees on Pensions and Patents of which he was a member, or the needs of some constituent. Whenever he interjected an inquiry or a comment it was in the direction of economy and regular procedure. But he took advantage of an opportunity to declare himself briefly on at least one important question of public policy. Shortly after the Christmas recess he introduced the following joint resolution, which was ordered to lie on the table:

"*Whereas*, An improved and cheaper maritime communication between the Atlantic and Pacific seaboards of the United States by means of a ship-canal through some

portion of the Central American isthmus has become important to the commercial interests of this country; and

Whereas, Congress deems it to be necessary and expedient that the national and public interests in such a
communication should be secured, rather than merely
private and speculative ends: Therefore,

Resolved by the Senate and House of Representatives, etc.,
That the President be requested, if he shall deem it expedient, to communicate to the governments of the principal
maritime nations of Europe the desire of this Government
to secure such public interests, and to invite the co-operation
of such governments in the selection of a route of isthmus
ship-transit, which shall be found to subserve most largely
the general interests of all the maritime nations, and also to
communicate to such governments the desire of the Government to come to a mutual understanding with reference
to the neutrality of such an interoceanic transit when it
shall have been opened by the enterprise and capital of
their respective citizens.

This resolution he succeeded in getting referred to
the Committee on Foreign Relations two months later,
but that was as far as it went. He lived to take part
in all the legislation which resulted ultimately in the
digging of the Isthmian Canal.

During this session also, Mr. Platt performed for the
first time a duty which he was called upon many times
to repeat during his twenty-six years of service—a delicate and difficult duty in which he always showed
rare taste and feeling. On the death of Rush Clark, a
Representative from Iowa, in the preceding spring, he
had been appointed a member of the committee to
accompany the body to the grave, and he was asked
to take part in the memorial exercises in the Senate
early in February. What he said should be recorded
here, not only for its excellence, but because it afforded

Mr. Platt his first opportunity to address the Senate in any but the briefest possible way:

The grave has at least one feature which somewhat modifies its gloom. There a man is truly judged by his fellows. The sharp antagonisms, the unjust judgments of life are buried there, before the coffin is lowered, and the abilities, the impress, and the true character of the one who is to be its occupant are there justly acknowledged.

The courtesies of the grave are accorded to all, but men do not there deceive themselves or others in the estimate which they place upon the life of a fallen comrade. There you may learn his true history, his innermost life, his true character. At the home of Rush Clark, from the moment we reached the station till the last sad rites had been tenderly and lovingly performed, the evidences of a great sorrow pervading the entire community were unmistakable. At the very borders of the State which he had adopted as his own, we were made to feel that his influence had extended beyond the limits of the district which he more immediately represented, and that the whole State mourned for one of its truest and noblest men. All along the route to the beautiful city which had been the scene of his more active labors, we were met by strong, true men, who grieved as if the deceased had been a brother. I shall never forget the hour of our arrival at Iowa City. It was night, but the whole population had gathered to pay its tribute of respect to the dead, to testify its sympathy for the bereaved. The saddened faces of the people, seen in the light of the torches which were to guide us; the whispered orders for the disposition of his remains; the tears which fell from the eyes of sturdy men, all spoke most emphatically of the character of the man and of the place he had won for himself in the hearts of all. If deep sorrow could have restored him to life he would have lived again. It was an hour to be remembered always, and its impressions were intensified by the obsequies of the next day, when a vast concourse gathered to attend with uncovered heads the impressive funeral ceremonies, and to follow in long procession to the tomb all that was left of him who had been their reliance and pride. Neither the falling rain nor the sharp thunder could deter those who honored him from the performance in minutest detail of the last solemn rites. So he was laid away to rest in the beautiful cemetery just outside of and overlooking the city he had chosen for his home. How appropriately such a resting place is called "God's acre." There we buried him, in the early springtime, when the opening bud, the sprouting grain, and the springing grass were nature's assurances of the life to come.

CHAPTER VI

DEVELOPMENT OF A LAWMAKER

Growth in the Senate—Personal Characteristics

TO those who look back now upon his service in the Senate it is plain that the traits which later gave him his peculiar hold were his in the beginning. From first to last there was a steady, even growth in qualities which make a well-poised legislator, and the germs were there at the outset in his patient industry, sound judgment, and rectitude. He liked to go slow and be sure; he was honest in his speech and in his mental processes; it has been said of him that he thought on oath. His early years in the Senate were marked by faithful attention to the duties of his place, by quiet observation of what was going on, by contented acceptance of responsibilities which gradually lengthening service brought upon him. Little known at the time of his election, he felt bound to justify it by being as good a Senator as he could. So he worked ploddingly on the committees of which he was a member until he mastered the business of each and investigated with scrupulous minuteness every question that came up to him. He could not rest contented with a thing half done, and his satisfaction came in the performance rather than in the resulting praise. "I have no ambitions," he wrote once; "what I do, I do because it is set me to do, and I have a feeling that I ought to do

it as thoroughly and as well as I can.   That is about
all of it "; and again: " There is a scriptural text somewhere in which Christ says of a woman, 'She hath done
what she could.'   I have never had any other motive."
In pronouncing a eulogy on Senator Gear of Iowa, he
unconsciously came very near describing himself:

All types of our people find their representatives here,
and it is well that it is so. Men of commanding intellect,
genius, eloquence, and brilliancy are both needed and
found in these senatorial seats, but other men equally
representing the people and equally useful, who do not
attract popular enthusiasm by reason of any unusual or
striking gifts, are quite as much needed here—men of
strong good sense, men of affairs, of great industry, and
unswerving devotion to the principles and the interests of
the Republic; men whose general characteristics can best
be described by three grand words—sturdy, faithful, and
true. Senator Gear was such a man. Sometimes I think
I would rather it should be written on my tombstone,
"He was sturdy, faithful, and true," than to have it
written, "he was eloquent, learned, and great."

Thus he went from session to session and term to
term, a little broader and stronger each year, a little
more confident in himself, a little better understood.
Gradually he became known among his brother Senators
as one who could always be relied upon, who had no
axes of his own to grind, and who thought and acted
truthfully.   It was not long before they found out that
he was a good lawyer and that his judgment was always
sure to be nearly right.   In the intimate association
which comes from continued service in a comparatively
small body they grew to trust him and to like him.   He
made no enemies in the Senate, any more than in
Meriden; and he did in the Senate exactly as in Meriden,

except that the things he had to do and the questions
he had to study carried a wider range. He had no
fads. He did not delude himself with the notion that
he was clothed with a mission. He attended to each
day's work religiously, and when one task was completed he laid it aside to take up another. To every
question big or little he gave the same painstaking
conscientious consideration, and tried to get at the
kernel of truth in it no matter how tough the rind,
without giving a thought to whether getting at it would
increase his reputation or not. He used to be in his
place whenever the Senate was in session, and those
who had questionable measures in hand learned to
dread his slowly spoken " Let that go over." Sometimes he was called a " watch-dog of the Treasury, " but
he did not like the name and it did not fairly belong to
him. He was not an indiscriminate objector, but he
wanted the Senate to know what it was doing before it
passed a bill. So it came about that Senators got in
the way of going to him for information and advice,
and of saying among themselves, "What does Platt
think of it?" before making up their minds. Years
before he gained much reputation outside the Senate
chamber, he was regarded there as one of the most
effective men in public life. When he died, Senator
Cullom, who had served with him more than twenty
years, expressed of him an opinion to which every other
Senator would doubtless give assent:

Senator Platt was capable in more ways to do what
the exigencies of the day from time to time put upon him,
than any other man in the Senate. He was always at
his post of duty,—always watchful in caring for the interests of the country, always just and fair to all alike,
and was always careful and conservative in determining

what his duty should be in the disposition of any public question; and his judgment was a little more exactly right than that of any other Senator.

It was only natural that he should be entrusted with work of steadily increasing importance as time went by. When Congress was ready for Federal supervision of railroads, he had been eight years a Senator and by common consent he was assigned to the special committee having that question in hand. When at the beginning of the tariff agitation of 1887 the Finance Committee were looking for help, they turned intuitively to Platt, because he was painstaking, thorough, and dependable, and even before the way was open to make him formally a member of the committee he was one of the props of the majority in everything relating to tariff and finance; when they were looking for somebody whom they could trust in the devious windings of Indian legislation, their eyes fell easily upon Platt; when the Judiciary Committee wanted a sane, careful, and tactful associate, they thought first of Platt; and every added responsibility he assumed without eagerness or protest, regardless of whether the new duties were likely to be congenial or not. He never pressed his claims for assignment to any particular committee, but was willing to let the regular processes of the Senate work in their own way. He was considerate of the feelings of others and never blocked the path of his more ambitious associates. So in course of years he gained authority among his fellows, begotten of understanding and confidence, and when the war with Spain came on with its weighty questions to be solved, the Senate turned to him with general assent as one well qualified to help in their solution. That his name should have been attached to the Platt Amendment and so become familiar everywhere was merely an incident; for his work in relation to the Platt Amendment was in line with what he had been doing right along, service which was valued by those who kept track of legislation, but which, owing to his own indifference to contemporary fame, never brought him the popular recognition he deserved. Had the Platt Amendment never been framed, he would have had a high place in the records of the Senate just the same.

He was no orator. He had no faculty for rousing enthusiasm, and was quite lacking in the personal magnetism which sways men in masses and which his colleague Hawley had in such generous measure. Public speaking had no glitter or charm for him. It was rarely that he experienced the responsive tingle that comes from popular applause. He regretted his own short-coming as he acknowledged Hawley's gift; but he never disclosed a trace of envy because Hawley had what he did not possess. He has been described as sitting in the Senate, almost lounging in his chair, which for years was in the front row directly under the eye of the presiding officer, his head often thrown back as if half asleep, or bent forward over his desk as though he were thinking of other things. But the questions he asked or the suggestions he made from time to time showed that he was following closely what was going on. When he rose to speak, he used slowly to stretch his arms over the desk, unbend his legs, and get to his feet by degrees, as if hesitating what to say or whether to speak at all. Whenever he had anything on his mind he said it without waiting to see whether the galleries were full or empty. He had a way of talking straight on, slowly and deliberately, using homely phrases and few adjectives, with a simplicity and directness that carried conviction of his sincerity no matter whether the listener agreed with him or not. He was never extravagant in statement, and after he had made a positive assertion there were few who were reckless enough to dispute it. Though having little of the art of oratory, yet in the scriptural dignity of his diction he sometimes rose to heights which could not be surpassed by those more skilled in rhetoric. He was not a frequent speaker. He never took the floor unless he had something pertinent to propose, some argument to elucidate, or some misunderstanding to set right. He seldom made a set speech. Outside an occasional eulogy, through all his service in the Senate, their number could almost be counted on one's fingers. Whatever he said was prompted by the circumstances of the moment; because he had something in his head which nobody else was likely to put exactly as he would like to see it expressed. When on the occasion of a public meeting or dinner he was obliged to prepare an address, he used to "agonize" over it, to borrow one of his own words, and even to the last he dreaded setting down in advance of delivery what he was expected to say. "Pumping water out of a dry well," he called it. As a lawyer, he would have appealed more effectively to a bench of judges than to a jury, and that, as it happens, is just the quality which gets a man a hearing in the Senate.

After his death, a writer who knew him well gave this truthful picture of his appearance in debate:

Physically Senator Platt was no less noteworthy than mentally. In his later years he used to be likened to a Hebrew prophet. Once suggested, that thought was never forgotten as one looked at him. There was a rugged strength in the sharp-cut features, strong and individual

as though chiselled in hard gray stone, an austerity in the
moulding of the mouth, in the outline of the jaw beneath the
short gray beard, in the whole pose of the man—he must
have stood six feet four inches tall—that stamped him a
ruler. He was slender and graceful, too, in his carriage
despite the slight bend that came with the years, and his
head was ever erect. His attitude as he addressed the
Senate was always the same. With one foot slightly
advanced, and with one hand pressed on the desk beside
him so that he leaned slightly from the shoulders, he
would stand with his head thrown back and speak slowly
and briefly without gesture, speaking distinctly but in a
quiet tone, looking upward rather than at his listeners, and
weighing each word as he uttered it, as if he had fused all
the factors of the problem in the crucible of his mind and
were but reporting in the minimum of words the conscientious result. There was no borrowed effect of impressive-
ness; he was naturally impressive or austere in the severe
simplicity of his manner. He often or commonly qualified
his statements with a slow "it seems to me" that added
rather than subtracted weight.[1]

As he continued in service and became one of the
veterans of the Senate, his unselfish helpfulness was
more and more in evidence, so that he had the affection
of his associates as well as their esteem. Sometimes
he felt that work was being heaped upon him beyond
his power to endure, but no matter what it was he never
thought of shirking. "I am nothing but a dray-horse
anyway," he said, "and I suppose that I must pull the
load as long as I can stand"; and another time he wrote:
"I would rather be an old work-horse drawing my daily
load than an old race-horse turned out to pasture."

After he had been in the Senate a good many years, a
newspaper asked him to answer the question:

[1] The Springfield *Republican*, April 22, 1905.

"What must a young man do to become a Senator of the United States?" The reply he made is suggestive of the spirit in which he carried on his work:

In reply to your question I would say: First, that a young man had better not have such an ambition, as he will only be disappointed if he achieves it; because the life of a United States Senator is one of hard work, which is never understood and never appreciated. If the young man simply desires to obtain the place for any credit or honor that may pertain to it, and if that fills his ambition without regard to what he may achieve as a Senator, that is one thing; but the Senate is much like the old-time schoolhouse—divided into classes. If a man is to get into the first class and sit on the first bench he has got to do it by intense study and work, and whatever class he may be in he only "goes up one" because of some superiority. This is an immense country; subjects of legislation embrace the widest range, and require the widest information; and to act intelligently a Senator must possess the widest information about every subject. The greater his information the more useful he becomes. Add to this that he is expected to be the agent of every one in his State who has business in Washington, legislative, political, or commercial—and you obtain a glimpse of what a Senator must do and be to obtain a successful reputation.

Second—If in spite of my advice any young man will persist in cherishing the ambition you name, his whole life should be a study of political affairs. The Senatorship may be thrust on him; it may come as the result of wealth, which follows business enterprise; but the clean and honorable road to it is through a study of public affairs, and the capacity to impress the people of his State with the idea that he possesses a thorough knowledge of them and will be their true representative.

Third—His idea of politics should be a lofty one. His motive for devotion to public life should be that he may render service to the people rather than to accomplish personal success. Few men will ever reach the Senate as a result of a talent for political manipulation, and those who thus succeed will be senatorial nonentities rather than senatorial leaders.

As he grew older he was spared the common failing of the old, a loss of mental elasticity. Instead, his faculties seemed constantly to expand so as to embrace new themes of national interest, and at his death, in all that goes to constitute a public servant he was intellectually younger than most of his associates who could not count so many years. He seemed to have learned the secret of perpetual youth, so that when the end came at the age of nearly fourscore the blow was as unexpected as though he had been a young man of promise just entering upon a new career.

When the venerable Henry Clay Trumbull congratulated him on his last election to the Senate, he replied:

You speak of growing old. Of course, the days are told off, one by one, and they go pretty rapidly sometimes, especially down here during a session of Congress, but so far as a man's actual age by years is concerned, that does not amount to much. I count no man old, who lives in the present, and thinks in the future.

CHAPTER VII

Chairman of the Patents Committee—Preserving the Patent System
—Speech of March 24, 1884—Friend of the American Inventor.

ILLUSTRATIVE of the spirit which guided the Senator through years of unselfish service was his work for the inventors of the United States. From the beginning almost to the very end of his career, he gladly gave himself without reserve to what to others might have seemed a thankless task, the shaping of patent legislation and the prevention of vicious patent laws. On all questions relating to these subjects, he spoke with unchallenged authority. It did not bring him general reputation; for newspapers do not advertise such quiet success. They save their headlines for spectacular effects, the melodrama and extravaganza of the legislative stage. But what he accomplished brought him the satisfaction of work far-reaching and well done, and that was all he cared for. If he lost the passing notoriety of the day, he wrote his name in shining letters in the history of American Invention where it will be read in years to come.

Beyond most men, he realized the poetry of patents, —invention's most effective stimulant and lure. The time in which we live he liked to call the age of machinery, and through it he believed the world was about to enter, if it had not already entered, a spiritual age when mind should triumph over matter, brain over muscle, when man should conquer nature's forces and make them all his slaves. For him the wonderful advancement in the realm of science and in the development of the mechanic arts was not the mark of a materialistic time; it was the evidence of higher things. For him an engine had the beauty of a sculptor's masterpiece; its rhythm was the music of the progress of mankind. Books without number had been written to tell us of the noble influence upon the character of man exerted by the scenes in which he dwells —" by mountain and forest, by brook and river and ocean, by clear sky and fleecy clouds, by the rare tints of sunset and dawn, by breaking billow and roaring blasts," but who should write, he asked, of that greater and subtler moulding influence exerted upon the character of man by his subjection of the forces of the earth and air to be his ministering spirits:

Compare the man who muses on nature, who drinks in the influence of the mountain from afar, with the man who pierces that mountain to make a highway for the distribution of the world's products, or digs out from their dungeon the imprisoned metals, to be wrought into implements for his own use, and tell me which man grows most and best. Which is the most of a man, he who gazes with awe on the dark storm-cloud and sees in the lightning only the manifestation of the wrath of an angry God, or he who subdues the lightning and makes it his servant and sends it to and fro on missions of mercy and sympathy to his fellow-man?[1]

Having this vision it is not strange that he discovered

[1] Address before the Congress in celebration of the beginning of the Second Century of the American Patent System, April 9, 1891.

the most significant event between the founding of the government and the Civil War, not in the crowded pages of political history, but in the little-known Act of 1836, which under the express authority of the Constitution created the Patent Office, and gave American inventors their first substantial recognition; nor was it to be wondered that he found congenial occupation in the task set for him of preserving the integrity of that act and blocking the schemes of those who would have done it to its death. He logically became a member of the Patents Committee at the beginning of his first Congress. There was a vacancy caused by the retirement of his predecessor, Barnum, and Platt was thought to be a good man for the place because his practice at home had much to do with patent law. It was natural, too, that Connecticut should be represented on the Committee, because in proportion to her population she stands at the head of all the States in the number of patents issued to her citizens. When the Republicans secured control in 1881, he became Chairman of the Committee and served as chairman ten years in all, one period of six years ending in 1887, when he went to the head of the Committee on Territories, the other period of four years terminating in 1899, when he was entrusted with the great responsibility of the newly created Committee on Relations with Cuba. He was a member of the Committee until 1903, and to the end of his service in the Senate he was looked upon as the highest authority in Congress on patent law. To reproduce his record would be to recite the catalogue of legislation during all that time, and he had to handle some of the most important measures affecting patents and copyrights enacted during the last three quarters of a century.

About the time he became Chairman of the Committee, the farmers of the West were up in arms on account of what they regarded as the extortions of those who held the patents on barbed wire and driven wells. The question was rapidly getting into politics, and there was danger that Congress would try to appease them by passing general legislation which would work hardship to innocent inventors not involved in the dispute. Mr. Platt was disturbed by the prospect, and tried to appease the discontent by moderate legislation. One of the first bills he introduced and reported as Chairman of the Committee in 1882 was to regulate practice in patent suits. It provided that where a defendant innocently bought a patented article or device for his own personal use and the plaintiff did not recover more than twenty dollars, no costs should be recovered of the plaintiff. He tried to get a vote on the bill in the Senate, but amendments were moved and objections interposed. "There are two sides to be considered here," he pleaded:

There are those who suffer from the acts of unprincipled men, and there are honest patentees throughout the country. The rights of both parties are to be considered, and I do not think that the people, particularly at the West, who have been imposed upon and made to pay money unreasonably and improperly, want to insist upon any bill or any amendment to this bill which will work a hardship to the honest patentee.

The bill went over; the pressure on Congress continued; but it was two years before anything else was done.

The first session of the Forty-eighth Congress in 1884 is memorable in the history of American invention. Mr. Platt was serving a second term as Chairman of the Patents Committee and it fell to him to save the patent system from serious injury. The House of Representatives early in the session passed a bill to regulate procedure in patent suits in cases of infringement by innocent users and purchasers of patented devices. It was intended to remedy the evils complained of by the farmers but its provisions were drastic. The true nature and effect of the measure do not seem to have been clearly understood. It passed the House without debate under suspension of the rules, and when it came to the Senate, the Patents Committee instructed the Chairman to report it favorably. No sooner did the inventors of the United States begin to realize what was going on than a storm of protest arose which soon reached the halls of Congress. It was contended that the suggested change would destroy the usefulness of the Patent Office and bring American inventive genius to a pause.

Mr. Platt, against the judgment of the majority of his committee, set to work to prevent the injury which was threatened. On March 24, 1884, hardly a month from the time the bill had been reported, he introduced a bill of his own which was intended to fix the attention of the Senate upon the patent system in a way which would react against unfriendly legislation. The bill proposed to make an independent department of the Patent Office, divorcing it from the Interior Department under which it was placed, and giving it a status like that of the Department of Agriculture, which at that time was presided over by a commissioner, and not by a cabinet officer. The bill also gave to the Patent Office exclusive control of the building now known as the Interior Department, and of the fund pertaining to the office. A few days after introducing this bill,

Mr. Platt delivered a speech in support of it which was regarded at the time as the best defence ever made of the American patent system, and which, betraying extraordinary thoroughness of research, remains to-day the most comprehensive and authoritative public utterance concerning its development.   He said:

The growth of our patent system, its vast importance, its intimate connection with and direct influence upon the property of the country demand that it shall receive a degree of attention which it can not and will not receive while it remains a merely subordinate bureau of the Interior Department.

After tracing the history of the patent system to its origin in the grant of enumerated powers in the Constitution, he declared that to his mind the passage of the Act of 1836, creating the Patent Office, was the most important event in the history of the Government, prior to the War of the Rebellion.   He presented pages of statistics to show that the unexampled progress of the United States had been dependent upon and co-incident with the growth and development of the patent system:

All history confirms us in the conclusion that it is the development, by the mechanic arts, of the industries of a country, which brings to it greatness and power and glory. No purely agricultural, pastoral people ever achieved any high standing among the nations of the earth.   It is only when the brain evolves and the cunning hand fashions labor-saving machines that a nation begins to throb with new energy and life and expands with a new growth.   It is only when thought wrings from nature her untold secret treasures that solid wealth and strength are accumulated by a people.   Especially is this true in a republic.   Under arbitrary forms of government kings may oppress the laborer, kings may conquer other nations, may oppress and degrade the men who till the soil, and they may thus acquire wealth; but in a republic it is only when the citizen conquers nature, appropriates her resources, and extorts her riches that you find real wealth and power.

We witness our development; we are proud of our success; we congratulate ourselves, we felicitate ourselves on all that we enjoy; but we scarcely ever stop to think of the cause of all this prosperity and enjoyment. Indeed, this prosperity has become so common that we expect it. Many men forget to what they owe it; many men I am sorry to say in these recent years deny the cause of it all. The truth is, we live in this atmosphere of invention; it surrounds us as does the light and the air; like light and air it is one of our greatest blessings; and yet we pass it by without thought. Some say that the cause of all this wealth, of all this influence in the world, springs from other sources; some say it is the result of our free institutions, of our Christian civilization, of our habits of industry, of our respect for the law, of the vastness of our natural resources, but I say inventive skill is the primal cause of all this progress and growth. I say the policy which found expression in the Constitution of the United States when this clause was enacted, giving Congress power "to promote the progress of science and useful arts by securing for limited times to authors and inventors the exclusive right to their respective writings and discoveries," has been the policy that has built up this fair fabric.

Concede all you claim: Free institutions, Christian civilization, industrious habits, great respect for law; acknowledge all our vast natural resources; and then deduct patents and patented inventions from the causes which have led to this development, and you have subtracted from material, yes, from moral, prosperity nearly all that is worth enjoying. Subtract invention from the causes which have led to our growth and our grandeur and you remit us, you remit our people, to the condition of the people of Italy, of Switzerland, of Russia. If "knowledge is power," invention is prosperity.

Let us turn a moment from the present and take one rapid glance at the past. Consider the country as it was fifty years ago. The cotton-gin, the steamboat, the railroad, the power-loom, the printing-press, were indeed in embryo, but their development was partial and their use was extremely limited. It was still the age of homespun; it was still the age of hand labor. Brain had not, so far as production was concerned, superseded muscle. We had then twenty-six States. When the commencement of our present patent system really began, there were twenty-six States in the Union. Twelve new ones and eight Territories added since are in my judgment a tribute to the inventive genius of this country and to the perfection of its patent system.

Three classes of men had made possible the advancement of the United States in material prosperity: First, the inventors; second, the manufacturers; third the skilled laborers. The farmer had become a skilled laborer. "He purchases a machine. He no longer toils with the rude implements of the past." Without patents, the agriculture of the day would be impossible, and a large proportion of the agricultural lands of the country would be inaccessible. Without the use of patents, the entire population capable of labor in the country could not raise the cereal productions and get the surplus to a market. He denied that inventions were opposed to the interests of labor. Whenever a labor-saving machine is invented, there is no destruction of labor, but redistribution. The man relieved from a particular kind of labor by the introduction of a mechanical device engages in some higher employment. New inventions open new fields of labor. Patents are educators. The man who lives in the atmosphere of

invention produces more than the one who does not.
The man who learns to operate a complicated machine
acquires education of as much real value as the man
who learns to conjugate Greek verbs. "There is an
education of the college; there is also an education of
the factory and the field. We may not despise or neglect either." He contended that the right of the
inventor was as much entitled to the protection of the
Government as any other species of property; that it
was excelled in point of dignity by no other property
right whatever, and was equalled in point of dignity
only by the rights which authors have in their copyrighted books. The property in patents was a property
which contained within itself the principle of the
reproduction of property, and that was a characteristic
which attached to no other species of property. Every
patent had in it the germ of a new patent, which in
time was property:

Nature is one vast storehouse of wealth, but it is a
locked storehouse, and the human brain alone can unlock
it. Invention is the magic key? Men seek gold in the
bowels of the earth, but it lies in the air, in light, in the
gases, in electricity. It needs no enchanter's wand, no
talismanic words to set it free—only the processes of
thought. . . .
We stand but in the very vestibule of the great store-
houses of nature's secrets. We have but gathered a
few pebbles along the shore on which beats a limitless sea.
. . . We live in a wonderland. The miracle of yesterday
is the commonplace of to-day. The dream of the present
is to be the fact of the immediate future.

He had heard it said that men would have invented
without regard to the encouragement given to them by
our patent laws; that, even if their property in patents

were not protected, they would have gone on inventing all the same; that there had been in some way a marvellous birth in this country of inventive capacity, and that it must grow whether protected or not.

It is not true [he declared]; the inventor is no more a philanthropist than is the agriculturist. He works for his support. He works to achieve a competency. He invents, if you please, to become rich; but he is no more a philanthropist than any other man in any other walk or avocation of life, and you have no right to demand of him that he shall be a mere philanthropist. He is entitled to his reward. He is a laborer entitled to his hire, entitled to it more if possible than any other laborer, as his labor is higher in dignity and grandeur than that of any other laborer.

Having thus dwelt upon the marvels of invention, he presented practical considerations in support of his bill. He said the Patent Office should be made an independent department, not only because of the vast importance of the interests which it must care for, but because of the treatment which it had received and must continue to receive so long as it remained a subordinate branch of the Interior Department. The Interior Department was overburdened. No one man could discharge its duties properly:

If the Secretary of the Interior had as many heads as the Hindoo divinity Siva, and as many arms as Briareus, he could not personally perform all the duties pertaining to his office that would be most acceptably performed if he could give them personal attention.

The duties to be performed by the Secretary in other branches of the Department would probably always lead in the future, as in the past, to the selection of a man for the place without special adaptation to the important work of the Patent Office:

Public opinion demands that the Secretary of the Interior must have defined ideas relating to the Indian policy; that he must have a knowledge of the laws relating to the Indian policy; that he must have a knowledge of the laws relating to public lands; that he must understand the operation of the railroads in their relation to the Government; that he must have a territorial knowledge which will enable him to administer, so far as his duty requires, the affairs of the Territories. He must have been trained in a different school from the man who should be selected for Commissioner of Patents or for the head of the Patent Department. Let me illustrate.

If the Secretary of the Interior is to be the superior officer, he must pass upon questions of administration which he cannot so well understand as the commissioner. Under the practice of the office he passes on most complicated questions affecting the right to inventions. There has been no Secretary of the Interior within my knowledge who has had any special adaptation to that office, who has been selected at all with reference to his mechanical judgment or mechanical skill, or because of his superior understanding of the complicated questions of patent law.

The head of the Patent Office should combine an accurate and almost universal knowledge of mechanical principles with a thorough knowledge of patent law and with rare executive and administrative ability. His position should be one of entire independence, as his duties are more judicial than executive. The office should be permanent and not subject to political changes.

Practical arguments there were why the entire building of the Interior Department should be turned over to the Patent Office:

The space which is allotted to the clerical employees of the Patent Office may be large enough for a dungeon, it may be large enough for a tomb, and it may be a little too large for a grave, but it is not a fit amount of room for a human being to live and do the work of this Government in. . . .

I have visited the Patent Office, and I undertake to say that, if any Senator will go there and see where the clerks are performing their duties, will see where the most skilled experts of the country, with the best scientific attainments, are performing their duties, down in the rooms which, until it became absolutely necessary to have more space, were used only for coal cellars, huddled together where the sunlight rarely or never shines in the room, where there is little or no ventilation, and where the air is so foul that I venture to say no Senator can stay an hour without becoming nauseated and sick, I think he would have little doubt that something should be done not only to increase the efficiency of the office, but to prevent the almost barbarous treatment of its employees.

And yet this " pauper whom nobody owns " was the only self-sustaining branch of the Government, with a fund to its credit of $2,727,107, " not including the amount that Congress took from its fund to help pay for the building, into the basement and coal cellars of which it has been largely crowded."

The bill which Mr. Platt introduced served only as a text for his speech. It never went farther on the legislative road, but that it was not framed in vain appears from the proceedings of April 21st, when Mr. McPherson of New Jersey, presenting a formidable array of remonstrances against the House and Senate bills to regulate practice in patent suits, moved to recommit the bills to the Patents Committee:

Considering [he said] the vast amount of interests involved in this matter, and considering also that all of these interests are to a great extent imperilled and held subject to the wisdom of Congress touching all matters relating to the patent laws, and considering further the very able and exhaustive argument made by the honorable Chairman of that Committee (Mr. Platt) upon this subject a few days ago, I have felt emboldened to ask the consent of this committee to review its work, and if possible present to the Senate some more equitable, some better mode of remedying the evils complained of than is found in the bills now before the Senate.

The motions were agreed to and the threatened peril was averted.

It was Mr. Platt's lot, during his long service, to aid in framing many acts relating to patents, so that there are few existing laws which do not bear his imprint, and even in the last days of his life he was in conference with the leaders of the American bar, with reference to reform in the patent laws still to be secured. But though he had done nothing else, the service he rendered in the Forty-eighth Congress would have been enough to earn him the lasting gratitude of American inventors.

CHAPTER VIII

International Copyright—A Legislative Triumph—Law of 1891—
Subsequent Legislation.

M R. PLATT'S name is justly associated more closely than that of any other legislator with the work done for bringing the United States into copyright relations with Europe. Under his skilful leadership, the campaign which for over half a century had been carried on without practical results by the publishers and authors of the United States, culminated in the enactment by the Fifty-first Congress of a law which for the first time assured to foreign authors protection in the United States for the property rights in their productions, and which secured at the same time reciprocal protection in Europe for the works of American authors.

The question of international copyright was first brought before Congress in 1837, when Henry Clay presented an address from certain authors of Great Britain representing the injury caused to their literary property and to their property interests, through the want of a law securing to them within the United States the exclusive control of their productions, and requesting, in behalf of the authors of Great Britain, a remedy through legislation. The address was referred to a select committee made up of Henry Clay, William

C. Preston, James Buchanan, Daniel Webster, Thomas Ewing, and John Ruggles, which committee reported a bill for the amendment of the copyright statute by the addition of an international provision. The bill drafted by Clay on the lines of the report of the committee remains one of the classics of legislative literature. Memorials urging its passage, signed by the leading writers of the United States, among them, Washington Irving, Edward Everett, Rufus Choate, John Quincy Adams, William Cullen Bryant, and Robert C. Winthrop, and further memorials signed by a publishers' committee, the representatives of which were William H. Appleton and George P. Putnam, were laid before Congress. Petitions were also submitted in opposition to the proposed legislation. Mr. Clay never succeeded in securing action upon his bill, the provisions of which were in accord with the statute passed in 1891, and with that which went into force in 1909, in requiring American manufacture for the books securing copyright. It was presented in the Senate five times, but was voted upon only once, in 1840, when it was ordered to lie upon the table.

Between 1837 and 1842, numerous petitions favoring international copyright were presented to Congress, petitions which included in addition to the signatures of nearly all the leading authors of the country, the names of the representatives of the Publishers' Copyright League.

In 1838, after the passing of the first international copyright act in Great Britain, Lord Palmerston invited the American Government to co-operate in shaping a copyright convention between the two countries.

In 1842, George P. Putnam brought again into activity the American Copyright League, and presented a memorial drafted by himself, and signed by ninety-seven publishers and printers, in which it was stated that the absence of an international copyright was "alike injurious to the business of publishing and to the best interests of the people at large."

In 1848, a memorial, drafted by George P. Putnam and signed by William C. Bryant, John Jay, and others, was presented to Congress, asking for a copyright measure similar in principle to that which was enacted in 1891. The memorial was ordered printed and was referred to a committee, from which no report was made.

In 1853, George P. Putnam, writing on behalf of the leading publishers of New York, including Charles Scribner, William H. Appleton, Mason Brothers, and others, addressed a letter to Mr. Everett, Secretary of State, recommending the framing of a copyright convention with Great Britain.

Charles Sumner, then Chairman of the Senate Committee on Foreign Affairs, interested himself in the subject, and reported to the Senate a treaty drafted by Edward Everett and himself. The proposal had the approval of President Fillmore, but it was met in Congress with a storm of remonstrance.

In 1854, President Pierce secured an additional article extending the time limit for the exchange of ratifications, but the Senate allowed the treaty to expire without action.

In 1867, Mr. Samuel M. Arnell, of Tennessee, secured the passage of a resolution in the House of Representatives directing the Joint Library Committee to inquire into the subject of international copyright, and to make a report. Such a report was presented to the House in 1868 by Mr. J. G. Baldwin, of Massachusetts, accompanied by a bill which was based upon a draft submitted from the Copyright Association of New York by W. C. Bryant, President, and George P. Putnam, Secretary. This bill secured copyright to foreign authors, with the condition that their books should be manufactured in the United States. It was referred to the Joint Committee on the Library, from which it never emerged.

In 1868, the American Copyright Association was reorganized in response to a letter headed " Justice to Authors and to Artists," which was issued by a committee comprising George P. Putnam, Dr. S. I. Prime, Henry Iverson, and James Parton. Of this Association, Mr. Bryant was made President. At the instance of this Association, a bill was prepared, which was introduced into the House in 1871 by S. S. Cox of Ohio, and in the Senate by John Sherman, also of Ohio. The bill, however, stirred up the usual flock of adverse petitions, as a result of which it was reported unfavorably by the Joint Committee on the Library, which at that time had charge of copyright business.

In 1870, the so-called Clarendon Treaty was proposed through Mr. Thornton, the British Minister at Washington. The proposed treaty gave to the authors and artists of each country the privilege of copyright in the other by registering the work within three months of the date of the original publication.

In 1872, a bill was again presented from the Publishers' Association, which provided that the American edition of the foreign work securing American copyright should be manufactured in this country, and that the American register of copyright should be made within one month of the date of the original publication. In the same year, the draft of a bill was submitted by Mr. John P. Morton, publisher of Louisville, under which any American publisher was to be at liberty to reprint the work of a foreign author on the condition of making payment to such author of a ten per cent. royalty.

Later in the same year a similar measure was introduced by Mr. Beck and Mr. Sherman providing that the royalty should be five per cent.   Both of these bills were buried in the Library Committee.

In 1873, Senator Lot M. Morrill of Maine, on behalf of the Library Committee, reported adversely to the consideration by Congress of any international copyright bill on the ground that "there was no unanimity of opinion among those interested in the measure."

In 1874, Mr. Henry B. Banning, of Ohio, introduced into the House the sixth international copyright bill, which secured copyright for foreign authors on the simple condition of reciprocity.   The bill was referred to the Committee on Patents where it remained.

In 1878, a project for a copyright convention or treaty was submitted on behalf of the Publishers' Association to Mr. Evarts, then Secretary of State, and in 1880, the draft of a convention in line with this scheme from the publishers was submitted by Mr. Lowell to Lord Granville.

In 1880, a petition was submitted to Congress, signed by President Woolsey, of Yale, and by a number of authors, publishers, and printers, asking for the enactment of a bill extending to foreign authors, composers, and designers the privilege of copyright in the United States.

In 1882, Mr. Robinson, of New York, presented a bill giving consideration to the whole subject of copyright, domestic and international.   It was referred to the Committee on Patents, where it was buried.

In 1883, the eighth international copyright bill was

introduced by Mr. Patrick A. Collins, of Massachusetts. This also was buried in the Committee on Patents.

In 1884, the ninth international copyright bill was introduced into the House by Mr. Dorsheimer, of New York. This provided simply for the extension to foreign authors of the privileges enjoyed by the citizens or residents of the United States. This bill was approved by the Copyright League, and was favorably reported to the House by the Committee on the Judiciary, to which it had been referred. It reached the stage of being discussed in the House, but a resolution to fix a date for its final consideration was defeated.

President Arthur, in his first annual message, reported to Congress that negotiations for an International Copyright Convention were in hopeful progress. The President, however, deemed it inadvisable to complete such negotiation until Congress should by statute fix the extent of the privileges to be secured in the United States by foreign holders of copyright. This country was accordingly not represented at the convention that was called in Berne in 1886, which resulted in bringing the states of Europe into copyright relations with each other.

In the same year a bill was introduced into the House by Mr. English dealing with international copyright in dramatic compositions. It was referred to the Judiciary Committee, which took no action.

In 1885, President Cleveland permitted the envoy of the United States to be present at the Berne Conference as a delegate, but without the power of committing the Government to any action.

In 1885, The American (Authors') Copyright League was reorganized with Mr. Lowell as President and Mr. Stedman as Vice-President. Mr. Platt had long shown a keen interest in the purpose of the Copyright Leagues and had come into personal relations with a number of those who were working to secure justice to authors. His first official connection with the movement, however, was when on the 13th of January, 1886, he secured unanimous consent for a resolution authorizing the Committee on Patents to take testimony relating to a bill introduced by his colleague General Hawley to establish an international copyright. The bill of Senator Hawley was substantially identical with that which had been introduced a year back by Mr. Dorsheimer. It was referred to the Senate Committee on Patents. A similar bill was introduced in the House by J. Randolph Tucker of Virginia, and was referred to the Committee on Judiciary.

Both committees failed to make any report, and the cause of copyright appeared, therefore, to be no further advanced than at the time when it was first brought to the attention of the Senate in 1837 by Henry Clay, but the leaven of half a century's teaching had been working both with the public and with Congress.

In 1886, President Cleveland, in his message of December 6th, gave to the movement a more emphatic endorsement than had been given by any of his predecessors. At the request of the representatives of the Publishers' Committee, Mr. Cleveland included in his message the following paragraph:

The drift of sentiment in civilized communities toward full recognition of the rights of property in the creations of the human intellect has brought about the adoption by many important nations of an international copyright convention, which was signed at Berne on the 18th of September, 1886. Inasmuch as the Constitution gives to Congress the power "to promote the progress of science and useful arts by securing for limited times to authors and inventors the exclusive right to their respective writings and discoveries," this Government did not feel warranted in becoming a signatory pending the`action of Congress upon measures of international copyright now before it, but the right of adhesion to the Berne Convention hereafter has been reserved. I trust the subject will receive at your hands the attention it deserves, and that the just claims of authors, so urgently pressed, will be duly heeded.

The action of the Convention of Berne in bringing into copyright relations with each other nearly all of the states of Europe unquestionably had its effect upon sentiment in the United States, and prepared the way for the work which was to be accomplished a little later by Mr. Platt and other leaders in Congress whose interest he had secured in the undertaking.

The Secretary of the American Publishers' Copyright League, from its re-organization in 1866 to the present time, has been George Haven Putnam. The Secretaries of the Authors' League have been successively George P. Lathrop, George W. Green, and Robert Underwood Johnson, who was elected in 1888. The two associations carried on a systematic campaign of "education," as a result of which the press throughout the country declared itself overwhelmingly in favor of the reform, and petitions urging copyright law rained in upon Congress from educators and leading citizens generally.

In 1888, a Joint Campaign Committee was formed, representing the authors, publishers, printers, the Typographical Union and other interests, which had arrived at an agreement upon a bill believed to be practicable. During the year ending March, 1891, Mr. Johnson acted as a secretary of this joint committee; and its Chairman was Dr. Edward Eggleston, whose

service and personal influence in Washington proved
very valuable. The publishers were represented on the
Committee by Charles Scribner and W. W. Appleton.
The labor of framing the successive bills fell chiefly
to the members and to the counsel of the Publishers'
Committee.

In 1888, Senator Chace, of Rhode Island, reported
favorably from the Patents Committee a bill that had
been introduced by himself, and a similar bill was reported from the Judiciary Committee of the House by
Patrick A. Collins, of Massachusetts. The Chace bill,
with some amendment, passed the Senate on the 9th of
May, 1888, by a vote of 35 to 10. It was reported
favorably by the Judiciary Committee of the House,
but no further action could be secured.

The first draft of the bill, which was submitted to
Senator Chace by the Joint Committee of the Authors
and Publishers, provided that foreign books securing
American copyright must be printed in the United
States, but permitted the importation of *clichés* of the
type, or of duplicates of the plates which had been
prepared for printing the original editions. It was
contended that for certain classes of books the necessity
of doing the typesetting twice instead of dividing this
cost between an English and an American edition,
would involve a wasteful expense, the burden of which
would have to be shared between the readers, the
authors, and the publishers. On the other hand, the
Typographical Unions insisted that a provision for
American typesetting was essential for their trade
interests, and that unless such a provision should be
inserted, they would be under the necessity of opposing
the bill.

It was the opinion of Senator Chace, and of other
of the Congressional friends of copyright, that the

co-operation of the Unions would be very important, while their influence against the bill in committee and through their friends in the House would probably be sufficiently powerful to prevent its passage, at least in the near future. It was, therefore, decided by the authors and publishers of the two leagues to accept on this point the contentions of the typographers and to utilize their co-operation. The International Typographical Union selected as its representative on the Joint Campaign Committee Mr. John L. Kennedy, of the Washington Union, whose service proved valuable in more ways than one.

The advocates of honest dealing in literary affairs, at the beginning of the new Republican administration of 1889, found their cause still far from success, but with the sentiment of the public appreciably aroused, and with an increasingly intelligent interest on the part of leaders in the two Houses.

President Harrison in his first message laconically expressed the opinion that the enactment of an international copyright law would be "eminently wise and just." Missionary work with Congress began at once, and the Copyright Leagues set about creating a sentiment at the capital commensurate with the feeling that had already been created outside.

In the Senate, Mr. Platt and Mr. Hoar, in the House Mr. Lodge, Mr. Simonds of Connecticut, Mr. McKinley of Ohio, Mr. Adams of Illinois, Mr. Breckenridge of Kentucky, Mr. Wilson of West Virginia, and Mr. Butterworth of Ohio, were strong advocates, while Speaker Reed lent his all-powerful aid. The most active opponents of the bill in the Senate were Beck of Kentucky, Daniel of Virginia, George of Mississippi, and Regan of Texas. Before the close of the year,

Mr. Chace resigned from the Senate, and on his urgent advice it was decided that Mr. Platt, who was then the second member of the Patents Committee, and oldest in point of committee service, should take charge of the Copyright bill. The selection was most fortunate. The task of the management of such a bill was difficult and delicate, calling for a full measure of patience, persistency, sagacity, and tact, familiarity with parliamentary procedure, sympathetic acquaintance with the personalities and foibles of his associates, and the capacity to deal both with the leaders of the Senate and the managers of the House.

The successful guidance of the bill to ultimate enactment on the very last night of the Congress was dependent on innumerable incidents, any one of which, bunglingly handled, would have contained potential disaster, and every one of which, under skilful pilotage, contributed to the final triumph. Mr. Platt on the very first working day of the session introduced a bill providing for international copyright. A little later he reported favorably from the Patents Committee another bill, differing only in the correction of informalities, and at the earliest opportunity he asked the Senate to consider this bill as in committee of the whole. But strategically he did not think it wise to press his measure in the Senate until it could be ascertained more clearly as to the sentiment of the House. So long as he could be instrumental in securing legislation, he was indifferent whether the measure bore his name. In the House, the Judiciary Committee and the Patents Committee each had reported bills. The Judiciary Committee's bill reported by Mr. Adams first got the ear of the House through a special order. It was badly amended and then beaten by a vote of 99 to 125. This

defeat served only as a guide to the friends of international copyright for future effort. A few days later
Mr. Simonds introduced another bill on the lines of the
bill originally introduced by Mr. Chace two years earlier,
in accordance with the programme of American writers,
typographers, and publishers. This new measure, in
effect, was promptly reported from the Patents Committee of which Mr. Simonds was a member. It was
not considered, however, during the strenuous days
of the first session of the Fifty-first Congress, and its
friends devoted the time until the next session should
meet in still further arousing public sentiment and
personally canvassing the members of the House.
President Harrison in his annual message of December 1, 1890, renewed his recommendation "in favor of
legislation affording just copyright protection to foreign
authors on a footing of reciprocal advantages for our
authors abroad," and on the very next day, the second
day of the session, on call of committees, Mr. Simonds,
on behalf of the Patents Committee, called up his bill.
In the face of every known device for parliamentary
obstruction the bill was passed on December 3, 1890, by
a vote of 139 to 95. As the Senate of the Fiftieth Congress, nearly identical in membership with the Senate
of the Fifty-first Congress, had passed substantially the
same measure two years before by a majority of over
three to one (35 to 10) the vote in the House was hailed
as a virtual achievement of the reform. It proved,
however, to be only the prelude of one of the hardest
contests in the Senate's history.

It was at this point that Mr. Platt assumed active
management of the campaign. The Senate was engaged in one of its historic struggles, precipitated by
the Democratic victory in November, and the deter-

mination of the Republican leaders, if possible, to secure
the enactment of the Federal Elections law before a
Democratic House should come into control.   There
were other important measures pressing for consideration which were earnestly desired by Senators on whom
the friends of international copyright depended for
support, and the time at the disposal of Congress before the 4th of March was distressingly meagre.   To
secure even an opportunity to discuss a measure was
no easy task, yet in face of the eagerness to get at the
Pure Food bill, the Nicaraguan Canal bill, and the
Revenue Cutter bill, Mr. Platt was called upon not only
to secure discussion, but to insure enactment of a bill
which was not popularly compelling, which was the
object of bitter and mercenary opposition, which was
objected to by certain publishers because it deprived
them of discreditable gain, and by a great mass of people
who had been cunningly convinced that international
copyright would mean an increase in the price of books
and would be a blow at the education of the poor.   In
the face of such opposition it was manifest that in order
to receive any consideration the bill must submit to
some amendment.   The delicate task with the Senator
who had it in charge was to distinguish where it would
be safe to yield without destroying altogether, and
where to remain steadfast without subjecting the
measure to the certainty of defeat.   A necessary first
step was to insure consideration for the bill.   Mr.
Johnson, secretary of the joint committee of the various
organizations favoring the measure, having reported
for duty, Mr. Platt counselled him to call upon the
members of the Steering Committee, on which were
Senators Hoar and Evarts, and secure for the bill as
high a position as possible in the regular order of

business. This was done, and the copyright bill was placed second, a labor bill having already been promised first place. This first move of Senator Platt was of the most vital importance.

On the 9th of February, 1891, less than a month before Congress must adjourn, Mr. Platt, watching his opportunity, moved to consider the House bill as in committee of the whole. Following his usual practice, he trespassed upon the patience of the Senate only to make the briefest necessary explanation of the purpose of the legislation. The bill, he reminded them, was practically the same as the Chace bill which had passed the Senate two years earlier, differing in principle only in that its application was to depend upon the adoption of similar legislation by foreign countries:

I will simply say that the bill proceeds upon one broad fundamental principle, and that is, that what a man fashions by his brain, his genius, his imagination, or his ingenuity, is property just as much as what he fashions by his hands or acquires by manual or other labor, and that being property, it should be property the world over and should be recognized as such. If an American writes a book, the right to publish that book should be recognized as property not only in this country, as it is now under the Constitution, but as property everywhere. If a citizen of another country writes a book, the right to publish that book should be as much property in this country as in his own country.

That is the broad principle upon which this bill rests— the protection of property, for which governments are instituted. The principle has been applied in the case of patents, and not a little of the growth and prosperity of the country is due to the fact of the recognition by this Government that a foreigner who invents a new machine or discovers a new process shall be entitled to secure a patent for the same in this country.

The Constitution puts authors first in saying that Congress may secure to them exclusive rights; it puts them before inventors; but the legislation of the country has extended the provisions of the Constitution in the matter of inventions very much further than it has in the matter of authorship and those who come in under the generic term of authors.

I believe, myself, no measure before this Congress is so calculated to enhance not only the intellectual but the material growth of this country as this Copyright bill, and I trust it will pass, and pass without amendment. As I said, we have waited fifty-three years for this opportunity, and this opportunity may be wholly lost by amendments in the Senate.

I do not know that I would say that this is a perfect bill, but it is a bill which has had long consideration by committees of the Senate and of the House of Representatives. It comes to us from the House, and now is our opportunity to obtain the passage of such a law. If there is anything in it which needs further examination, which would call for further legislation, the way for the people who desire international copyright to obtain it is to pass the bill while we have the opportunity to pass it, and establish the principle. Then if it needs further application, we can trust to the future that justice will be done.

In spite of his appeal for the passage of the bill in the form in which it came from the House, Mr. Platt was obliged to yield to several amendments, which, in the opinion of friends of the bill, detracted from its efficacy, but which were essential to securing its passage through the Senate. For more than a week, with measures of urgent importance pressing upon the Senate, and with the end of Congress in sight, Mr. Platt held the Senate to the consideration of the Copyright bill, arguing, placating, urging, pleading. He

spoke as seldom as possible, but a few things he felt
that he must say. For one, he could not tolerate the
lax notions prevailing about the rights of property:

People see the acquisition of property in large amounts
and then jump to the conclusion that some man whom they
call a millionaire has not acquired his property by direct
and honest methods, and the result is that they have no
respect for that man's property any more than they have
for the gambler's. But they do not draw the line between
property honestly acquired and property which has been
acquired dishonestly. They do not draw the line between
property for which a good fair equivalent has been given
and property for which an honest and fair equivalent has
not been given. So there has arisen in this country a
tendency which, if not checked, will bring us to ruin sooner
than is generally supposed—a sentiment not to regard the
rights of property honestly acquired.

Of all the property which is the subject of acquisition,
literary and intellectual and artistic property is the most
honestly acquired. A man who has devoted his life to
letters, a man who has devoted his life to art, who has
been its slave and its devotee, is as honestly possessed of
the property which he produces in that way as any man
in the United States is honestly possessed of any property.

I wish to touch right here on the idea that a copyright
is a monopoly. It is not a monopoly in the strict sense
or in the legal sense, or in the right sense of that word.
It is rather a property right. The right of a man to publish
his book and to control the publication of his book, to
publish his engraving and to control the publication of his
engraving, to reproduce and control the reproduction of his
painting, is a right, and a right of property, just as, when
my friend from Michigan breeds a fine horse, that horse is
his property, and no other man can use it; he has a right
to control the use of it.

It is not in the sense in which the term is used a monopoly.

It is the right to use one's property.   A man buys a house. He alone has the right to use it.   He has a right to say who shall use it; he has a right to rent it to a tenant, and no other man shall set his foot in it; no other man can come to it; it is his castle; he may kill the man who ruthlessly tries to enter it.   And yet no one calls him a monopolist. This copyright is simply protecting men in their property rights.

With the argument for cheap books he was equally out of patience.   He declared that no man had a right to set up a cry for cheap books, if insisting that they must be cheaper, whether stolen or not:

No man has a right to put up the cry for cheap books if that cheapness depends upon appropriation without consent of the owner, any more than he has for cheap horses if to insure that cheapness the rights of the owner are in any way to be interfered with or limited or restricted. You can have everything cheap if you appropriate it without the consent of the owner; there is no trouble about that. There is no species of property in the world which you cannot cheapen by appropriation.   Sometimes I think that the moral sense of the community is entirely dulled on this subject.

Finally he made his appeal for international copyright on broad and general grounds because he believed it was just and beneficial.

I believe this Congress cannot be engaged in any work nobler, or grander, or more beneficial, or more calculated to develop this nation than to protect its literature and its art, and to so act and to so legislate that its literature and its art shall be protected wherever the sun shines, in other countries as well as in this country.   I believe by that means you will build up a literature, a standard of thought, a standard of intellectual effort, that you will build up a standard of art in this country, which will elevate our whole people.

What is this country for? Is it for the mere matter of getting things cheap for the people? Is that all there is for government in these days to think of? Has it come to this, that all the wheels of government must be turned to get things cheap for the people at the expense of the property and the rights of others if need be? Is not the Government to build up, is it not to develop, is it not to make a higher and nobler race of our people, and how can we reach that any better than by protecting, by stimulating, by encouraging intellectual effort and artistic effort?

I want to tell Senators that the brain of our people is the true and I might say the only source of our national wealth. It is what our people think. When they think on a higher plane they are the richer. The higher the plane of intellectual development, and the higher the plane of artistic development the richer are our people with a wealth that is not evanescent, but a wealth that endures, and a wealth that endures not only in this world, but is the only wealth that a man can take out of it.

Senator Platt's most serious embarrassment came from amendments offered by Frye and Sherman. The bill as it passed the House provided that the two copies of books required to be deposited in the Library of Congress for purposes of international copyright should be "printed from type set within the United States or from plates made therefrom." Frye moved to include in this requirement, maps, charts, dramatical and musical compositions, engravings, cuts, prints, photographs, chromos, and lithographs. Sherman moved to amend the clause prohibiting the importation of books printed abroad, enjoying the privilege of amended copyright, by striking out the word "prohibited" and inserting in lieu thereof "subject to the duties

provided by law." The Frye amendment was adopted
by a vote of 27 to 24, the Sherman amendment by a
vote of 25 to 24. Either one of these amendments, had
they not been attended to in Conference, would have
seriously affected the chances of passing the bill, and if
the Sherman amendment had become a law, it would
have practically nullified the purpose of the legislation.
Frye's amendment was subsequently modified so as
to apply only to lithographs and photographs, and the
Sherman amendment went out altogether.

At last, on February 18th, he secured a vote on the
bill, and it was passed by a majority of 36 to 14, badly
amended it is true, but in such form as to give some
hope of an adjustment. A conference with the House
was asked, and Mr. Platt, Mr. Hiscock, and Mr. Gray
were appointed conferees for the Senate. Only four-
teen days remained before the statutory adjournment
of Congress, and ten days elapsed before the House took
the question up and acceded to the Senate's request.
It is an interesting coincidence that the leading member
of the Conference Committee on the part of the House,
Mr. Simonds, should have been a Connecticut man, so
that it fell to the lot of two representatives of a single
State to play the most important part in the culmina-
tion of fifty years' endeavor. It is to be remembered,
too, that General Hawley of Connecticut was the first
to introduce a pure and simple copyright bill in 1885.
Even after the bill had gone to Conference the fight
against it was continued, and it was then that some
of the most skilful manœuvres were resorted to. On
March 2d, the House adopted the report of the Conference Committee, which eliminated some of the objectionable Senate amendments, but the Senate refused
to recede. There was a further struggle for twenty-

four hours, one proposition for compromise after another being made, and finally after midnight on the 3d of March, the Senate accepted the Conference report and about 2 A.M. passed the bill. Having been signed by the Vice-President, the bill was taken by Mr. Lodge to the House for consideration. After its passage in the House (at about 3 A.M.) and the signature by the Speaker, the bill was hurriedly engrossed (under the immediate supervision of Mr. Lodge, who stood over the clerks until they had finished their work) in order that it might be sent to the President at the White House. According to the usual routine, this would have been the end of the matter, but the opponents of international copyright were not yet prepared to give up the fight. Before the Senate had received information of the passage of the bill by the House, Senator Pasco moved to reconsider, and when the Senate adjourned at 4 A.M. that motion was pending. The Senate re-assembled some hours later, and about 11 A. M., March 4th, voted down Senator Pasco's motion, and the President, being then at the Capitol, signed the bill.

In the history of legislation, there have been few measures which clutched success so narrowly from the hands of opportunity.

At the moment Mr. Platt received the full measure of appreciation for the work he had so faithfully performed; he was a guest of honor at a banquet given in New York on April 13th, to celebrate the abolition of literary piracy,[1] and his services were recognized in other ways.

[1] At this dinner, which was presided over by E. C. Stedman, and at which were present George William Curtis, Henry Cabot Lodge, and Count Emile de Kératry, Robert Underwood Johnson in the course of a response to a toast said:

"I could name a dozen men at this board and a dozen elsewhere, but for the aid of any one of whom at some critical time we should

The leaders of the movement were generous in their acknowledgment. The decoration of the French Legion of Honor which was conferred upon Messrs. Adams and Simonds, who retired from the House of Representatives on the day the bill was passed, was offered to him but could not be accepted because he was still in office; but the Cercle de la Librairie and the Syndicat de la Propriété Littéraire et Artistique of Paris sent to him by special messenger a gold medal struck in recognition of his services to the cause of literature. The medal was brought to this country by Count E. de Kératry in June, 1891, who delivered also a letter, of which the following is a translation:

PARIS, June 16, 1891.

Senator PLATT of Connecticut.
          Washington.

Senator:

You have decided by your influence the vote of the American Senate upon copyright in international relations. You have affirmed "that a product of a man's brain is his property"; you have caused it to be recognized "that there can no longer be any difference between an American and a

---

not have had the happy fortune that brings us here to-night. There was at least one time, however, when the identification of oné man with the success or failure of this movement was complete, when in fact its fortune appeared to rest wholly and for many days upon the tact and devotion of one Senator. I can think of no parallel to the situation save the anecdote of Col. Jones's body servant in St. Mary's Parish in Louisiana. A visitor conveyed through the bayous of the Teche inquired of his darkey boatman, Wesley, whether his former master was connected with the White League.

"'Cunnel Jones connect wid de White League?' queried Wesley in unaffected astonishment. 'Yes, a member of the League.' 'Cunnel Jones a member ob de White League? Cunnel Jones? Why, bress de Lord, Massa, Cunnel Jones *am* de White League.' In those last despairing days in the Senate, Senator Platt was not merely in charge of the Copyright bill, he *was* the copyright cause."

foreign author and that the latter henceforth ought to be placed, with you, on the same footing with the native author." You have said with regard to France that the hour has long since come to grant reciprocity for her decree of 1852, which declared all piracy of a foreign work, a crime.

It is our duty to express our keen gratitude for the great part you have taken "in this triumph of a just cause."

Our Cercle de la Librairie and Syndicat des Associations Protectrices des Œuvres de l'Esprit et de l'Art have had made in your name a medal to bear witness to this legitimate sentiment, and we are happy to have been commissioned to transmit it to you.

Will the Senator accept the expression of our high regard.

> (The President of the Cercle de la Librairie
> and the Syndicat de la Propriété
> Littéraire et Artistique.)
>
> (*Signed*) A. TEMPLIER.

(The Secretary General of the Syndicat.)
(*Signed*) GERMOND DE LAVIGNE.

To Robert Underwood Johnson, Secretary of the American (Authors') Copyright League, who had written him an expression of thanks, he replied a few days after the adjournment of Congress:

The fact that I am still fighting over again night by night, in my sleep, the copyright struggle, will show you how deeply it took hold of me, and how nearly it came to upsetting me. I have a feeling that I was not very courteous to its friends while the contest was in progress, so morose and irritable, all of which I know they will forgive me for. I am very glad that it resulted in success. As I have written some of the publishers, the fate of copyright is now in their hands. The sentiment that it was a bill for the benefit of the publishers and against the interests of the people took a much deeper root than we at the time realized, although we felt its strength in a measure. But in talking

with people since the close of Congress I am surprised to
see how thoroughly and completely that idea has per-
meated the country.   There is no way of meeting it except
by publishing editions of books copyrighted by foreign
authors at a low figure.   The publishers ought to see this,
and ought to make a point of it.   A twenty-five cent edition of a popular foreign author's copyrighted book, fairly
executed, scattered as far as the market can be reached,
with attention called to it in the public press as being one
of the first results of the copyright law, will do more for
copyright than anything else.   I don't believe that you,
living in a publisher's atmosphere, can realize fully the
force of this, but you can to some extent.

To Dana Estes, the Boston publisher, he wrote:

I confess that there were times when the passage of
the Copyright bill seemed hopeless, and I do think that
persistent and patient work had something to do with the
final result, over which I think I was as much gratified
as any of the persons interested in the passage of the bill.
Indeed, it is either my misfortune or good fortune always
to feel more keenly than those directly concerned, an
interest in whatever I undertake.   It is wearing work
under such circumstances, and sometimes I got irritable
and cross, and as I look back over this contest, I feel as if
I had not always been patient and courteous to those who
were here looking after it, so perhaps you have a better
opinion of me for having stayed away.

I think copyright has come to stay, unless publishers
put up the price of books or make some combination which
will be stigmatized as a trust.   I don't believe they intend
to do this or that it would be for their advantage to do it,
and I trust you may steer clear of it.   The publisher who
first gets control of the work of a popular English author
and publishes a cheap edition of it, and forces a wide circulation, will do more for the copyright law than we have
been able to do in passing it.   The objection which made

votes against it was the cry of monopoly and dearer books.
The publishers can silence that cry, and it is very important
that they should do so if possible, before the next session
of Congress.   I need not say to you that the spirit of socialism is rampant in the country, and the regard for property
rights of all kinds is being weakened by demagogues and
by great masses of people who want to get something that
does n't belong to them, and the right of property in the book
or other creation of man's intellect or genius is harder to
understand and appreciate, and therefore less likely to be
respected than the property right to real estate or to
other kinds of personal property.   It is right along this
line that the danger lies.   It will not do to aggravate this
sentiment in respect to copyright.   I want to see some
publisher try the experiment of publishing the copyright
work of a foreign author for the million.

Great as were his services to the cause of international
copyright in 1891, they did not by any means mark
the extent of his achievements.   Throughout his life
he remained the steadfast friend of those who were
interested in improving the copyright laws, and they
invariably turned to him in the hour of need.   The
law of March 4, 1891 was far from adequate, but it
was the establishment of the principle for which the
authors of the English-speaking world had been striving.   It proved possible by means of the reciprocity
provisions in the statute to bring the United States
into copyright relations with all important European
countries.

In 1897, when the playwrights of America planned
to secure the enactment of an improved law for the
protection of dramatic copyrights they turned instinc-
tively to Mr. Platt, and in the Fifty-fourth Congress,
largely through his efforts, a bill was enacted which
elicited from Bronson Howard, the President of the

American Dramatists Club, the following appreciative letter:

201 WEST 78TH STREET, NEW YORK,
January 11, 1897.

Honorable O. H. PLATT,
    United States Senate.

DEAR SIR:

I beg to thank you most earnestly on behalf of the American Dramatists Club for the great interest you have taken, with other members of the committee of which you are chairman, in the passage of the new law, giving protection to dramatic writers and to managers in America. The importance of the new act reaches beyond even the justice it extends to your fellow American citizens. It will raise the standard of the American theatre in every respect, and so work a great public good. Especially it will tend strongly and with certainty to the development of a national dramatic literature worthy of the country; something impossible to establish under the old law.

In due season, the defects which were inevitable in the law of 1891 began to assert themselves. Complaints arose from authors of Germany, France, Italy, and other European states, against provisions of the law, which, in effect, discriminated against all writers whose works originated in any other language than English. In the Fifty-eighth Congress, although no longer a member of the Patents Committee, at the request of George Haven Putnam, Secretary of the American Publishers' Copyright League, he introduced a bill, which had been drafted under the instructions of the Executive Committee of the League, to remedy this injustice, which threatened to lead to the abrogation of the international copyright arrangements between Germany and France and the United States. The purpose of the bill was to relieve the foreign author in the difficulty he experienced in complying with the typesetting clause, by reason of the fact that his book was in a foreign language. The act gave him complete copyright for one year, including the absolute right of translation, but in order to continue the term of protection beyond the year, he was obliged to typeset his work in the original language in the United States, or to typeset a translation of it, in which case he was protected both in the translation and in the original work. If he complied with the typesetting clause as to the original work he secured the absolute right of translation for the entire term of the copyright.

It was no light task to secure the enactment of any kind of copyright legislation, and on a smaller scale this measure underwent some of the vicissitudes which beset the original bill in the Fifty-first Congress, but finally during the last week of the Congress, it became a law, thus proving to be almost the last public act of Mr. Platt's life. On March 3, 1905, he received from George Haven Putnam, Secretary of the American Publishers' Copyright League, this letter:

DEAR MR. SENATOR:

I desire to extend, on behalf of the Publishers' Copyright League and of others on both sides of the Atlantic, authors and publishers, who are interested in the protection of literary property, our cordial and appreciative thanks for the patient, capable, and all effective service that has been rendered by the Senior Senator from Connecticut during the past three years in connection with the measure that has now secured enactment in Congress. I have this morning a report from the President that the bill shall receive his signature. Your friendly co-operation in this particular undertaking is in line with a long series of similar services that you have been able to render to the cause of literary property and of national ethics.

Mr. Putnam was able later to report to Mr. Platt that if the serious injustice of which the Continental authors and their representatives had complained had not been remedied by the amendment in question, the copyright convention between Germany and the United States would probably have been terminated. The first steps towards such cancellation of the convention had, in fact, at the instance of the German Copyright League, already been taken in the Reichstag.

That the world of letters gratefully remembered the service he had done the cause of literature was shown only a few weeks later, when the word passed over the wires that the end had come. Among the messages received at the house of mourning in Judea, was this:

The American Copyright League respectfully offers you its sympathy. Your honored husband was the father of international copyright, and deserves to be gratefully remembered by all lovers of justice and of letters. This organization will be represented on Tuesday.

EDMUND CLARENCE STEDMAN,

President,

ROBERT UNDERWOOD JOHNSON,

Secretary.

Resolutions were also adopted by the American Publishers' Copyright League, as follows:

The Executive Committee of the American Publishers' Copyright League feels that in the death of the Honorable Orville H. Platt, of Connecticut, the friends of copyright have lost one of their most efficient and steadfast supporters, and one upon whose judgment and experience they could always rely.

The passage of the International Copyright act of 1891 was chiefly due to Senator Platt, and his interest in the cause of copyright continued until his death.

The Executive Committee records upon its minutes the gratitude of the American Publishers' Copyright League to Senator Platt, and its appreciation of his great ability as a statesman, his high sense of public duty, and will never forget the kindness and consideration he has always shown to all members of the League. The President is directed to send a copy of this resolution to the family of Senator Platt, and to offer them the sincere sympathy of the League.

W. W. APPLETON, *President.*

GEO. HAVEN PUTNAM, *Secretary.*

A few days after Mr. Platt's death, the following appreciative letter from the pen of Robert Underwood Johnson, Secretary of the American (Authors') Copyright League, appeared in the New York *Evening Post:*

Senator O. H. Platt and International Copyright

TO THE EDITOR OF THE " EVENING POST ":

SIR: In the press notices of the death of Senator Orville H. Platt I find in the enumeration of his public services little or, in some cases, no mention of his activity in the campaign for the International Copyright bill of 1891.

No one who knows the facts will dispute the statement that the passage of the bill was due first of all to Senator Platt. His high character, his mastery of the subject, his good humor, his tact, and his parliamentary experience brought the bill through the numerous vicissitudes which beset it in the last eight weeks of the session. It was inspiriting to note his undemonstrative but unwearying devotion—rallying the friends of the bill again and again, gently mollifying the opposition of many enemies, exhorting to patience supporters whose favored measure was being blocked by the bill, and who as the session drew to a close were threatening to side-track it if it did not get out of their way.   Our era of literary piracy was memorable for the many statesmen who were enlisted in the defence of literary property, but the one man more than any other who accomplished the reform was Orville H. Platt.

In view of the fact that in the press reports of the obsequies of Senator Platt no mention has been made of the participation of authors or publishers, I may be pardoned for saying that since his death the two copyright leagues have done what they could to honor his memory by recognizing his extraordinary services to the cause of justice to literary property.   Both the American Publishers' Copyright League and the American (Authors') Copyright League sent to Mrs. Platt telegrams of sympathy and of grateful acknowledgment, and both were officially represented at the funeral—the former by its President, Mr. William W. Appleton, and, in the absence in Europe of its Secretary, Mr. Putnam, by Mr. Frank H. Dodd of the Executive Committee; the latter by its Secretary.   It was a matter of great regret to Mr. Stedman, the President, that it was impossible for him to attend.   The Executive Council of the Authors' League also sent a wreath.

I beg the space for these facts lest it might be thought that those who know Senator Platt's pre-eminent service were singularly indifferent to his death.

It is said that republics are ungrateful.   This ought, least of all, to be true of the republic of letters.

R. U. JOHNSON,
Secretary American Copyright League.

NEW YORK, April 26th.

On the personal side of Mr. Platt's work in behalf of American publishers and authors during this period, Mr. George Haven Putnam writes:

It was my good fortune, in connection with my work on behalf of literary property, to come into personal relations in Washington and in New York with Senator Platt, relations which covered a long series of years. I found myself holding the Senator in increasing regard not only for clear-headed and wise-minded statesmanship, but for his absolute integrity of purpose, freedom from self-seeking, and general sweetness of nature. It was this combination of sweetness and force in his character, combined, of course, during the later years of his work in Washington, with his wide experience in affairs and knowledge of men, that secured for him so exceptional an influence over the opinions and the actions of his associates. He was held in affectionate regard not only by those with whom he was in accord on the political issues of the day, but by practically all of his political opponents, that is to say, by all with whom he came into any personal relations. The responsibility came upon him during the years between 1884 and 1891 of presenting before successive committees of the House and of the Senate the arguments in behalf of international copyright, arguments which were, as it was claimed, simply a contention on behalf not only of national ethics but of the highest intellectual interests of the community. In addition to the formal arguments presented in the committee rooms, there was, of course, much to be done in the matter of personal words with senators and representatives, to many of whom the subject was entirely unfamiliar. It was in this matter of personal relation and in the task of withstanding prejudices that were mainly based upon ignorance of the subject, that Senator Platt's influence and service were of inestimable value.

I recall one occasion, in 1904, when the Committee on Patents, of which the Senator had for years been Chairman, had, in giving their approval to a provision for a fuller measure of protection for works originating on the Continent, through a clerical error, connected with this amendment certain provisions taken from the statute book of 1891. The result of this action would have been a recommendation on the part of the Committee on Patents for rescinding the international copyright that had been secured in 1891. I was permitted to accompany Senator Platt to a meeting of the Committee, of which at that time Senator McComas, of Maryland, was Chairman. To Senator McComas the subject of copyright was comparatively new, and he had not had direct touch with the previous proceedings. Senator Platt began to explain to the Committee the error that had been made in its previous action. He was interrupted by the Chairman and by one or two members: "There is no necessity for any detailed explanation, Senator; if you say the action was wrong, it will, of course, be rescinded. Tell us what you want, and you shall have our approval." Each man in the room knew not only that Senator Platt understood the subject of copyright, but that any word that he had to give on this or on any other matter could be absolutely trusted. The people are fortunate when their legislative business can be in the hands of men like Orville H. Platt who are not only capable leaders but also great citizens. The standard set by him for the conduct of the nation's business will prove of inestimable service for legislators, and for the nation back of the legislators, for the years to come.

CHAPTER IX

PROTECTOR OF THE INDIAN

The Red Man's Most Practical and Useful Friend—Fourteen Years with the Committee on Indian Affairs—Prevents Mischievous Legislation.

IT was almost a matter of chance that so much of the Connecticut Senator's activity in public life should have been turned to a question which up to the time of his arrival in Washington had hardly engaged his thoughts and which would seem to have as little interest for his immediate constituency as any in the numerous group of governmental problems. After he had been eight years a Senator, he found himself a member of the Committee on Indian Affairs, an assignment which few sought, and for which he had no special inclination. The Chairman of the Committee was Henry L. Dawes of Massachusetts, a serious-minded and industrious man, who, after distinguished service in the House as Chairman of the Ways and Means Committee, had found his peculiar sphere of usefulness in the Senate to be the conscientious guardianship of the interests of the nation's wards. It was probably at his request that Mr. Platt, who by that time was known as a painstaking and unbeguilable Senator, became a member. It is a curious circumstance that for many years the fortunes of the Indian should have been so largely in the keeping of two Senators who were almost neighbors in the Berkshire and Litchfield hills, and it was a lucky chance that two high-minded men of such capacity should have been ready to devote their time and talents to a thankless task.

Except to a limited number of Senators, most of them from far western States, matters concerning the Indians were of only casual interest, unless, through neglect and indifference, something in the nature of a scandal developed, as was not infrequently the case; yet the questions growing out of the relations of the United States with its Indian wards, especially the five civilized tribes in the Indian Territory, were for many years among the most complicated and difficult problems with which Congress had to deal. The treaties and agreements with the Indian tribes, some of them dating back nearly a century, were continually calling for the best legal ability in their interpretation and application to constantly arising questions of administration. The never-ending conflict between the friends of the Indian and the white settlers and avaricious corporations encroaching on the reservation forced tangled problems upon the legislative branch of the Government. The opulent soil of the territory occupied by the Indians has always been a lure to the white man, inciting him to violence, bribery, and theft; while the extraordinary spectacle of nations within a nation, presented by the republics of the Indian Territory for many years, afforded limitless opportunity not only to evil-minded persons, but also to the conscientious legislator. It was Mr. Platt's difficult task for nearly twenty years to stand between the despoilers of the Indian on the one hand, and his super-serviceable friends on the other, —to thwart the schemes of grafters and thieves, while tempering the zeal of importunate reformers. It was a burden from which he often sought relief, but never successfully until a few months before he died, when he was able to plead his assignment to the Chairmanship of the Judiciary Committee as an excuse from further service. So he plodded along, examining with religious scrutiny every piece of proposed legislation and the wearisome details of every appropriation bill. He was scrupulously accurate in his knowledge of the ramifications of the Indian question, knew every provision of every treaty and agreement, and all the circumstances relating to every reservation.

After Mr. Dawes's retirement from the Senate in 1893, Platt was, by common consent, regarded as the one man on the Committee to whom other Senators must look for guidance in Indian legislation, and the one upon whom other leaders depended to see that no improper measures were enacted.

James K. Jones of Arkansas became Chairman under the Democratic régime of the Fifty-third Congress in 1893, but when the Republicans returned to control, there was an insistent demand that the Chairmanship of the Committee should go to Mr. Platt. He received letters from bishops, college presidents, and friends of the Indian everywhere, urging him to take the Chairmanship, to which he was in line of succession. Mr. Dawes, then Chairman of the Dawes Commission, wrote him:

When I was at Mohonk there was a great deal of talk about your taking the Chairmanship of Indian Affairs, and the cry was universal that you *must* take it. I told them the reasons of your reluctance, which I thought I knew pretty well. But the friends of the Indian the country over know the situation, and will sorely grieve if you disappoint them. Now I do not know that you owe them anything, but I want earnestly to commend to your consideration the question whether you are not called upon to make the sacrifice, both for the good name of the Republican party, and for the good of the Indian. You know what I mean. There is no need of further word between you and me, or to induce you to do what you think is right.

He was not moved by these appeals, and chose instead the Chairmanship of the Committee on Patents, which was much more to his liking, and which would not be so great a drain upon his energies at a time when he was to be occupied in the work of the Committees on Judiciary and Finance.

Into the details of his work on the Indian Affairs Committee, it is hardly profitable to go. Important though it was, it cuts little figure in the significant history of the time, and is of interest now chiefly as an illustration of the conscientious treatment of a strangely difficult and evanescent problem. He took an important part in all legislation affecting the Indians for nearly twenty years. His judgment prevailed with his associates in innumerable complicated questions which the great majority of Senators had neither time nor inclination to study. He had a part in the legislation relating to the opening of the " Cherokee Outlet " in 1893, and the withdrawal of government aid to sectarian schools. He urged, so far as practicable, the allotment of lands among the Indians, but he believed that the Indian ought to work his land and not rent it or sell it, as many were inclined to do, with the idea of living in idleness upon the proceeds. The manner in which his work impressed his associates is shown in the words spoken after his death by Mr. Nelson of Minnesota, a sagacious Senator, who had unusual opportunities for appraising it:

For sixteen years he was a member of the Committee on Indian Affairs, where he rendered most valuable and efficient service. No one was better versed than he in all the intricacies of Indian legislation, and no one was more alive than he to the true welfare of the Indians—always on guard to protect and defend them against open and insidious inroads on their rights and interests, but never a block or impediment to the opening and settlement of our vast public domain. His heart went out to the frontiersman, as well as to the Indians. He had none of those hazy and transcendent notions of so-called "Indian rights" or "Indian character" possessed by a school of closet reformers. He gauged the Indian at his true worth and at his real aptitude and ability, and hence he was the most practical and useful friend the Indian had.

One of the first measures which came out of the Indian Committee after he became a member did not meet with his approval. It was a bill " For the relief and civilization of the Chippewa Indians in the State of Minnesota "—briefly, a proposal to sell for the Chippewas the pine timber on their land, valued anywhere from $5,000,000 to $10,000,000, and devote the proceeds to the uses of the Indians, capitalizing the timber for them so that they should receive a fixed income for fifty years, and in certain emergencies five per cent. of the principal. Mr. Platt's reasons for opposing this plan betrayed an intimate knowledge of the Indian character. He declared that the very worst thing that could be done for the Indians was to create such a fund:

I think the result will be that at the end of fifty years these Indians will not be a particle more advanced toward civilization than they are to-day. The truth is that the hardest Indians in the United States to civilize are the richest ones, and in proportion to the amount of their riches. You cannot break up the tribal relations of a rich tribe of Indians with one half the ease that you can among Indians that have no money. Riches bring a kind of aristocracy among them, and they maintain their manners and their customs and resist every possible attempt to civilize them. You may take their children and send them to school at Carlisle, and when they go back to the tribe they have either to be driven out or to go and adopt the customs and submit themselves to the regulations of the tribe.

This reference to Carlisle touched a phase of the Indian problem upon which he held a decided opinion. For many years he was convinced of the futility of bringing Indian youth East for education with a view to their return to their own people. In the few instances where they had the strength to adhere to their Eastern training, they were cast off by their tribe. More often they returned to the tribe, enfeebled physically and morally, fell back into the old ways, and became the most worthless Indians on the reservation. He held that the missionaries who had gone out and spent their lives among the Indians had done far more good than the Eastern schools or professional philanthropists, although as time went by he grew to value the work done at Carlisle by Capt. R. H. Pratt.

The operation of the treaties with the five civilized tribes he regarded with deep disgust. They had worked in practice to the injury of the Indians, for whose benefit they were originally framed, and their flagrant abuse had resulted in the control of the affairs of the tribes by unscrupulous white men and half-breeds who occupied the most productive lands and profited by a fictitious or mongrel relationship. He held that, under these conditions, the United States was not bound to

abide by the treaties which had been so scandalously
diverted from their beneficent purpose. He expressed
this opinion forcibly on more than one occasion.
During the discussion of the Indian Appropriation bill
in April, 1896, he undertook to secure the insertion of
an amendment, which would have greatly strengthened
the prestige and authority of the Dawes Commission
with the five tribes with whom they were empowered
to negotiate. The amendment, although favorably
reported by the Indian Committee, was opposed by a
persistent lobby, and was finally ruled out on a point of
order. Some of those who opposed the amendment
referred unctuously to the spires of the Indian churches
ascending to heaven, "showing that they are followers
of that meek and lowly Nazarene, that Man of Galilee,
to whom we all bow." The character of the opposition
filled the soul of the Connecticut Senator with wrath.
He declared that neither in Russia nor Turkey was the
despotism of the so-called government in the Indian
Territory equalled, and that neither in Cuba nor anywhere else were their atrocities surpassed. The objections to the amendment he said were made, not in
the interest of the Indians, but in the interest of white
men "who have not a drop of Indian blood in their
veins, yet who dominate these tribes and these nations
with as heavy a hand as the feudal baron ever domi-
nated the people of his barony." He asserted that in
the Indian Territory five hundred men, largely white,
with scarcely a half-blood Indian among them, had
"seized, appropriated, and hold nine tenths of the
agricultural land to the exclusion of those who are
entitled equally as citizens of the Territory to the use
and benefit of that land; and the moment any
measure is proposed looking to a remedy for that

awful injustice, that unholy spoliation of the Indians, our wards, whom we are bound to protect, then Senators are shocked lest some rule of the Senate should be transgressed." Self-government in the Territory, he declared, was more than a failure:

It is a shame, a disgrace, an intolerable nuisance, the five hundred men who have seized the land control it by the corruption of the Legislatures, by the corruption of courts, by the terrorizing of those whose lands they have seized. . . . If it be necessary to override treaties, if in the opinion of any Senator there is anything in the amendment which by any construction or by any stretch of construction can be held as not living up to the letter of the treaties, then I am prepared to say that no more solemn obligation ever rested upon the Senate of the United States than to disregard those treaties. When we make a treaty with an Indian nation, we make it not only for ourselves but for the Indians. We make it with our wards. We make it with a people whose interests we are bound to protect, and when the letter of the treaty is used for the oppression of those people by men who have thrust themselves into the situation for gain and for personal advancement, it becomes our duty to see that the spirit in which the treaty was made is carried out. Five hundred people of the sixty thousand so-called Indians have appropriated the property which belongs to the whole number. Civilization is arrested, progress is arrested, the real Indian is retrograding; he is going back to a state of savagery and barbarism, and all in order that the five hundred robbers and despoilers may be kept in their unlawful possessions. I would not hesitate to disregard a treaty if it were necessary to do so for that purpose.

That these words were not spoken on impulse or without full consideration, is shown by the fact that earlier in the session Mr. Platt had introduced a joint resolution, declaring:

That the condition of the Indian Territory as regards population, occupation of land, and the absence of adequate government for the security of life and property has so changed since the making of treaties with the five civilized tribes that the United States is no longer under either legal or moral obligation to guarantee or permit tribal Indian government in said Territory, and should at once take such steps as may be necessary to protect the rights and liberties of all the inhabitants of said Territory.

In preparing his first annual message, President McKinley sent for Mr. Platt and asked him to prepare a paragraph covering the condition of affairs in the Indian Territory, with special reference to the ratification of the agreement recently effected by the Dawes Commission with the Choctaws and Chickasaws. Instead of complying literally with this request, Mr. Platt outlined his opinion of the whole Indian problem in a letter to the President, dated December 2, 1897, in the course of which he said:

The condition of affairs in the Indian Territory is a disgrace to our government and our civilization. I do not believe that so unjust, iniquitous, and utterly indefensible a condition of affairs exists in any civilized community in the world. Under the guise of Indian self-government, supposed to be guaranteed by the United States, we permit practical despotism and the perpetration of unbounded injustice.

The treaties made with the Indians dating back to 1838 or thereabouts, with modifications and perhaps sanctions since that date, were made upon the understood agreement between the Indians and the United States, that the Indians should be provided with a territory and a home where they

should live apart from the whites and govern themselves
as Indians, having a common tribal title to the land in
which every Indian should have an equal interest with
every other Indian. . . . The whole situation has been
changed not by the United States, but by the action of the
Indians themselves.

A territory, nearly equal in extent and fertility to the
State of Indiana, has, by operation of Indian laws and
the action of Indian governments, been given practically
into the possession of a few persons who have little or no
Indian blood in their veins, but are recognized as members
of the different tribes or nations. And the methods by
which they have become possessed, and the Indian enact-
ments under which they hold this vast tract or territory,
amount almost to giving them a fee-simple title and occupation. The real Indians, whose interests should be just
as much the care of the United States now as when the
treaties were made, have been despoiled, their use of lands
which have any value has been denied, and their whole
condition made more pitiable, I think, than the condition
of any other Indians in the United States. . . .

To allow a few persons, recognized indeed by special
enactment as Indian citizens, but who are either purely
white or with only a small proportion of Indian blood,
longer to monopolize these lands, would be an unpardon-
able neglect of duty on the part of the United States.
In making the treaties and conveying the lands to the
different tribes, the United States imposed a trust upon
the tribal governments, and those governments assumed
the obligations of the trust, which were that all the
members should have equal rights in the use and occupation of the lands. That trust has been disregarded and
wantonly violated by the Indians, and no pettifogging with
regard to the language of the treaties and the powers
given to the different governments can absolve the United
States from its obligation to see that the trust is properly
executed. The Indians who have no lands, and can obtain

none, because they have been appropriated by the few so-called Indians, must be protected in their rights and put in possession of their fair share of the tribal property. This can only be done by allotment, either of the use and occupation, or of a full title to the land. . . .

Meanwhile the condition of the white people who have been not only permitted but encouraged to go into the Territory by the Indians, demands the attention of our Government. It is the Indians alone, who are responsible for the presence of the white people, amounting probably to 250,000 domiciled in the Indian Territory, as against less than 70,000 Indians. They are without local govern-ment, without the privileges of American civilization, without the opportunity in any way to participate in the government of the country where they are located; white American citizens occupying a country where, by law, so far as the local affairs are concerned, there is only a govern-ment of Indians, by Indians, and for Indians in existence. The United States Government certainly owes to these citizens the duty of providing for them the opportunity which other citizens of the United States enjoy, to have a voice in their own government. So that both the interests of the Indians and the protection and the development of our own white citizens imperatively demand that our Government should, without further delay, change the existing conditions in the Indian Territory. There is nothing in the spirit of the treaties to prevent. If it is supposed in the letter of the treaties the United States Government has surrendered its rights both to care for the Indians and protect its own citizens, it is sufficient answer to say to those who insist that nothing shall be done, "that the letter killeth, but the spirit giveth life."

One hobby he had—the appointment of fit persons in the Indian service. He was especially intolerant of the debauching of the service during the second Cleve-land administration, under Secretary Hoke Smith.

On one occasion, when the Indian Rights Association urged him to assist the confirmation of some
of Smith's appointments, he replied hotly to Herbert
Welsh:

If the Secretary of the Interior has in any way reformed,
I am glad to hear of it. He has been, with reference to the
Indian service and the Territorial service in general, utterly
shameless in the matter of his appointments, not that I
mean he has always gotten bad men; a man cannot do that
always, but he has made them very largely upon political
grounds and for political purposes, this last more with
regard to officials in Oklahoma, perhaps, than elsewhere. I
think it is susceptible of proof that he has said that he proposed to hold the Territory of Oklahoma by his appointments until he brought it in as a Democratic State. I don't
want to say harsh things about any one, but I have no
patience with the way the Secretary of the Interior has
administered his office wherever there has been an opportunity to appoint an impecunious and worthless Democrat.
If of late he has done any better than formerly, we ought
to be thankful for it. I have not yet seen the evidence of it.
The States in which there are Indian reservations are mostly
represented by Republican Senators and Representatives, so
that under what they call the "Home-rule System" not one
of them could have the slightest influence in the matter of
appointments. When Mr. Harrison was President, I
believe that without exception he appointed men from the
States and Territories where the reservations were situated,
and by comparison he got a very much better set of officials.
I am not sure that it is a rule we ought to follow in all
instances. The suggestion, that these men who are now
nominated have done well and that their appointment is
something in the nature of a promotion, has great force.
But as between the practice of appointing from the States
and sending carpet-baggers there, I can have but one opinion. I have known a man, appointed and confirmed by

the Senate,—yes, more than one,—whose reputation was
that the first inquiry they made on their rounds as Indian
inspectors, was for an Indian girl to sleep with. I have
known men who were thieves and seducers at home, confirmed by the Senate, when the record was plain. I have
been so absolutely disheartened and disgusted with the
character of men that were sent from other States to be
Indian agents and inspectors, that I am ready to turn to
almost anything with the belief that it cannot be worse than
what has been done. The appointment of army officers
relieved the trouble somewhat so far as character is concerned, but an army officer does not make the best agent
always, or indeed usually.

He never hesitated to address himself, with wholesome frankness, to the well-intentioned people who had
voluntarily taken upon themselves the responsibility
for the proper settlement of the Indian question.
When the *Outlook* in March, 1902, published an article
on "The Lease of the Standing Rock Reservation,"
taking Congress and the administration severely to
task, he wrote promptly to Dr. Lyman Abbott:

Some one has sent me the *Outlook* for March 29th, with
a marked article by Mr. Kinman, "The Lease of the Standing Rock Reservation." I regret to say that I do not
remember to have ever seen, within the same space, so
much of statement and insinuation calculated to give an
entirely erroneous impression as to the facts as in that
article. Surely you cannot suppose that the Secretary
of the Interior, and the Indian Commissioner, and Committees of Congress, are either corruptly or stupidly trying
to despoil the Indians of their rights.

In the winter of 1900–01, a proposition was brought
into the Senate, looking to the construction of a dam
across the Gila River, near San Carlos, Arizona, to

store the waters of the river for the benefit of the
Pima Indian reservation. The Pima Indians from
time immemorial had supported themselves largely
by agriculture under irrigation. White settlers on the
upper portion of the Gila River, having taken up their
lands under government laws, had diverted the water
so that the Indians were deprived of its use. Mr.
Platt believed that the Government ought, at any
practicable cost, to supply water to the reservation
for the benefit of the Indians, but he believed also that
all the water needed for irrigating lands upon their
reservation could be obtained without resorting to the
expedient of building a dam 130 miles above the reservation, at an estimated cost of $1,000,000 to $2,000,000.

He recognized in the proposed amendment a scheme
to commit the Government to a system of national
irrigation—a system to which he was not necessarily
opposed, but which he felt should not be entered upon
without the most careful consideration. The National
Irrigation Association and the Geological Survey earnestly advocated the legislation, and, to supplement
their work, the friends of the Indian were rounded up
and induced to pelt sympathetic Senators with petitions
and appeals. To one of these philanthropists, Mr.
Platt responded:

I have an idea, and I may as well express it frankly,
that your board, and other people throughout the United
States who are friends of the Indians, have overestimated
the necessity of spending a couple of million of dollars,
more or less, to irrigate the Pima reservation. The plan
is being pushed from two sources: One, philanthropic
people who desire to subserve the interests of the Indians,
and the other, the National Irrigation Association, that has
fixed upon this plan to commit the Government to a system

of national irrigation, which if once entered into will cost hundreds, and possibly thousands, of millions of dollars. I myself believe that all the irrigation needed at present by these Indians can be provided without embarking in this very expensive enterprise. I think the sufferings of the Indians have been very much overdrawn. We were told last year that they were in a starving condition, and that it would take at least $50,000 to support them for the year. We appropriated $30,000, of which only $7,000 has been used, and I think that the use of that money has relieved any actual suffering. I believe that with $10,000 expenditure, the work to be performed by the Indians, their lands can be irrigated, for the present at least, and I think that the philanthropic friends of the Indians throughout the United States ought to be very careful that they are not made use of to try to commit the Government to a system of national irrigation.

While he at no time relished the irksome work on the Indian Committee, he nevertheless took quiet satisfaction in the thought that he was rendering a valuable service both to the Indian and to his own Government. When in 1902 he secured an amendment to a bill opening to settlement the Rosebud reservation in South Dakota, by which settlers, instead of obtaining free entry, were required to buy at the rate of $2.50 an acre for their lands, he wrote home to a friend in Meriden:

I suppose the world would go on if I should die, but while I am here in the Senate there is always something depending on me especially. Just now it is the Indian Appropriation bill; next week it will probably be Cuba, if the House passes some bill, and so it goes. What a man does quietly is never known or appreciated. For instance—I put an amendment into a bill to-day for the opening of an Indian reservation which is likely to save the

Government, first and last, if the same policy is continued with reference to other matters of a similar kind, at least $50,000,000. I feel that I have to watch these things, but still I am looking forward to trying to find the time when I can get to Connecticut; wish I could get there on Good-Friday.

When he became Chairman of the Committee on Cuban Relations, he endeavored to escape further service on the Indian Committee, but the urgency of those interested in the integrity of Indian legislation prevailed upon him to remain. To one of these friendly advisers, F. J. Kingsbury, of Waterbury, Connecticut, he wrote, on March 10, 1901:

The Indian question, as it is called, is one of great difficulty. If it is considered from the sympathetic side merely, that is one thing. If it is considered from the practical side, that is often an entirely different thing. It perplexes the wisest and best to know what is to be done in given instances. There is enough work on the Indian Committee to take the entire time of any Senator, and then he would be as uncertain as to the best practical thing to be done as he is now. I have felt that I ought to go off from the Indian Committee, and yet I think it is no egotism to say that for some years I have stood between the Indians and a disposition in a good many quarters to consider the wishes of white people rather than the interests of the Indians. You cannot look at an Indian reservation in this country without seeing a case for the Supreme Court of the United States. The questions arising are most perplexing and complicated. I really have not the time to give to them. I am second on the Judiciary Committee, third on Finance, Chairman of the Committee on Relations with Cuba, either one of which, to say nothing of the Indian Committee, involves great labor, and I feel as if I ought to give some attention, indeed careful consideration, to the great public questions which loom up now as never before. I do not know what to do about staying on the Indian Committee. Nothing that I can do will satisfy either side, for both the benevolent Indian sympathizers, and those who have no regard for the Indians when the white man's interest is involved, are extremists. Truth here, as in most all matters, lies in the middle.

But with all his discriminating conscientiousness in legislation, it was through the personal side of his relations to the Indian that his service on the Committee had its peculiar value. For twenty years he was the real friend and champion of the Indians, and they regarded him as they would a father. From all over the country the Indians seemed to know that Senator Platt would befriend them, and see that justice would be done, and they always felt free to write him. Of this phase of his experience, one who had peculiarly close relations with Mr. Platt during the last years of his life says:

One characteristic letter, I remember, came from "Mak She Ka Tan No," who made his mark, which was witnessed by "Wm. Myer" and "Sal Williams." This was written from Shawnee, O. T., March 4, 1903, and reads:

"Honorable O. H. Platt, United States Senate, Washington, D. C. Dear Sir: I have been told you know a great deal about Indians and the Indian business, that you are one of the Senate council for that purpose. I am a poor Kickapoo Indian boy. A few years ago when the Government allotted land to the Kickapoo Indians in Oklahoma some of us were left out and got no land. I am a full blood Indian, my father and mother were full blood Kickapoo Indians, and the letter I hand you herewith, which I ask you to transmit to the Secretary of the Interior with such recommendations as you may deem proper, explains to you that it is in the power of the Government to yet give me an allotment. Trusting you will be kind enough to do something for me, I am

"MAK SHE KA TAN No."

Senator Platt took as much trouble and pains with this Indian as he would have taken with any man in Connecticut; he took it up with the Secretary of the Interior, and the matter covered most of the summer; the "Kicking Kickapoo" band was involved, and finally this Indian received his allotment, as well as others shown to be entitled, on the diminished Kickapoo reserve in Kansas.

Even when Senator Platt was obliged to give up his membership on the Committee on Indian Affairs he still helped to scrutinize the Appropriation bill, and was looked to for advice in the Senate, and appealed to by Indians without number or limit.

I think one of the most affecting scenes I witnessed, in connection with his official life, was during the session towards the end of 1903, or 1904. As usual the Indians were in Washington to look after their interests. They had been going to see the Senator, and sending him messages, and going through the regular evolutions, to all of which he gave patient attention. One day a delegation of braves, probably numbering fifty, possibly more, were at the Capitol to see him. He was much pressed for time, as usual, was working on an important amendment to the Indian bill, together with other matters, but he left the Senate floor, and came to his committee-room, walked over and sank down in a chair by the window. An interpreter was present, who seated himself near the Senator, and all the balance ranged themselves around the room, close to the walls, hunched up, watching the Senator intently, who surely was the personification of the "Big White Father."

All he said was: "Now tell me all about it," turning to the interpreter, who proceeded to make explanations, while the Senator sat as silent as the Indians. He asked some questions, pointing first to one and then to another of the Indians, saying, "Just what is it you want—and why?" He spent a couple of hours, and then rose up, while all those in the room did likewise, and in precisely the same fashion, and then he said, first directly to one and then to another, "That you cannot have; it is not right; you are not entitled to it; the Government does not owe it to you." To another, "I will look into it." To another, always pointing to the one intended, and never confusing any particular request or demand, "you shall have it," and so on. Finally, "I say to you—you shall have justice; I shall look after you." Then straight to the door he walked without a word further or gesture, while the entire delegation muttered the Indian grunt of satisfaction and approval—"Ugh! Ugh! Big Chief! Big White Father!" and all slowly passed out after him, single file. They had formed a line down which he passed much after the fashion of the Indians at the little Catholic Church up at Wequetonsing, Michigan, when the Father passes out from celebrating Mass on Sunday mornings.

Among the eulogies delivered after his death, there was none more fitting than that of Senator Morgan of Alabama, a political opponent, who had seen years of service with him on the Indian Committee:

As the great and proud race of Indians are disappearing from their fatherland, which no Indian would ever desert nor be driven from it save by forces that made death the penalty of resistance, none of them will forget the sympathy of Senator Platt in his patient, just, and humane devotion to the rights that remained to them after more than two centuries of warfare for the maintenance of their original independence. He provided for them in their necessitous condition almost as a father would provide for his family. His great abilities and industrious labors were always engaged in their service when needed, so that none were neglected; and the records of the Senate are a history of his work that carries honor to his memory on every page that relates to Indian affairs.

His only possible reward was the consciousness of duty well and honestly performed.

The proud and silent nod of the grateful Indian in approbation of the equally proud and silent assistance of the great Senator was the only token of friendship between men who were sternly just in their actions, and neither of them asked nor expected nor granted favors.

CHAPTER X

Chairman of Committee on Territories—Instrumental in Admitting Six New States—In Close Touch with the West.

A SYMPATHY as broad as the Continent, an understanding which comprehended the needs and aspirations of every State and Territory helped to make Platt of Connecticut in all the name implies a Senator of the United States. A New Englander of Puritan descent, he was an American citizen first of all, and the star that represented California on the flag was as significant to him as that which marked his native State. His connection with the Indian Committee brought him in close touch with the country beyond the Mississippi, and years of service with the Committee on Territories gave him an acquaintance with the Far West which gained him recognition as the Eastern Senator most conversant with its problems and sympathetic with its aims. He watched the growth of the Western country with satisfaction and pride. It carried to him no message of apprehension for the future of his own region. The threatened encroachments upon the influence of New England did not disturb him. "New England has no fears for the future," he said. "She has heard the cries of 'cotton is king', 'wheat is king,' 'iron is king'; and has heard them unmoved.

134

She knows there is no real kingship in the United States but the sovereignty of ideas."[1]

Western men learned to trust him and confide in him. He bore toward some of the younger of them an almost paternal relationship, and they went to him like children for encouragement and help. The affection with which they grew to regard him seemed, at times, incongruous with the practical workings of the legislative machine, yet it contributed subtly and oftentimes indispensably to its effective operation. Since his death no one has quite taken the peculiar place he occupied as a link between the East and West.[2]

[1] Speech advocating the admission of Washington, March 3, 1886.

[2] Western men are fond of telling about the positive way in which he handled questions relating to their part of the country, disclosing a shrewd and appreciative understanding of the Western character.

Once when the Utah question was up before the Territories Committee he asked a man who appeared in behalf of the Mormon side: "Do you know Abbott R. Heywood of Ogden? Is he a truthful man?" Heywood was Chairman of the Liberal party in Utah and Mr. Platt was palpably toying with a letter which from the heading evidently came from him. The answer was: "Yes, I know Mr. Abbott R. Heywood and I think that he is a truthful man." The Senator chuckled drily, opened the letter, and said: "You have made a lucky reply. I guess you are a truthful man too. Abbott Heywood says that you are all right and he takes your view of this particular part of the case." Later when statehood was on the point of gaining or losing and his decision was likely to settle the question, he asked for Abbott R. Heywood's opinion and got it. When overzealous friends of statehood had made rash assertions in their eagerness to gain his support he sent for the man whom he had once before tested on Heywood's letter and said: "I 'll take your word and no one else's among the Mormons on this question. Have these people, any of them, been living with their plural wives since the manifesto?" "Yes, Senator," was. the reply, "there has been a case now and then, but the Gentiles have not chosen to prosecute it because they believe the Church will discountenance the practice and if the pulpit will range itself with the law it cannot go on." "Well," was Mr. Platt's comment,

It was partly a matter of chance that he had so much
to do with the admission of new States to the Union,
but while he was Chairman of the Committee on Territories it happened that six stars were added to the flag
and that it fell to him to secure the enactment of the
bills creating six commonwealths,—a record which
stands to the credit of no other public man since the
beginning of the Government. It is true that Idaho,
Montana, North Dakota, South Dakota, Washington,
and Wyoming would sooner or later have been admitted
to the sisterhood of States, for the times were ripening
for the change, but the date and manner of their
admission might have been far different had it not been
for the tact and integrity of the Senator who had their
fortunes in charge, and for the confidence which he
inspired. A narrow-minded partisan in his position
might have been a serious obstacle in the way. But
Platt was broad enough to grasp the true significance of
the development of the West. He believed with
Seward that Territories should be transformed into
States just as soon as local circumstances justified the
change. He held to the conviction that the sooner a
Territory emerges from its provincial condition the
better, and the sooner the people are admitted to
participate in the responsibilities of government, the
stronger and more vigorous the State those people
form will be; that the longer the process of pupilage
the greater will be the effect of federal patronage and
federal influence upon them. To his mind there were
four conditions of admission. First, there must be
sufficient territory; second, that territory must have

"they say that you are New England folks out in Utah. If you
are and will live up to New England traditions you will soon get
into line for the country and you will stand by it to the death."

the requisite population; third, it must have resources
which promise development; fourth, it must have a
people whose character is a guarantee of a republican
form of government.   Throughout his career in the
Senate, he favored the admission of new States whenever these conditions were fulfilled.   In advocating the
admission of the State of Washington in 1886, he said:

Whatever the future may develop with regard to the
acquisition of territory—whatever we may think with
regard to Alaska, which is territory acquired outside of
what I may call our integral territory, it seems to me that
with reference to the territory which we have, which is now
circumscribed by the lines which bound upon the north
what is called "The United States," there can be no
question, but that the same rule of admission is to be
applied now with regard to those territories as has been
applied in the past. The people of those Territories are
not full American citizens, are not fully entitled to the
rights of other citizens of the United States, do not fully
illustrate the principles of self-government, until they are
admitted to become participants in the general union of
States.

It has been said that in this admission of new Western
States he saw no reason to fear for the influence of New
England.   He recognized that, as the country grew in
wealth and population, New England of necessity would
count for less and less in a material way and that her
influence must depend upon the character of her people
and her representatives.   But he took an even broader
view than that.   He saw with a prophet's eye that her
real supremacy must be maintained through the right
development of the country to the West, and he pro-
tested earnestly against the theory advanced by some
that her true policy was to prevent if possible any

addition to the existing number of States lest she should be shorn of a portion of the strength she then possessed. Pleading for Washington in 1886, and speaking for New England, he said her Senators were haunted by no such fear:

The policy of New England with respect to national growth has never been one of exclusion or repression; on the contrary, it has been the policy of the admission of new States and the consequent enhancement of national strength. Examine the record, and you will find that opposition to the admission of States has not come from New England either in the Senate or House. We have learned, and we know full well, that we cannot maintain our place and influence in the national household by numerical power. It takes but a few years in the great march of national progress to build up new communities that in population and wealth and numerical representation can more than compete with New England. No, sir; we understand if, as we hope and trust, New England is to maintain in the future as she has in the past a conspicuous, if not potential, place in the councils of the nation she must base her claim to such notice on something besides numbers or wealth.

We have learned, indeed we have always realized, that there are invisible forces which can make a small State great; that the true sources of power are in the brains and hearts of a people, be they many or few. So long as New England can maintain for her citizens a high standard of intelligence, of virtue, and national love, I have no misgivings as to the position she will occupy in the Republic. If her Senators can truly and worthily represent a people with such characteristics, they need never fear that their voice will be unheeded. Once New England cast exactly one third of the votes in this branch of the national legislature. Now she casts less than one sixth of them, and yet she does not feel that she has been shorn of her strength or that her influence has departed or waned. . . .

Why should New England be thought to fear or regret the admission of new States? Cast your eye along the parallels of latitude which stretch from the Atlantic coast to the Pacific shore. Study the characteristics of that marvellous civilization which has redeemed the land and subjugated the forces of nature along those parallels. Take note of the people who along those lengthened lines have builded cities, developed agriculture, penetrated the deep recesses of the earth, created a highway, yes, highways for the nation, established the institutions of education and religion, elevated and glorified mankind. Who are they? Are they not bone of our bone and flesh of our flesh? The blood of New England courses along every artery of national life. Put your finger on the pulse of enterprise as it beats in Walla Walla, or Seattle, or Tacoma, or Port Townsend, and you will feel the heart-throb of New England. Who are these men who to-day are asking the Senate permission to enjoy the full privileges of American citizenship in the new State of Washington? True, they have gathered from many States; they have come even from foreign lands, from lands beyond the sea; a new people indeed, but how many of them can trace back their vigor and force to the ancestral cottage which stood on the New England hillside, their patriotism to the village green, and their virtue to the New England church? The voice which I bring to them to-day from their ancestral States is, "Come in, and welcome."

Washington was not admitted as a State during the Forty-ninth Congress. The bill for its admission passed the Senate, providing for the incorporation of the Panhandle of Idaho into the new State, but the measure did not pass the House. When the proposal came again in the Fiftieth Congress, in 1888, Mr. Platt favored the admission of a State containing the original boundaries of Washington and leaving Idaho undisturbed, a provision which finally prevailed, although not favored by the majority of the Territories Committee. In the Fiftieth Congress, the Committee on Territories reported favorably four bills looking to the admission of new States into the Union—Washington, Montana, and the two Dakotas. It had been proposed to admit the northern half of the Territory of Dakota as a State under the name of "Lincoln." The people of the Territory objected, and several Democratic Senators, among them Mr. Butler of South Carolina, took them to task for what was termed a lack of reverence for the name of the great emancipator. Mr. Platt confessed his sympathy with the people of the Territory in this.

"The condition is such," he said, "that the name of Dakota cannot be taken away from either portion of the Territory without injustice, and without doing violence to the wishes and feelings of the Territory."

As for the charge of irreverence brought by Mr. Butler, he said:

Suppose that some one should propose to change the name of the Senator and call him by the name of the most illustrious of all Presidents, the father of his country, and that his name henceforth, instead of being Matthew C. Butler should be Matthew C. Washington, and that he should object and say, "My name is Butler; I do not desire to change it." Would he be held lacking in respect and admiration for the great name of Washington? Not at all. And no more are the soldiers of North Dakota, who followed the flag and carried the musket, who, under the lead of the great Lincoln, preserved the Government when it was assailed—no more are they to be charged with being wanting in respect to the name of Lincoln. I congratulate the Senator from South Carolina, and I congratulate the country on his new-born zeal and admiration for the memory of Lincoln.

The Democrats in the House, having a majority there, and enjoying the support of a Democratic administration, not unnaturally undertook to prevent the admission of four Republican States on the eve of an election for President, and made an issue by proposing the admission of Dakota as one State while New Mexico was to be brought in as a Democratic balance. A caucus of the Democrats of the House adopted this resolution:

Resolved, That it is the sense of the caucus that an enabling act for the Territories of Dakota, Montana, Washington, and New Mexico should be passed at this session, providing for constitutional conventions in each Territory, and the submission of those constitutions for ratification at an election in November, 1888, substantially as provided for in the bill reported by the Committee on Territories at this session.

Mr. Platt contended that the people of the southern part of Dakota had a right to participate in the next election for President; that they ought to have been admitted long ago. He declared that Congress had been derelict in its duty, that it had temporized and postponed the creation of the State until it had become 400,000 strong, a population greater than that of Rhode Island, Vermont, New Hampshire, Delaware, Florida, Oregon, Nebraska, Nevada, or Colorado, and that the fact that another presidential election was approaching was no reason why they should now be denied admission into the Union as quickly as it could be done. He quoted the treaty with France ceding the Territory of Louisiana of which Dakota was a part, and the Northwest Ordinance of 1787, as extended in 1834, to show that the people of the Territory had morally a right to be admitted to the Union. At the same time he contended that the Territory was too large to be admitted as one State. It was larger by 27,000 square miles than England, Ireland, Scotland, and Wales—practically as large as New York, Pennsylvania, New Jersey, Maryland, and Virginia, and capable of supporting as large a population:

Even if the sentimei t of the people were not adverse to it and the people had a dream of empire to grow out of the admission of such a great State, yet Congress, having reference to the physical equality of all the States, ought not to think of admitting one State into the Union so capable of sustaining a dense population.

The idea of proper self-government repelled the notion that such a State would not be too large. It was impossible for the common people to take part in the concerns of a State of that size. The expense of travel to conventions and to the Legislature would practically shut them out from a participation in the privileges of government, relegating the conduct of affairs to the rich or unscrupulous. It would amount also to a practical denial of the administration of justice in the courts. Poor people must have their courts near at hand:

Good statesmanship will avoid the creation of imperial States. I heard it said during the discussion last year that if we would divide Dakota and divide other Territories the Senate would become a mob. At most it could not have more than one hundred members if we admitted all the Territories, dividing Dakota, and, I think, splitting up Texas into five States besides; but it is better that the Senate should be so enlarged, that it should represent the popular will and feel the popular pulse, than that a State should be admitted which would have an abnormally large representation in the House of Representatives. It is to the danger, it is to the disadvantage of smaller States and medium-sized States that any State should have an abnormally large representation in the House of Representatives.

The act enabling the people of the two Dakotas, Montana, and Washington, to form constitutions and State governments, was passed in the next session, and was approved by President Cleveland on February 22, 1889.

In the first session of the Fifty-first Congress in 1890, Mr. Platt as Chairman of the Committee on Territories, secured the enactment of bills admitting to statehood Idaho and Wyoming. There was a Republican majority in both Senate and House, and the opposition to these bills was perfunctory, though, in the case of Wyoming, there was a question as to the advisability of admitting to full participation in the privileges of statehood a community where women would be permitted to vote under the constitution. To this Mr. Platt responded that while he had never been an advocate of woman suffrage, he would not keep a Territory out of the Union because its constitution allowed women to vote, nor would he force upon a Territory any restriction or qualification as to what the vote should be in that respect. Both the Idaho and Wyoming bills were passed and the two new States were admitted, one on July 3, 1890, the other on July 11th.

It was six years before the admission of another State. Utah was admitted in 1896, and Oklahoma in 1907. In the first session of the Fifty-second Congress, in 1892, the Committee on Territories reported a bill for the admission of New Mexico. Mr. Platt did not join in the report, and questioned whether, in view of statistics and facts, New Mexico was entitled to admission. When the attempt was made ten years later to admit Arizona and New Mexico, with Oklahoma and the Indian Territory, Mr. Platt, although not then a member of the Committee, strongly opposed the admission of the four new States. He was ready to admit Oklahoma and the Indian Territory as one State, and that finally came about, but his influence, which was very powerful, was exerted against any other conclusion than this. To his friend, L. F. Parker of St. Louis, who favored giving the Indian Territory a delegate in Congress, he wrote, on March 25, 1903:

There is much in what you say in your letter of November 20th, but I do not feel like doing anything which may seem to have the apparent effect of looking toward statehood for the Indian Territory alone. I have pretty decided notions on that subject. Oklahoma and the Indian Territory have, of course, sufficient population for statehood, when compared with many States we have admitted, but I believe it is best for the country and best for both Oklahoma and the Indian Territory, that when they do come in, they shall come as one State. States are made altogether too easily and thoughtlessly now. I do not know that the allowance of a delegate would affect the matter, but Alaska is asking for one, as well as the Indian Territory—both are in somewhat unorganized condition, and between us, I do not think there is any necessity for one from either. I do not mean by this to say that I would oppose it, but am merely expressing my own feeling about it.

During all his association with the Committee on Territories and the Committee on Indian Affairs, Mr. Platt scrupulously refrained from interfering in the purely local questions involved, save where it was necessary in the enactment of legislation. Above all

he kept himself aloof from the scrambles for office.
His reply in 1889 to one who wrote him in behalf
of an applicant for the governorship of New Mexico is
typical of his attitude in all such things:

I have felt that it would be a mistake for me to recommend particular persons for appointment in Territories
—in any of them. By reason of my position as Chairman
of the Senate Committee on Territories, and the very severe
struggle to get the four Territories admitted, viz.: Washington, Montana, and the two Dakotas, I have come to occupy
a position where my endorsement is very much sought by
applicants for positions in those Territories. I am in no way
qualified to recommend the persons to fill the offices, and
if I should recommend one, I would displease the others.
So I have thought that the best interests of the Territories
required that I should not make recommendations. I
am very much interested in having President Harrison
adopt the policy of immediate change of officers and make
appointments from the Territories and not from the outside. I have told him that I have no men to push, but
that I do believe that the interests of the Republican party
require immediate action. And I have even declined to
express an opinion when asked by him, as to the comparative merits of candidates—not in New Mexico, but in one
of the other Territories. I think I can do more for the
Territories in that position than to try to get this or that
man appointed, and there is no middle ground. I must
either make recommendations in all the Territories or in
none. I think you will coincide with me in saying this is the
wisest thing to do. But if not, I have already taken this
position with the President, and do not see how I can
change.

His service with the Committee on Territories lasted
for twelve years,—from 1883 to 1895. During the first
four years Benjamin Harrison was Chairman of the

Committee and Platt sat next to him at the table; during the six years from 1887 to 1893, Platt was Chairman of the Committee; from 1893 to 1895, the Democrats were in control. The work which he did during this period gave him great satisfaction, and on the rare occasions when he enumerated his achievements in legislation he always laid stress upon the new States he had a hand in creating; but perhaps the greatest value of his service was in the experience it gave him with the practical problems of territorial government which came so well in play when the time arrived to consider the graver questions growing out of the organization of strange territory through the war with Spain.

CHAPTER XI

THE FOREIGN-BORN AMERICAN

Restriction of Immigration—Advocate of Reasonable Legislation—
His Opinion of the Adopted Citizen.

THE preservation of the quality of American citizenship was a thing which all his life appealed powerfully to this typical American of English ancestry. At the same time, he was broad enough in his humanity to understand the aspirations of the alien seeking to better his condition by migrating to our shores, and practical enough to recognize the economic value of the implement thus thrust into our hands. He believed in immigration and was for welcoming every worthy stranger who wandered this way for a home. It is true that in his early manhood he had been affiliated with the American or "Know-Nothing" party and had served as Chairman of its State Committee, but this was not because he subscribed to the party's bigoted anti-foreign creed. It was because he saw in its organization the most effective agency then at hand to advance the Anti-Slavery cause. As time went by and he saw the deserted homesteads in the Litchfield hills gradually renewing their life through the influx of thrifty Swedes, he grew to appreciate the value of the healthy blood infused into the veins of a thinning countryside, and he appreciated also the importance of maintaining the wholesomeness of the inflowing stream. For the

147

French-Canadians who had come to the mill towns of the Connecticut valley in great numbers, he had a high regard. He seized more than one occasion in the Senate to record his commendation of their sterling qualities:

I have known these people for forty years in the city where I reside [he said in the course of the debate on the Wilson-Gorman Tariff bill in 1894], and I am proud to number among them very many valued acquaintances, social acquaintances, with whom I am as glad to associate as with any of the citizens of my town. They are, as a rule, intelligent, industrious, thrifty, and conservative; they make good citizens; they accumulate property, they are mechanics, agriculturists, and merchants, and among them are many scholars, authors, and men representing the different professions; they assimilate with our native population; their children intermarry with ours; they are quiet and unostentatious; they make no trouble, and after a period of residence here they can scarcely be distinguished from our own native population.

Their children attend our schools, take prizes in competition with the children of the old inhabitants of Connecticut, and in no respect can they be taunted with being an inferior or undesirable people. Usually they accumulate property, and they do not return to Canada carrying away the money which they have earned here. They do not supplant our American workman by accepting lower wages. They work for the same wages that the native workman receives; they work beside him at the same bench or on the same machine. There is no prejudice against them. They are a church-going and a religious people, moral as well as industrious. They do not appear in our police courts, but they do take part, as they should, in our town meetings.

But he was not blind to the fact that all immigrants were not of the character of the Swedes and French-

Canadians who settled in his own State, and throughout his service in the Senate he invariably supported measures to exclude the undesirable.

In the second session of the Forty-eighth Congress in 1884, a law was enacted to prohibit the importation and migration of foreigners and aliens under contract or agreement to perform labor in the United States, its Territories, and the District of Columbia. Mr. Platt not only voted for it but spoke for it:

It is a bill [he said] which proposes to declare, as I understand, two things, and therefore I am in favor of it: First, that the policy of this Government is to protect its laboring men, its workers, to protect them to the extent that they shall be elevated rather than degraded, that they shall be educated rather than made ignorant, that they shall be honored rather than despised; and second, I understand the principle of this bill to be that labor in this country belongs of right to the laborers who are now resident here, and to such other laborers as shall voluntarily come here to join those resident here in the performance of that labor, and I have no hesitation in saying that a practice which contradicts and violates these principles is a crime against the Republic, a crime against its social order, and a crime against its system of government.

It is impossible to bring foreign laborers here under contract without assailing all these principles which I have been enunciating. I am opposed to importing laborers as we import horses and cattle. I am opposed to what may be called involuntary immigration into this country. I am not opposed to voluntary immigration. I regard voluntary immigration as one of the chief sources of our strength, as a factor which has developed and is further to develop the grandest civilization that this continent or the world has ever known, and to make our own the most prosperous, the most powerful, and the most beneficent of all the nations of the earth. I believe that the admixture with our native races of those who come here imbued with the principles of this Government, seeking to better their condition, honestly desiring to work in this land of freedom, tends to build us up as a people and to ennoble all our citizens.

I have never been in favor of involuntary immigration. I voted against the Chinese bill, not because I was in favor of Chinamen being brought here under contract for labor, but simply because I thought that there were in that bill sections and clauses which prohibited voluntary immigration into this country, which shut out the man who desired of his own accord, of his own free will, to come here and become a part of us; because men were shut out from this country by that bill, as I understood it, simply on account of their being laborers who wanted to labor in this country. I will go as far as any other man to prohibit bringing contract labor here, whether it be Chinese, or Italian, or Hungarian, or English, or French, or Irish.

It is that principle against which I contend, and in so doing I recognize and uphold the right of any human being on this globe who himself, of his own motive, of his own desire, his own free will, wishes to come here and become part of us, and honestly partake of the benefits of labor in this country, to come without hindrance or restriction. My doctrine is that no importation of laborers to lower the rate of American wages should be permitted, and no voluntary immigration of honest laborers should be prevented.

He supported the bill which became a law on March 3, 1891, amending and systematizing the immigration laws, and he voted for the bill which was vetoed by President Cleveland on March 2, 1897, establishing an educational test. Beyond those regulations he did not see how it was possible to restrict immigration without excluding people who ought not to be excluded. During the consideration of the Immigration bill which

became a law on March 4, 1903, he was instrumental
in securing an amendment, the absence of which might
have proved embarrassing to the enforcement of the
law, when he caused the word "immigrant" to be
stricken out after the word "alien."   Had the original
expression been retained, it would have been possible
for any alien coming to the United States to escape the
provisions of the law by declaring his intention to return
to his own country.

His creed with regard to immigration he expounded
in the course of the speech which he made during the
debate on the Chinese Exclusion bill, September 7, 1888:

I hold that a citizen of any country on the face of this
earth has a right to leave that country and to transfer his
allegiance to another country with the consent of the
Government to which he endeavors to transfer his allegiance.
That right, I think, is too sacred in American history to be
denied or impeached or in any way invaded.

I hold just as firmly to our right not to receive a man
who may thus expatriate himself and desire to come to
this country as I do to his right to come with our consent.
I hold that we have a right to so regulate, restrain, restrict,
or prohibit immigration into this country, as that our own
country and our own people shall not suffer by that immigration, as that the character of our own people shall not
be in any sense degraded or suffer by such immigration.   I
hold that we ought to receive any person who thus desires
to leave a foreign country and come to our shores and who
can comply with certain conditions which are necessary
to be complied with in order that our civilization, our labor,
and the character of our people shall be in no sense lessened,
interfered with, or degraded.

If, then, a man coming from another country is honest,
is reputable, is able to take care of himself, is healthy, is
the head of a family, is of capacity to understand our

system of government, and is sincerely desirous of casting
in his lot with us and ultimately becoming a citizen of this
Government, I hold we have no right to exclude him.   But
if on the other hand that person belongs to the criminal,
or to the pauper, or the diseased or vicious class, we ought
to exclude him.   We have no room here for that class of
immigrants.   We have no room for criminals, paupers,
diseased, vicious people in all our wide domain.   We ought
also to exclude people who have no sympathy with us
or with our form of government or with our institutions.

The very clause in our statute of naturalization is a guide
to us in this respect.   Before an alien can become a naturalized citizen he must make it appear to the satisfaction of
the court admitting him to citizenship that during his
residence in the United States "he has behaved as a man
of good moral character, is attached to the principles of
the Constitution of the United States, and well disposed to
the good order and happiness of the same."   I would not
admit to these shores, if I could apply the test, a single
individual who had not capacity enough to understand
something of our system of government, and to have an aspiration for the liberty and independence and the dignity
which a man may acquire and achieve under our system of
government.   No anarchists, no communists, no persons,
from wherever they may come, who do not come here
imbued with the principles first laid down, in the history
of the world, in that glorious Declaration of Independence,
should be permitted to come, if I could apply the individual
test which would keep them away.

CHAPTER XII

FAIR PLAY TOWARDS CHINA

Chinese Exclusion—Opposes Act of 1882—Unsuccessful Attempt
to Amend Geary Act—Legislation of 1888—Prevents
Drastic Legislation in 1902 and 1904.

DENNIS KEARNY, the sand lots agitator of San
Francisco, was in the midst of his crusade against
the Chinese, at the time Mr. Platt entered the Senate.
The anti-Chinese cry in California had been growing in
volume for a long time. In 1876, it had reached such
proportions that both political parties inserted in their
platforms planks regarding it; the Democrats demanding legislation to prevent further Mongolian immigration, the Republicans calling upon Congress to investigate the effects of the immigration and importation of
Mongolians upon the moral and material interests of
the country. In 1878, Congress had passed an act
"to restrict the immigration of Chinese into the United
States," which President Hayes had vetoed, on the
ground that the legislation was in violation of the
existing treaty negotiated in 1868 by Mr. Seward and
Mr. Burlingame. The House declined to pass the bill
over the veto. President Hayes thereupon proceeded
to negotiate two treaties with China—one relating to
commercial intercourse, the other relieving the United
States from the provisions of the Burlingame treaty and
permitting the exclusion of Chinese laborers. This
treaty, signed in 1880, was ratified July 19, 1881, and at

the next session of Congress a bill was introduced by Senator Miller of California, the avowed object of which was "to enforce treaty stipulations relating to the Chinese." The bill forbade the coming of Chinese into the United States for a period of twenty years, and was drastic in its provisions. Mr. Platt could not bring himself to vote for it. He believed it violated the spirit of the treaty as well as the principles of natural rights and justice. On March 8, 1882, he delivered a speech in opposition to the measure, which was emphatic and comprehensive. "To prevent possible damage or alleviate a real misfortune," he said, "I cannot consent to the infraction even of the spirit of a treaty, while professing to be bound by it." He reminded the Senate that a treaty was "a contract between nations" and should be kept like every other contract, in the spirit in which it was made:

We made this contract which we call a treaty with the Chinese Government, and we must keep it. We must keep it or stand forever disgraced in the eyes of the world. There is no way in which an individual can so soon and so thoroughly forfeit the respect of the community in which he lives as to be sharp in making a contract and sharp in taking an unfair advantage under the contract which the other contracting party never expected that he would take. There is no way in which a nation can so surely forfeit the respect of all other nations as to make that contract called a treaty in shrewdness, and then as shrewdly take advantage of the technical terms of that treaty to accomplish what the other contracting party never intended should be accomplished.

But aside from the fact that the bill was in violation of the treaty, Mr. Platt opposed it because:

The true intent and meaning of it is to declare that

henceforth, excepting only the Chinese now here, and the colored people now here, no man shall work in the United States except he be a white man.

He could not give his adherence to such a principle:

In the right to work honestly, the Chinaman is your equal and my equal and the equal of every living man, and I will never consent to the passage of any bill which contravenes that principle. Do not misunderstand me. I do not say the Chinaman is the equal of the Anglo-Saxon socially or intellectually. What I do say is that, other conditions being equal, he has the same right to come to this country and work that any white foreigner has.

Mr. President, it will not do to put this legislation on that ground. It will not do to say that a white man who has all the characteristics and habits of a Chinaman and who will work as cheap as a Chinaman may come and labor here and a Chinaman may not, because, forsooth, he is a Mongolian. It will not do to invite white men to come and labor, no matter how cheap they may labor, and forbid a Chinaman to come and labor at the same wages. You must put this legislation on some other ground than the ground of race or color.

Having given the reasons for his opposition to the bill, Mr. Platt went on to suggest certain conditions under which he could vote for legislation on the subject:

I would vote for a bill which did not improperly regulate or limit, or unreasonably suspend the immigration of Chinese laborers. I would vote for a bill which should prevent them coming to this country in such numbers as to endanger our political and social institutions. I would vote for a bill which would prevent their coming here as laborers in such numbers as to ruin labor. I would vote for a bill which should prevent their coming here, if they

degrade labor or make it dishonorable. But I cannot
vote for a bill which has for its only object, for its only
aim and result, the extirpation and the exclusion of the
Chinaman from this country. . . . I am willing, and I put
on record my willingness, to vote for any law we may
properly pass, any law we can pass without violation of
treaty obligations, to the end that the labor market of this
country shall not be over-supplied by immigration from
any quarter; that there shall be no undue and ruinous
competition in labor; that honest labor shall not be dishonored or degraded anywhere; that the standard of labor
shall be fairly remunerative everywhere; that the man who
is willing to do honest work with hand or brain, or both,
shall receive wages enough to enable him to live respectably,
to educate his children, and respect himself.

But the tide of sentiment was too strong. The
Senate voted down an amendment reducing the period
of exclusion from twenty years to ten, and on March
9, 1882, passed the bill in all its criminal enormity, by
a vote of 29 to 15. Mr. Platt had a general pair with
Mr. Johnston of Virginia, and so could not be recorded,
but in announcing his pair, he said: "I regret very much
that I am not permitted, by reason of the pair, to vote
against the bill." He had respectable company in the
minority: Aldrich, Allison, David Davis, Dawes,
Edmunds, Frye, Hoar, Ingalls, and Morrill, among
others.

The bill passed the House a little later, and President
Arthur vetoed it, in his message of April 4th, on the
ground that both good faith and good policy forbade
the suspension of Chinese immigration for so long a
period as twenty years. The Senate refused to pass the
bill over the veto. A few weeks later, a bill was passed
providing for suspension for ten years, instead of twenty,

and making other modifications. Mr. Platt was one of fifteen Senators to vote against this bill, but it was signed by the President on May 6, 1882.

For six years there was comparative quiet in Washington, so far as anti-Chinese legislation was concerned, although the feeling in the West became more and more intense. In the Cleveland administration a treaty was negotiated with China, under which the Chinese Government was to prohibit the emigration of laborers, and the United States was to protect from violence those already in this country. While this treaty was still pending, one of the most disgraceful episodes of American politics was written into the records of Congress. Mr. Cleveland had been renominated and the Presidential campaign was on. William L. Scott of Pennsylvania, a leading member of the House, was also a leading member of the Executive Committee of the Democratic National Committee. He was regarded as President Cleveland's spokesman in Congress. On Monday, September 3, 1888, without previous notice, an extraordinary bill was brought into the House by Mr. Scott, the President's friend, amending the Act of 1882, by striking out all permission for a Chinese to return to this country for any purpose, after having once left it, and declaring all return certificates void—in fact, barring the United States to any Chinese workman once outside its boundaries. The bill, which was thought to have been prepared at the White House, was rushed through the House that Monday morning within half an hour of its introduction. It was a spectacular political trick, so timed that neither party in Congress could afford to oppose it in the face of a Presidential election. Mr. Platt voted for the bill under protest, and voiced his protest in the Senate:

If a vote is now pressed upon this bill I shall vote for it, and I desire to state the reasons, and I desire also to state some reasons why I shall do it under protest, for I do not intend that any action of mine shall be misunderstood or misrepresented.

I do not like the way this bill has come before Congress, and I want to say so as emphatically as I know how. In May last the Senate of the United States advised and consented to a treaty which had been negotiated with China and communicated to the Senate by the President. We were told by those representing the Pacific Coast, and we have heard it over and over again, that the treaty as it came to the Senate was not satisfactory and would not accomplish the object in view, namely, the exclusion of Chinese laborers from this country. Being told that, the Senate amended the treaty in a way which was proposed by the representatives of the Pacific Coast and in a manner which they told us would be entirely satisfactory and would have the effect of preventing Chinese laborers from coming to this country in competition with our home labor. The treaty was so amended and passed the Senate. Following that treaty the Senate passed a bill on the 8th of August, 1888, to carry into effect the provisions of that treaty when ratifications should be exchanged—a bill which I think received the unanimous support of the Senate, a bill which I approved and which I still approve. . . . The treaty has been submitted to the Chinese authorities for the exchange of ratifications. The bill, after having passed the Senate, went to the House of Representatives, was concurred in by the House, and on the first day of September, 1888, was taken to the President of the United States for his approval, and remains before him at the present time. This was last Saturday. With that bill, which, if the treaty is to be ratified by the Chinese Government, goes as far as any human being in the United States has asked Congress to go in the exclusion of Chinese laborers—with that bill passed by both Houses, now in the hands of the President of the United States for approval or rejection, there comes here another act, based upon the assumption that this treaty is not to be ratified. As I say, the bill passed by both Houses of Congress was delivered to the President of the United States last Saturday, the first day of September. On last Monday, the third day of September, there came to us from the House of Representatives the bill now under consideration.

If, as every Senator here thinks, if, as the whole country believes, the bill under consideration emanated from the Executive Department, and was started in hot haste immediately after the laying before the President of the United States of a bill passed by Congress upon the subject, it seems to me to be an Executive interference with the legislative branch of the Government, and I am bound in my character as a Senator to make that remark. . . .

I can not say that this bill is written upon the paper of the Executive Department. I know it is generally believed in both Houses of this Congress that it is. I can not say that the most potential man in the Democratic National Committee in the management of this campaign came from the White House to the Capitol with this bill; but it is generally believed in this chamber and throughout the Union. If there has been no official notice or unofficial intimation that this treaty has been rejected or is to be rejected by the Chinese Government, why this hot haste to override the act now lying before the Executive for his approval, and to pass this bill, which under such circumstances would be a direct insult to a nation with whom at least we are desirous of continuing friendly commercial relations? Is this a vote-catching performance? Has it come to this that public office is to be prostituted for Democratic electioneering purposes? And if not, what other reason is there for thrusting in this untimely way this bill upon the attention of Congress? . . .

This bill being here, being bound as a Senator, in spite of all the circumstances which point to other conclusions, to assume that the Executive and the State Department and the Democratic National Committee have some knowledge which has not been communicated to us, that this treaty is not to be ratified, I am going to vote for the bill, and I am going to do so because I am heartily and sincerely in favor of prohibiting and preventing any immigration into this country of a character which we ought not to receive. . . . I put my vote for this bill solely on the ground that I can not assume that there is no necessity for it. If the treaty which we agreed to here is to be ratified by the Chinese Government, and if the bill which we have already passed to carry the treaty into effect is to be approved by the President of the United States, I can not see the necessity for this bill. But I will not, as a Senator, assume that this bill has no necessity behind it, and that it is simply and purely an electioneering trick, a performance on the part of the Democratic party and its high officials to catch votes in certain quarters of the United States.

Only three members of the Senate, Hoar of Massachusetts, Brown of Georgia, and Wilson·of Iowa, voted against the bill, and many of those who voted for it under the stress of what was represented by the administration spokesmen to be a great emergency, lived to regret their record. One of these was Mr. Platt, who later took advantage of the opportunity to make amends.

In 1892, when the ten years' period specified in the Act of 1882 was approaching an end, Mr. Geary of California presented in the House a bill to prohibit absolutely the coming of Chinese persons into the United States. The bill, having passed the House, came up for action in the Senate, April 25, 1892. Mr. Platt offered an amendment, providing that the Act of October 1, 1888, should be excepted from the laws then in force, prohibiting and regulating Chinese immigration, which should be "continued in force for a period of ten years from the passage of this act."

The Scott law had met with remonstrance from the Chinese Government, as in contravention of the treaty of 1880, and strong representations against it had been made to our Government, which persistently ignored them. Mr. Platt declared that he could not vote for the bill without his amendment, and explained that he had voted for the Scott bill under protest. His amendment was rejected by a vote of eight to forty-five, and the bill was passed without a roll-call.

At the end of a second ten-year period, in 1902, Mr. Platt again had an opportunity to make an impress on Chinese legislation. A convention with China of October 8, 1894, had restored the conditions of return to the earlier status. In 1902, a bill passed the House to prohibit the coming into, and to regulate the residence within, the United States, of Chinese and persons of Chinese descent. It was a long bill, putting into law all Treasury regulations and drastic provisions with regard to the way the law should be administered. When the bill came to the Senate, it gave rise to long debate and grave differences. The bill was pending for months. Mr. Platt finally solved the difficulties by presenting a substitute for the bill, which, with some modifications, was accepted by Congress. The effect was to continue all laws then in force, with a provision that the laws were "re-enacted, extended, and continued, so far as the same are not inconsistent with treaty obligations."

In January, 1904, the Chinese Government gave notice of the termination on December 7th, of the treaty of 1894, not because she wished to secure admission for her laborers into the United States, but because she

wished to make a new treaty which should define
more specifically the word "laborers" and thus accord
to the higher classes the privilege of coming into the
United States. Mr. Patterson of Colorado introduced
a bill with the avowed object of meeting the situation
thus created. The bill was complicated, technical,
and stringent. Its effect would have been to exclude
bankers, commercial brokers, and all persons of the
higher classes, as well as laborers; to give to immigration officers additional means to harass the Chinese,
and still further to widen the breach between China and
the United States. For one thing, it provided that the
words "Chinese person" or "persons of Chinese descent"
should be construed to mean any person descended
from an ancestor of the Mongolian race, "which ancestor is now, or was at any time subsequent to the year
1800, a subject of the Emperor of China."

Mr. Platt took the lead in opposing the bill. He
pointed out that it would exclude "a great many
Japanese, all Koreans, a very large proportion of
Filipinos," for they had Mongolian ancestors who were
subjects of the Emperor of China within the last one
hundred years:

If they have one particle of Chinese blood from an ancestor of 110 years ago, they are to be excluded on the statement of the inspector that he believes they had such an
ancestor, unless right then and there they can prove the
contrary.

Mr. Platt dissected the bill section by section. He
was in constant communication with the White House,
restraining the President, who had it in mind to send a
special message to Congress, and keeping him advised
as to developments in the Senate. The bill failed to

become a law, and Mr. Platt's part in chloroforming it was generously recognized. Among the letters of approval, he had this from a former Secretary of State:

I congratulate you and the country on your effective effort respecting the Chinese Exclusion amendment. You have saved us from some very discreditable legislation.

CHAPTER XIII

SOUND FINANCE

First Essays in Finance—Refunding Bill of 1881—Speech of February 17th—Proposes Abolition of Tax on Bank Circulation.

FINANCIAL questions are proverbially among the most troublesome topics which come before Congress. They lead to bitter differences of opinion, to unreasoning debate, to sectional and class hatred. Beyond all other subjects of legislation, those affecting the coinage, banking, loans, and currency should be religiously divorced from politics, yet they can generally be depended upon to excite political feeling and accentuate party alignments, so that it is impossible to consider them in accordance with simple business principles, to say nothing of recognized principles of finance. There have been few questions about which charlatans have so freely had their say or about which men conspicuously lacking in the qualities which inspire confidence have presumed so cheerfully to meddle with the operations of a complex governmental machine. Not only does public finance have a curious fascination for theorists and those with badly balanced minds, but it too often weaves a spell on public men devoted to its study, deluding them with some fantastic scheme impossible to execute, even though it were to take the place of the admittedly imperfect system now in force. The wonder is that on the whole, through years of turmoil, compromise, and blind experiment, the government has waxed strong financially, and that a system which, like Topsy, has "just growed," should have so many merits and so few defects. That chaos has not sprung from ceaseless agitation and the promulgation of queer ideas is due in no small measure to the influence of men of common sense like Platt, who, while pretending to no mastery of the theories of finance, have kept more eager spirits from plunging into rash extremes. Platt never claimed to be a financier, and he was quite content to leave to others the authoritative exposition of monetary principles. It was many years before he attained a position on the Finance Committee, yet it may be doubted whether the judgment of any other member of the Senate went farther on the subjects with which that Committee has to deal. "It is not more money we need," he wrote once, when the question of an elastic currency was under discussion, "it is more sense about money,"[1] and that remark illustrates the way in which he always approached the subject.

In concluding the first long speech he ever made in the Senate, he thus expressed his modest judgment of his own attainments:

I have ventured to make these observations with great diffidence in the presence and hearing of Senators who, from study and long observation and experience, are so much better qualified to discuss this subject than I am. I do not pretend to be a financier, but I have thought that the suggestions which I have tried to make, some of them at least, might claim the merit of being in accordance with common sense; and, if so, what I have said will not be an entirely unworthy contribution to this discussion.

[1] Letter to John H. Flagg, August, 1903.

This was his habit—to appeal to the every-day experience of the average man. He made no pretence to expert knowledge. So far as he was able, he applied the ordinary rules of private business to the consideration of public affairs. He had always been a "sound-money" man, and it happened that his first serious discussion of an important measure helped to fix his place in the Senate as a pillar of conservative finance.

In the first session of the Forty-sixth Congress, in 1880, Fernando Wood, from the Committee on Ways and Means, of which he was Chairman, had reported to the House a bill "To facilitate the refunding of the national debt." As originally reported, it provided that, in lieu of the bonds authorized by the refunding act of July 14, 1870, bearing 5, 4½, and 4 per cent. interest, bonds bearing interest at the rate of 3½ per cent., to the amount of $500,000,000, redeemable at the pleasure of the United States, and also Treasury notes in the amount of $200,000,000, bearing interest at the rate of 3½ per cent., redeemable at the pleasure of the United States after two years, and payable in ten years, be issued.

The Secretary of the Treasury was authorized to issue any of these bonds or notes for any of the bonds of the United States as they became redeemable, par for par, the 3½ bonds to be the only bonds receivable as security for national bank circulation.

The bill as introduced and reported was in harmony with the recommendations made by Secretary Sherman in his annual report, and if it had been passed in that form it would have saved the United States great sums of money, and would have measurably strengthened the public credit. But the Democratic House tore the bill to pieces. All sorts of queer and erratic

amendments were offered, and the Ways and Means
Committee acquiesced in so many of them, that, in
the judgment of the Secretary of the Treasury, the
execution of the law, had it been passed, would have
been out of the question. The rate of interest was
reduced to 3 per cent., and a provision was made that
no bonds should be taken as security for bank circulation, or government deposits, except the 3 per cent.
bonds thus provided. The bill, distorted, passed the
House on January 19, 1881. The Senate Committee
on Finance amended it so as to eliminate the more
objectionable features, restoring the rate of interest
to 3½ per cent. The bill was taken up in the Senate
on February 15th. It was important that some
sensible legislation should be had. In a little more
than sixty days from that time, bonds bearing interest at 5 per cent., to the amount of $469,651,050,
would become payable at the option of the Government.
On the thirtieth of June two other loans, each bearing
6 per cent., the first for $145,786,500, the second for
$57,787,250, would also mature, at the option of the
Government. This extravagant rate of interest might
have been exchanged for the then reasonable rate of
3½ per cent., if the impossible elements of Congress
had been willing to listen to reason. It was felt by
the masters of finance that a bond of a lower rate
than 3½ per cent. could not be floated under conditions
then existing, but the radicals in the Senate and in
the House insisted that the rate should be at least
as low as 3 per cent. It was in the days of fanatical
opposition to the national banks, many of which were
approaching the end of the twenty years' period for
which they were originally chartered, and nothing
was regarded as unreasonable which would compel

the banks to accept a low rate of interest for the bonds required to be deposited for circulation. Twenty years later, it was found possible to float over $600,-000,000 of 2 per cent. consols, and Mr. Platt was among those who favored that rate of interest in 1900. But that low rate of interest could not have been obtained had it not been for artificial devices, the wisdom of resorting to which is now seriously in question.

In speaking of the funding bill of February 17, 1881, Mr. Platt began by quoting the homely phrase, "It is better to be safe than to be sorry." He asked:

What is a fair rate of interest? It is certainly not the highest rate which the lender would take if he could get it. It may not be the lowest rate at which the Government can induce the lender to part with his money. What is a fair rate of interest, if we consider only this day and this hour, may be a very unfair rate of interest before the five years' option shall expire, or before the twenty years shall have expired when these bonds mature. If it be found to be an unfair rate of interest, the result will be that these bonds will go below par, a disaster I think which would more than overbalance all the benefits to be derived from the saving which the Government might make in the difference between $3\frac{1}{2}$ and 3 per cent. I believe that rate to be fairest and wisest and best which, during the whole period that these bonds are to remain outstanding, will maintain them at or substantially at par, always excepting times of panic, against which we can not provide, and the coming of which we can not certainly foretell.

He then asked a question which reads somewhat strangely in view of the ease with which the $200,-000,000 Spanish War loan was floated in 1898 at three per cent., and $730,000,000 in consols and Panama bonds have been floated since 1900:

Does any one who does not listen to the interested specu-
lators of Wall Street, and whose eyes are not blinded with
the glamour of stock speculation, believe that a three per
cent. bond or a three and one quarter per cent. bond is to remain at par in this country during the next five, ten, or
twenty years? I think I may safely assume that the answer to that question must be in the negative; and I suggest
to those who desire to win a cheap glory for this Government in placing this bond at a lower rate of interest than
any other government has ever been able to place its bonds,
to consider the probability of these bonds at a three per
cent. interest being at 90 or 85, and to ask themselves
whether the whole country will not then point to the un-
wisdom of their position of to-day.

He could not tolerate the inference that, because the
banks were largely to take the bonds, it was of no
consequence at how low a rate of interest Congress
could compel the banks to accept the bonds and be
satisfied:

I have no interest in national banks; I do not own a
dollar of stock in a bank, and therefore I may say that I
have no patience with the sentiment abroad in this country
which cries "Down with the national banks!" We should
not have a country to-day if the banking system had not
been adopted and put in operation; we should not have
prosperous business to-day; we should not have good times
to-day, if it had not been for that wise system of banking—
the wisest and the best in my judgment that exists on
the face of the earth—a system which furnishes absolute
security to the bill holder. No man in this broad land ever
lost one dollar upon the bills of a national bank, and no
man ever will.

He did not believe that, even at $3\frac{1}{2}$ per cent. interest,
the bonds then held by national banks would be fully
replaced by new bonds, and he suggested that any

Senator put the question to "his conservative banking friend, as every Senator has such a friend in whom he places implicit confidence." He believed that there must be a sudden and violent contraction of the national bank circulation:

If it were not for that fact I should regard the issue of Treasury notes as a dangerous measure, in that it would inflate suddenly the currency of the country, and then as suddenly, when interest had accumulated upon them, contract it again. It will be my hope that to some degree they may supply the place made by the retirement of the national bank circulation under this act.

He would rather pay four per cent. than three per cent. and he believed that with the exception of the men in Wall Street who, for purposes of speculation, were running government bonds up beyond their intrinsic value, the business men of the country would prefer that the rate should be four per cent. rather than less than three and a half per cent.:

This Government, if the bond is really worth more than par at three and a half per cent., will reap its advantage in the increased premium; the Government will lose nothing; and it will thus prevent a loss falling eventually upon that class of people who are least able to bear it, to a great extent, and whom we least desire should bear the loss, if any there is to be.

But the rate of interest that is to be paid in business transactions during the next five, ten, or twenty years, is to be largely affected by the rate of interest which the Government places upon this loan. I know that the government rate of interest is not the only thing which influences the business rate of interest; but it does influence it; it does have its effect upon it. When you reduce the government interest, there follows or goes along with it a reduction in the business rate of interest. The business rate of interest is a most important factor in the future prosperity of this country. If it be too low there is danger in it as surely as if it be too high. If the rate of interest be too high, what is the result? It eats up capital, it eats up the capital invested in all business enterprises, and bankruptcy follows, hard times follow. And what if it be too low? The capitalists seek other avenues for investment, they are tempted into speculative enterprises, and they will do what they are doing to-day—put their money at risk for the sake of obtaining a higher rate of interest than the current rate. What is the result of that? Overspeculation, overtrading, followed by panic, by depression, by hard times. What this country needs, what the business of the country needs, is a stable, fair rate of interest, one which shall neither be too high nor too low; and I think in fixing the rate of this government loan we should have in view the influence that the government rate of interest is to have upon the business rate of interest.

Mr. President, all these considerations lead me to hope that the recommendation of the Committee will be adopted; that we shall neither make the rate 3 per cent., nor $3\frac{1}{2}$ per cent., nor shall we change the recommendation of the Committee by saying at a rate not exceeding $3\frac{1}{2}$ per cent. I think there is great force in the fact that when you are dealing with the men of Wall Street, as you must to a certain extent deal with them in placing this loan, it is not wise to say to them: "We will sell our bonds at 3 per cent. if you will take them; if not, we will let you have them at $3\frac{1}{2}$." I believe that the legislative branch of the Government should fix a rate at which it knows, as well as it can be assured of anything, that the loan will be placed, and placed quickly, and that rate should be certain, not left to the discretion of the Secretary of the Treasury.

In spite of the attitude of the administration and the arguments of some of the most influential Democratic Senators, among them Mr. Bayard, Chairman of the Finance Committee, the Senate, after long debate, disagreed to the amendments of the Committee and passed the bill substantially as it came from the House. Had the bill become a law in this form, it would have imperilled the national banking system, and the fear of this result caused a serious flurry in the money market during the last week in February, while the country was awaiting the action of the President. On the 3d of March the President returned the bill with his veto. "Under Section 5 of the bill," he said:

It is obvious that no additional banks will hereafter be organized except possibly in a few cities or localities where the prevailing rates of interest in ordinary business are extremely low. No new banks can be organized and no increase of the capital of existing banks can be obtained, except by the purchase and deposit of 3 per cent. bonds. No other bonds of the United States can be used for the purpose. The one thousand millions of other bonds recently issued by the United States, and bearing a higher interest than 3 per cent., and therefore a better security for the bill holders, cannot, after the first of July next, be received as security for bank circulation. This is a radical change in the banking law. It takes from the banks the right they heretofore had under the law to purchase and deposit as security for the circulation any of the bonds issued by the United States, and deprives the bill holder of the best security which the banks are able to give, by requiring them to deposit bonds having the least value of any bonds issued by the Government.

Two years later, on February 10, 1883, during the second session of the Forty-seventh Congress, during the debate on a bill reducing internal-revenue duties,

Mr. Platt made a proposition to abolish the tax on national-bank circulation, thus bringing down on his head the reproaches of Mr. Sherman and Mr. Morrill, then at the head of the Finance Committee. The bill, which became a law on March 3, 1883, described, among other taxes to be abolished, the tax on bank checks, bank capital, and bank deposits. During its consideration in the Senate, Mr. Platt moved to amend, by inserting the words:

"And on bank circulation, as provided in the third clause of Section 3408 of the Revised Statutes of the United States."

In advocating this amendment, he said:

If we are to remove all the internal-revenue taxes except the tax on whiskey and a portion of the tax on tobacco, I can see no reason why the tax should be left upon the circulation of banks. I can see no reason why the tax should be removed from bank deposits and bank capital, and be left upon bank circulation. There are, to my mind, many reasons why, if a discrimination is to be made, the tax upon circulation should be repealed, and not upon deposits; and I will state them very briefly:

The deposit tax is the tax easiest paid by the banks. The repeal of the tax on deposits will relieve the banks which least need relief. The repeal of the tax upon circulation will relieve the banks which most need relief. Of course the city banks are the great deposit banks of the country; they have deposits many times in excess of their capital, and they are banks of small circulation. When you go into the country, the conditions are reversed. The country banks are banks of small deposits and of large circulation. . . . If there is to be any tax left on banks it should be the tax on deposits, and the tax on circulation should be repealed for the benefit of the country banks, the weak banks, the conservative banks, the banks that never indulge in or countenance speculation, and are conducted for the benefit of the people and the business interests of the communities where they are located.

Mr. Sherman denounced this proposition as monstrous, and Mr. Morrill expressed regret that the subject had been introduced. No vote was taken on the amendment, and nothing more was ever heard of it. The tax on circulation remained at one per cent. until the passage of the law of 1900, which reduced the tax to one-half per cent., when circulation is secured by two per cent. consols. Recent proposals to abolish altogether the tax on circulation secured by two per cents. have not been denounced as "monstrous."

CHAPTER XIV

THE FREE-SILVER DELUSION

A Genuine Bimetallist—Opposes Coin Certificates in 1888—The Sherman Law of 1890—Opponent of Free Silver—Objects to Hasty Repeal—Retaliation against Great Britain.

WHEN Platt became a Senator, free silver was a dormant issue. The Greenback heresy had seen its day, and its devotees had shifted their allegiance to the "dollar of the Fathers" as the next worst thing. The Democratic party, from force of habit, had accepted the new doctrine, and they were reinforced by Republicans from silver-mining States, while other Republicans weakly wavered. The issue had been joined in Congress, resulting in a compromise upon the so-called Bland-Allison Silver Act of 1878, which was as far from satisfying the advocates of free-silver coinage as the friends of a stable medium of exchange, but which for a time served as a makeshift to keep the silver question out of Congress except for sporadic outbursts of debate.[1] Though the question was kept out of Congress, the friends of silver were not idle. After the election of Cleveland in 1884, they made a vigorous demonstration, which was held in check only by the President's firm stand against the majority of his own

[1] The Democratic House had passed a straight free-coinage bill under suspension of the rules by a vote of 163 to 34. The measure was modified by the Senate, which had a Republican majority.

party, and which so impressed itself upon the politics of the day, that when the Republicans returned to power in 1888 they found it necessary to consider further legislation which, stopping short of free coinage, should mollify prevailing sentiment by providing for a larger use of silver.

Platt had been a sturdy antagonist of the Greenback propaganda. He was opposed not only to inflation but to the greenback in itself, and up to the end he seldom touched upon the currency in any form without uttering a note of warning against that survival of the operation of Civil War finance. He was just as sturdy an opponent of free silver at the ratio of 16 to 1, but he had no prejudice against silver as a medium of exchange. He was an international bimetallist, and so he always remained. With him bimetallism was not a political evasion, it was a serious economic proposition. He believed there was a place for both silver and gold in the currency of the world, if the great commercial nations would agree, and he believed that the danger of silver coinage would be greatly mitigated if the coin itself were used in the currency instead of silver certificates issued by the Government. Holding these views, it fell to his lot to be of material service in bringing hostile forces together and so preventing the enactment of a free-coinage law, when that peril was imminent in 1890.

He first declared his position in the Senate on the silver question in the course of a debate during the first session of the Fiftieth Congress in 1888 on an amendment offered by Stewart of Nevada to a bill "To provide for the purchase of United States bonds by the Secretary of the Treasury." Stewart proposed to authorize the issue of coin certificates at United

States mints and assay offices in return for deposits
of gold and silver bullion, the price of silver bullion
to be stated by the Secretary of the Treasury on the
first and fifteenth of each calendar month, but not to
exceed $1 for 412½ grains of silver, nine-tenths fine.
In the opinion of Mr. Platt this proposition reeked
with financial heresy, and he spoke with force and
earnestness against it.   The decline in the price of
silver, after the enactment of the Bland-Allison act,
had been responsible largely for the continued agitation of the silver question, and the advocates of the
pending amendment insisted that its enactment would
put silver at par.   Mr. Platt reminded them that silver
had declined, as all other things declined, because there
had been an over-production of it in the world—more
than was required for coinage and other uses, including
manufacturing and the arts:

Why should the adoption of the proposed measure put
silver at par?   Because it will furnish a customer for all
the silver that can be mined in the whole world.   And
what will be the effect of that?   Simply that mining will
be more profitable, will attract new capital, will enlist
new enterprise, and the more it is produced the more the
Government must take of it and issue the coin certificates for it, and this not only in the United States, but
throughout the world.   There is nothing to prevent the
bringing of silver to this country, and there is nothing
to prevent any foreigner, anybody on the whole face of the
wide globe, from bringing all his surplus silver to the
Treasury of the United States and taking the coin certificates of this Government for it.

If this bill passes, the Senator from Nevada may well
say there will be prosperity.   There will, but it will be the
prosperity which comes with inflation, to be followed at
last by worse adversity.   The history of the world has

shown that when a government begins, upon the demand
for more money, to increase its paper money, there is no
end of that increase and inflation except absolute bankruptcy and financial ruin.

The Stewart amendment was absorbed in an amendment offered by Mr. Beck, of Kentucky, substituting
coin certificates for the existing gold and silver
certificates. The Beck amendment was adopted
by a vote of 38 to 13 and Mr. Platt was enrolled with
the small minority. The bill, thus amended, passed
the Senate on April 5, 1888, without division. It
never became a law but the popular call for free coinage
continued. It became so strong that at the beginning
of the new administration in 1889, Secretary Windom,
with the approval of President Harrison, submitted
to Congress, in his first annual report, his plan for
increasing the use of silver in circulation. This plan
provided that the Treasury Department should purchase silver bullion every month to a limited extent,
paying therefor Treasury notes receivable for government dues, and payable on demand in gold, or in
silver bullion at the current market rate, at the time
of payment, and that the purchase of silver bullion
and the compulsory coinage of silver dollars under the
Act of 1878 should close. On the twenty-eighth of
January, 1890, Senator Morrill, Chairman of the
Finance Committee, introduced a bill prepared by the
Secretary of the Treasury and embodying his views.
The bill was reported favorably by the Finance Committee with certain amendments. Its important section was the first, which authorized the Secretary of
the Treasury to purchase $4,500,000 worth of silver
bullion each month and to issue in payment therefor
Treasury notes receivable for customs and all public

dues, and redeemable on demand in lawful money of the United States; when so redeemed to be cancelled. A similar bill had been passed by the House, the principal difference being that under the House bill the notes to be issued were full legal tender, and the Secretary of the Treasury was authorized to redeem them in gold coin or silver bullion at the market rate.

The Senate considered these measures at intervals for over three months in a notable debate, into which entered every question connected with the financial operations of the Government since the war.

The debate was carried on largely by the friends of free silver, who declaimed at great length of the iniquity of the "Crime of '73"; for the proposal of the Finance Committee and the bill passed by the House were a long way from meeting their demands. The opponents of free silver contented themselves, as a rule, with replying to the arguments advanced, and with taking up, point by point, questions as they arose during the discussion. Mr. Platt had little to say except to interpolate an occasional query. Toward the end of the debate, on June 13, 1890, he interrupted a speech of Mr. Stewart with the following comment:

Does the Senator believe—and he has paid great attention to this subject, and his opinion is entitled to great weight—that if the maximum amount now provided by law to be coined into silver dollars were to be coined, the result of that would be to restore the equivalency in value between the gold and silver dollar? Because if he does and is correct in his supposition, I confess that it seems to me that is a ground upon which we might all come together. . . .

If the Senator will permit me one other word, some of us have this difficulty: We feel that if we use the two metals as money—and we feel that we ought to do it—the material of which a dollar is composed in each metal ought to be the same. I do not suppose that in 1878, if it had been an original proposition, anybody would have thought of coining a silver dollar of which the material was not of the same commercial value as the material in the gold dollar; but it was thought that a great wrong had been done, that silver had been demonetized when the material of which the dollar was composed was worth as much as the gold dollar, and that wrong ought to be righted, and that we ought to take the same ratio although the value of the silver had depreciated; and that, I understand, was the ground upon which the bill of 1878 was passed.

Now, if there is any way in which we can get back so as to have the material of which one dollar is composed of the same value of which the other dollar is composed, then we should all get back upon a common platform.

Four days later, on June 17th, an amendment proposed by Senator Plumb, striking out the first section of the bill and inserting in its place an unqualified provision for the free coinage of silver at 16 to 1, was adopted by a vote of 43 to 24, the favoring votes coming from the Democratic side of the chamber, and from Republican Senators of silver-producing States.

The ultimate result was the Sherman Silver act. Mr. Sherman was at the head of the Conference Committee for the Senate and Mr. Conger of Iowa for the House. It took nearly three weeks for the Conference Committee to approach a reconciliation of the wide differences between the two sides, and Senator Platt had more to do than almost any other man in bringing the free silver Senators to accept a compromise. When the report was finally made, on July 7th, Senator Harris of Tennessee, and Representative Bland of Missouri, the Democratic free silver members of the conference, refused to sign it. The bill as finally passed provided for the purchase of 4,500,000 ounces of silver bullion per month, instead of $4,500,000, a change, which, owing to the subsequent fall in the price of silver, reduced the amount to be purchased. It also contained an important new clause, declaring the purpose of the Government to maintain the parity of the metals.

Mr. Sherman, from whom the act took its name, although he was not primarily responsible for it, declared a few years later that he was ready to repeal it the day it became a law, if repeal could have been had without substituting in its place absolute free coinage. Mr. Platt, while no more nearly satisfied with the act than others, was never carried away with the clamor against it which began almost immediately, grew in volume after the election of Cleveland in 1892, and continued unabated until after the repeal of the purchasing clause in the following autumn. Having voted for the law as a compromise, and worked for it to avoid the evil of free coinage, which was threatening, and which would surely have carried in the House after passing the Senate, had it not been for the superb courage of Speaker Reed, he was never ready to denounce it as an unquestioned evil in itself, although with other Republican Senators in 1893, he upheld the hands of President Cleveland in voting for the repeal.

During the winter of 1892-93, succeeding the second election of President Cleveland, Eastern Democratic and Mugwump newspapers and periodicals, unwilling to acknowledge the threat of tariff revision to be responsible for the then impending financial disturbance, entered upon a crusade for the repeal of the Sherman

law, demanding that the Congress then in session
enter at once upon that imperative task, and ignoring
the obvious fact that no legislation of such importance
could be agreed upon by a Republican Senate and a
Democratic House in the few weeks remaining before the
fourth of March, when a single free silver Senator,
with stout lungs, was physically capable of preventing
any legislation whatever. One of those who joined
in the cry was Henry C. Bowen, editor of the New
York *Independent*, who sent to his old friend, Mr.
Platt, a galley proof of an editorial entitled "Repeal
the Silver Law" which was going to appear in his publication. Mr. Platt wrote him a letter of mild reproof,
which contained food for thought:

A galley proof of the article in *The Independent* of
January fifth, entitled "Repeal the Silver Law," has been
sent me. I suppose it reflects your views as well as the
views of the paper.

In my opinion, however, some things ought to be considered, which do not seem to have attracted the attention
of people who are so earnestly urging the repeal of that law.

First. By means of it the country has been furnished
with a circulation amounting to practically $4,500,000 a
month since August, 1890. That this addition has not
been more than was needed is shown conclusively, I think,
by the fact that it has not resulted in an increase of prices,
and therefore is not in any sense inflation. I believe,
moreover, that the prosperity of the country has been
full as much due to this increase of currency—which somewhat keeps pace with our increase of population and
business—as to our tariff legislation or any other thing.
Without it we should have had relative contraction, and,
I think, more or less financial distress. And now when
the Treasury is running on a somewhat narrow margin,
and every little scare operates to make a squeeze in money,

can we afford to cut off this circulation without putting
something in its place?

I see your article suggests that this should be done. To
that I reply that the substitution of any other form of
circulation is a practical impossibility. Three methods
are spoken of:

First,—the increase of national bank circulation, which
is absolutely hopeless. New York does not realize the
temper of the country, which is much more likely in the next
administration to prohibit the issue of currency by national
banks than to increase it. Of course, I regret this temper.
But the increased issue of national bank circulation cannot,
in my judgment, get the vote of one third of the Senate
or House.

Second,—a return to the "Bland" act. I would rather
buy four and a half million ounces of silver a month, and
issue treasury notes to the exact amount of purchase,
than to buy two millions a month and coin it into three
millions, and issue silver certificates to the amount of
three millions for the purchase of two.

Third,—the repeal of the tax on State bank circulation,
which is the only probable method of continuing the increase of currency, if the so-called Sherman law should
be repealed. I am convinced that the Democratic party,
with Mr. Cleveland at its head, does intend to do this, if
it can repeal the present law; and I would rather continue
the Sherman law than resort to that.

Have you thought of the probable effect of repealing
or suspending the Sherman law, upon the price of silver,
and if it should result in a further serious fall whether
that would not precipitate a premium on gold quicker than
a further continuance of silver purchases? The present
law makes a market for more than one third of the world's
product of silver. Suppose that demand to be withdrawn, and that silver should fall from its price of about
67 cents on the dollar of gold to, say, 50 cents on the dollar,
how long would it be before the Treasury notes which have

been issued since August, 1890, payable in "coin," would
be presented at the Treasury for redemption? The Treasury would feel bound to pay them in gold as long as it
could, and how long could it?

The silver certificates issued upon the coined dollars are
redeemable only in silver by law. But would they continue
to circulate at par with a gold dollar, if silver should fall
to 50 cents on the dollar? In the downward course of
silver a point would be reached where gold would go to a
premium. It might not be at 50 cents on the dollar; but
there is a point somewhere in the downward price of silver
when the silver certificates and the silver dollar would not
pass for the equal of the gold dollar, and then gold would
be immediately at a premium.

There is but one answer to this, and that is that the
situation is not to be ultimately relieved by a further continuance of silver purchases. But I have thought that
perhaps the production of silver was now being reduced
by the low price, and that except for the fact that the
Sherman law might be repealed in the near future, silver
would be likely to advance to a price where the entire
amount purchased under that law would be equal to all the
certificates that have been issued.

The problem is one of great difficulty. I believe the
evil day can be longer postponed by continuing the purchase of silver than by immediate cessation, without the
possibility of putting into circulation a similar amount of
currency in the place of that now being issued.

Finally. We are still bound until next May in good
faith to try to bring about an international agreement
for the enlarged use of silver, or for an international coinage arrangement; and it would be discreditable to a nation
that has solicited the conference to attempt to bulldoze
the conference by refusing to use silver at all. My own
judgment is that it is better to wait till that conference re-
assembles next May, and then if we cannot get some international agreement for the enlarged use of silver or for an

international coinage agreement, to tell the conference that the United States would be compelled in self-defence to change its policy with regard to its use.

My view, too, is that when that change is made, it should be a gradual cessation of purchase rather than a total suspension.

These expressions of mine are purely tentative. I do not know how I should vote on a given bill, which might come up for action. But it seems strange to me that people who assume such financial wisdom should apparently have never thought of these things.

In spite of obvious reasons for letting the currency alone during the short session, the unthinking demand persisted, inspired chiefly by doctrinaires with heads in the clouds, profoundly oblivious to parliamentary possibilities. Politicians, to ingratiate themselves with the newspapers, feigned acquiescence in the demand. David B. Hill, of New York, introduced a bill to repeal the purchasing clause of the Sherman act, and on February 6, 1893, less than a month before Congress must come to an end, he moved to take it up for consideration. It was a political play, and every Senator knew it, but, confronted with the issue, most of the gold standard Republicans, for the sake of the record, felt compelled to vote in the affirmative. Mr. Platt could not bring himself to do this, but joined the free silver Republicans and the Democrats in defeating the motion. To his friend John Flagg he wrote:

I fear that I displeased my Connecticut friends to-day in not voting to take up the silver question, but the thing was so plainly and manifestly a mere fencing for political advantage, that I was sick of the whole matter. Every Senator who voted to take it up knew there was not the slightest opportunity to get it to a vote, and I did not propose to vote to embarrass the business of the session. I am not quite sure that I am in favor of a repeal of the Sherman law anyway. I should vote against it at this session, but possibly next session I should vote for it. I don't think it is just fair to nations that we have asked to take part in the conference to change the situation while the conference continues. I think it would have an unfavorable effect upon the conference, and what I sincerely desire is an international agreement for the free coinage of silver. I confess I don't know what is going to happen if we can't get it. I think to discontinue the use of silver as money absolutely, would send it down to a point where we would be quite as likely to get on to a silver basis as we shall by continuing the law.

The pressure continued, the expected financial panic arrived, President Cleveland called Congress in special session to repeal the purchasing clause of the Sherman law, and after many dreary weeks of debate, the clause was repealed. Mr. Platt and the majority of Republican Senators voted for the repeal, in company with a few Democrats, but it has never yet been demonstrated that the repeal of the act materially relieved the financial distress which continued until a succession of Republican victories had at last assured the great industrial interests of an end to experimental legislation.

The next opportunity which Mr. Platt accepted to discuss the silver question was during the debate on the Wilson-Gorman Tariff bill in the spring of 1894. Mr. Lodge, at that time one of the youngest members of the Senate, had introduced the following amendment to the bill:

Except that when not in contravention of any existing treaty, any article made dutiable in the following sections shall, if it is the product or manufacture of Great Britain or of any of the colonies of Great Britain, pay a duty double that herein imposed; and any article upon the free list in the preceding section shall, if the product or manufacture of Great Britain or of any of the colonies of Great Britain, pay a duty of 35% ad valorem; and such additional and discriminating duties shall remain in force until Great Britain shall assent to, and take part in, an international agreement with the United States for the coinage and use of silver and shall close whenever Great Britain shall assent to, and take part in, such international agreement for the coinage of silver.

This proposed amendment, which attracted much attention at the time, was in line with the professions of the Republican party as declared in its platforms, and was intended to demonstrate the sincerity of the demand for an international agreement, which hitherto had been rendered ineffectual through the immobility of British statesmanship.

Mr. Platt, as has been said, was a constant advocate of bimetallism under an international agreement, and on May 2, 1894, he spoke in support of the Lodge amendment:

I believe myself to be and claim to be a bimetallist. I know that there is a difference in the definition of that word. I know that my friends who are in favor of the free coinage of silver by the United States alone, do not admit that any one is a bimetallist unless he agrees with them and supports the free coinage of silver by the United States alone. I am a bimetallist and honestly so in the sense that I desire, if it be possible with safety to the country, that we shall have free coinage of silver. If that be not possible I desire to use all the silver that we may safely use in this country as a legal-tender money.

The difference between myself and those who insist

upon free coinage by the United States alone is that they believe it would be better for the United States acting independently to adopt the free coinage and use of silver. I believe that that would be more disastrous to the United States than to pursue our present policy of keeping the silver which we have in use and waiting until such time as the world will engage in the free coinage of silver or the limited use of silver.

I recognize the fact that all that stands in the way to-day of the free coinage of silver by the commercial nations of the world at a ratio of 16 to 1 or 15½ to 1 is the attitude of Great Britain, and I think that the passage of this amendment, passed as it ought to be by both sides of the chamber, would be an admonition and a voice which Great Britain could not refuse to hear.

I agree to a certain extent with those whom I may call my silver friends, that the scarcity of gold in the world for many purposes has been productive of great disaster, has been to a large extent responsible for falling prices and unremunerative business. Perhaps I would disagree with them as to the extent to which that cause has operated. I have no doubt I should disagree with them in supposing that other causes were potent in the fall of prices and the unremunerative character of business; but that the appreciation of gold and its ever-increasing scarcity for money uses have to a great extent destroyed values and made business unprofitable I do agree. That Great Britain stands directly in the path of the use of silver and stands there almost alone, I think is unquestionable. Therefore, I desire by the passage of this amendment that we may do something which will convince England that it is no longer to her interest to stand in the position of the usurious creditor of the world, something which may open her eyes to the fact that there is for her a path of greatness and prosperity aside from the mere lending of money and taking the interest in gold, and cheapening the prices of these commodities and things which she desires to buy and must buy.

CHAPTER XV

PAPER MONEY

Continued Agitation for Free Silver—Opposes Fictitious "Seigniorage" in 1895—Criticism of the Greenbacks—For Sound
Money in 1896.

OF course, nobody of political intelligence expected
that the repeal of the purchasing clause of the
Sherman act would settle the silver question. The
controversy was bound to persist until it had furnished
the compelling issue in a campaign for the Presidency,
and until, through an unforeseen increase in the production of gold, with a consequent expansion of the circulating medium, it became merely an academic dispute.
The friends of silver would not acknowledge defeat,
nor could they rest. They tantalized jaded industries
with one and another alluring bait, seeking fatuously
to tease their way to recognition. It was only a little
more than a year after the repeal, at a time when no
significant financial legislation by any chance could be
enacted, that the Democratic majority of the Senate
Finance Committee reported a bill with no other apparent purpose than to play for political position. The
bill as originally introduced was to provide "for the
issue of bonds, the coinage of silver, and for other
purposes." Under the merciless pruning of the Finance
Committee it was reduced to a single paragraph, which
meant in simple English that any owner of silver bullion,

without limit of quantity, might sell it to the United
States at its market price, receiving for it silver dollars
and certificates issued upon the silver dollars, and that
the United States should make a profit of the difference
between the market value and the coinage of the silver
which it purchased—a fictitious "seigniorage." The
bill was defended by its advocates, but there was
practically no argument in opposition, until Mr. Platt,
on February 19, 1895, took the floor. He declared that
of all the measures suggested to Congress for a larger
use of silver, this was the most indefensible, and that
"of all the foolish, illogical, impracticable methods for
the use of silver" none had ever equalled it. He
declared, moreover, that there was not a Senator in
the chamber who really wanted the bill to become a
law. He derided the so-called "seigniorage" in the
bill. The provision by which the Government of the
United States was to pay for the silver delivered to it,
and that moment have it worth twice as much as it
was in the hands of the seller, was not a seigniorage:

No government in the world has ever, to my knowledge,
attempted the making of money out of the business of
coining money except the Government of the United
States. It would not be tolerated, I think, anywhere else.

If the bill should pass, he said the very pleasing
fiction that by thus dealing with silver bullion the
Government was making one hundred per cent. profit
at the present price of silver would disappear:

It will prove not to have been a profit at all. If the
time should ever come when, by reason of the extent of
its purchases of silver, gold and silver should part company
as to value, and the gold dollar should become more valuable
in purchasing and debt-paying power than the silver dollar,

the moment that occurs, if it does occur, then it will be seen that all this supposed advantage of one hundred per cent. profit in the purchase of silver was not a profit after all; and the loss will fall not upon the Government, not upon the man who sold the silver to the Government, but upon the man who holds the coins which the Government issues in the purchase of the silver, or which it coined after having paid for the silver and used it, for other purposes.

He acknowledged that he was a bimetallist and expressed his belief that, if we could have an international agreement among the commercial nations, the world could use as money all the silver produced, without in any way impairing the value of the silver money:

I have not lost hope of international bimetallism. I think we may be very much encouraged at the present time to hope that international bimetallism is a thing of the not very remote future.

If it should be shown that England and Germany utterly and absolutely for all time refused to engage with the United States in an international agreement for the enlarged use of silver, he would be willing, and would advocate, that the United States join with such commercial nations as were willing to engage in an international monetary conference for that purpose.

The most significant passage of the speech was that in which he impressed upon his hearers a few wholesome truths about the currency system of the United States, and outlined what, in his opinion, would be genuine currency reform. His conclusions are as valid now as then:

I believe the vice of our whole financial situation lies in our paper currency. . . . I regard it as one of the most unfortunate epochs in the history of the United States when under a supposed and a real necessity we departed from the ancient methods and practices and customs of the Government to simply coin the metals, silver and gold, and resorted to a paper currency. No country ever did it, whether the paper was redeemable or irredeemable, that did not suffer for it in the end.

When we resorted to the greenback I venture to say that there were not ten public men in the United States who claimed that it was a sound financial measure. The men who advocated it, the men who insisted upon it, resorted to it upon the plea of necessity only, acknowledging that it was unsound finance, promising that when the war should be over and our great expenses arising from the war should no longer have to be met, greenbacks would be retired from circulation, never for a moment admitting or supposing that they could pass into our financial system; but they have been incorporated in our system.

In addition to that amount of paper money, the greenbacks, we have about $480,000,000 of silver paper. We have in this country, then, about $875,000,000 of paper money. That money is responsible for the growth of paternalism in this country. The people from coming to believe that it was not sound finance, that the only function of government with regard to money was to coin gold and silver, placing the government stamp upon the metal and delivering it to the person who should bring it to the mint, and regulating the value of it, have come now to believe that in some way or other it is the function of government to furnish money to the people, to believe that it is one of the functions of government to make every man's business as profitable as the man himself shall desire it to be. It is the inherent vice of government paper money that the people look to the government to furnish them with money and to regulate the money of the government so that they can be prosperous in their business. . . .

The whole country has become demoralized with this idea that the Government may properly and wisely issue paper money, and regulate not alone the value of money, but the value and conduct of all business throughout the country thereby. There never was a more fatal governmental heresy than that national benefit is to be derived from issues of governmental paper. . . . Any nation that issues its promise-to-pay as money has embarked on a road where it is almost impossible to turn about, the end of which is disaster and financial distress and ruin.

My greatest objection to the use of silver is in the issuing of paper money upon it. There is where the danger lies. We can maintain at a parity with gold coin all the silver coin at a ratio of 16 to 1 which the people will use as coin, but I firmly believe that we cannot maintain at a parity with gold all the silver upon which we can issue paper money in this country. . . . One thing is true, and that is that if there are two kinds of money the bullion value of which differs materially the cheaper kind will drive out the more valuable kind if it becomes sufficiently redundant. That is denied by no one. If we continue the purchase of silver, the bullion of which has only a gold value of fifty cents to the dollar, and continue putting out paper upon it without limitation, we shall finally arrive at that point where the cheaper money will drive out the more valuable money and where gold will go to a premium. . . . You can use two metals of different bullion value together to a certain extent. If the United States Government should stamp $412\frac{1}{2}$ grains of copper as a dollar, receive it for government dues, make it a legal tender, and put no more of it in circulation than was fairly required for the payment of government dues, and to meet perhaps the views of some few people who believe that the stamp of the Government is all that is needed, it could carry copper dollars of $412\frac{1}{2}$ grains to a certain extent just as well as it can silver dollars of $412\frac{1}{2}$ grains, when the bullion in the dollar is only worth half as much as the gold dollar. But, if you kept that process up, and issued those copper dollars until they were vastly in excess of what was required to be used for the payment of the government dues, and in excess of the amount used by those who believed that the Government stamp will carry anything as a dollar, when the amount exceeded those requirements, then those dollars would become valuable only as copper. So, if by this system of issuing paper upon silver you get into circulation more silver than is required for the use of payments to be made to the Government, and up to a point where a majority believe that there is too much of it, then the silver which the paper represents will be valuable as silver only. . . .

The trouble is that the Government has gone into the banking business, and no financial measure which does not look to the retirement of the Government from the banking business is going to be of anything but temporary avail. When we settle this question, we must settle it upon sound financial principles. That is our trouble now. With $875,000,000 of paper money out, $346,000,000 of which is directly redeemable, if not by law, by our customs, in gold, and $155,000,000 more of what are called "Sherman-purchase-act notes" which have also been treated as being redeemable in gold, we have in round numbers nearly $500,000,000 of paper money to be redeemed in gold, and in addition to that are the national bank notes, which may come in for gold redemption. I do not speak of that, however, because I am speaking of the absolute government paper money. What does that involve, Mr. President? It involves our keeping a fund of gold in the United States Treasury all the while lying idle, until demand may be made upon the Treasury for redemption. It involves our keeping sufficient gold there so that every one will be satisfied that there can be redemption under all circumstances.

We have by law put it out of our power to get a dollar of gold into the Treasury except by borrowing it. Then comes the necessity of meeting a demand for gold in our foreign payments, and so the gold is gradually or rapidly depleted from the Treasury, when we fill it up, as it were, with a sufficient reserve fund. This thing is to go on forever. So long as our present system of paper money continues there is no relief from it. . . .

If we had not departed from the old system of coining gold and silver for the persons who brought it to the mint and in paying our own obligations in coin, or in the checks and bills of exchange which make up so large a proportion of the payments of this country, we should have no trouble. All this idea that the people have a right to depend upon the Government through its money transactions and its issue of paper money to regulate their affairs to their liking would not be present, and this paternalism, socialism, and populism, latent or rampant, would never have got such a foothold in this country if it had not been encouraged by the false financial system of paper money which we have inaugurated.

I know that in the minds of a great many people I am talking financial heresy. I remember when I first came into the Senate a message was received from the President in favor of the continued retirement of greenbacks, and I saw the remarkable spectacle of the Secretary of the Treasury recommending that there should be no further retirement of greenbacks.

The difficulty with this question is to get rid of our paper money without disturbing the financial condition of the country. That is a serious question. It requires the attention and study of the best, the most careful, and most thoughtful financiers; but that we ought to do it in such a way and as rapidly as possible, without disturbing the financial conditions and dealing a serious blow to business, I have not the least doubt.

This road of Government paper issues can lead only to disaster in the end, and the worst feature about this bill is that it goes on adding, adding, forever adding, to the volume of our paper money.

As the conventions of 1896 approached, Mr. Platt became greatly concerned about the currency plank of the Republican platform. The nomination of Mr. McKinley was assured several weeks before the meeting of the Convention at St. Louis, and those who had his fortunes in charge were arranging already the declaration of principles upon which he was to go before the people. Mark Hanna was determined that the issue of the campaign should be the tariff; for he felt that his candidate would make his strongest appeal as "the advance agent of prosperity," just as he had already won his way in the Republican primaries in that character. Both Hanna and McKinley thought it would be good politics to minimize the currency question so that the Western Republican adherents of the cause of free silver might not be driven to new party alignments. The Eastern leaders, most of whom had been supporters of Speaker Reed, were determined, on the other hand, that there should be no evasion of the currency issue, and that the party should place itself squarely on a platform declaring for the maintenance of the gold standard. It fell to the delegations from New England and New York to make this fight, and Mr. Platt, although not a delegate to the Convention, exerted his influence in behalf of an unequivocal declaration. On June 11th, he wrote emphatically to Samuel Fessenden:

We who represent States like Connecticut here in Washington feel very nervous and anxious with reference to what the platform shall be in St. Louis. There is nothing that I can urge upon you, and yet I feel as if I must say something. Here in Washington, where we are supposed to catch public sentiment, there is a feeling that the delegates who will apparently nominate McKinley will want to tone down the platform so that it may not be entirely unacceptable to the free-coinage delegates. I cannot help feeling that a platform which can possibly be interpreted as favorable to silver would be disastrous. As it looks to me now, we have got to fight in the next campaign Democrats, Populists and the bolting silver Republicans, and we ought to make the money issue plain and distinct and unequivocal. If we can't win on such a platform, let us go down. We can at least lay the foundation for the party of the future, and I believe that we can carry more States on a square sound money platform than we can on one which can even be claimed to be equivocal. If we have an equivocal platform or one which any considerable number of people say is equivocal, we shall get no Democratic sound-money votes. If we have a square, honest declaration against free coinage and for the maintenance of the existing standard, we shall carry New York, New Jersey, and Connecticut by very large majorities, and I believe we can do better even in the States where the silver movement is feared by Republicans than we can upon a hesitating or evasive platform. I don't know what the Committee on Platform is likely to do, but, if it does not come up to the mark which we believe it should, I think some one in the Convention should make the fight. And looking the Convention over, I don't see but three men in the Convention who can make it. There may be others, but it seems to me that the fight will have to be made on the floor of the Convention by Warner Miller, Mr. Lodge, and yourself.

I hope you won't think that I am unduly frightened or exercised, but what I have heard in Washington the last few days has induced me to fear very much that our success may be imperilled by an attempt to placate the free-coinage Republicans.

The issue was joined at St. Louis under the leadership of Senator Lodge of Massachusetts, and Thomas C.

Platt of New York. Mr. Hanna, greatly against his
will, was induced to put in the platform a straight out
declaration for gold, on a threat that otherwise the
fight would be carried to the floor of the convention.
The subsequent campaign was conducted almost solely
on the money issue, after a futile attempt to force the
tariff to the front. Free silver was overwhelmingly
beaten, and the way was clear for the formal legislative
endorsement of the gold standard, which came at last
with the Law of July, 1900.

CHAPTER XVI

REAL CURRENCY REFORM

The Finance Committee—Helps to Frame Law of 1900—Letter to
Timothy Dwight—Consideration of Additional Measures of
Relief—Opposed to Asset Currency—The Aldrich Bill—Con-
ference at Warwick—A Central Bank.

COINCIDENT with the election of President Mc-
Kinley the currency question assumed a new
phase. Hitherto the advocates of a debased coinage
had been in the aggressive, while the friends of a stable
currency had as a rule contented themselves with
resisting the encroachments of unsound finance. Now
the tables were about to be turned. In the winter
succeeding Mr. McKinley's election a group of business
men, financial students and economists, entered upon a
systematic campaign with a view to securing legislation
which would insure the maintenance of the gold standard, the ultimate retirement of all classes of United
States notes, and a banking system which should furnish
credit facilities to every portion of the country with
a safe and elastic circulation. Hugh H. Hanna of
Indianapolis was the intelligent organizer who brought
the scattered elements together, resulting in the
Indianapolis Convention of January, 1897, and the
Monetary Commission convened in Washington the
following autumn. The general movement of which
the Indianapolis Convention and the Monetary Com-

mission were conspicuous manifestations resulted in
the enactment of the Law of March 14, 1900, and in an
education of the public along the lines of sane finance,
undoubtedly wholesome in effect, although accompanied,
as was inevitable, by quixotic suggestions and unreasoning insistence on ideal schemes, impracticable in face
of the necessity for legislative compromise.

Mr. Platt while sympathizing with the general movement, did not allow himself to be carried away by
enthusiasm for any particular remedy. "I am not
sure whether I can support the proposition for a monetary commission," he wrote on March 17th, 1897:

Ever since I have been in the Senate, especially since
the Tariff Commission of 1882, I have had very decided
views as to the impolicy of commissions appointed outside
of Congress to formulate legislation on given subjects, and
have frequently taken occasion to express myself in the
Senate on that subject. While entirely in sympathy with
the advocates of a reformed currency system, I doubt
very much whether anything is to be gained by a monetary
commission. If we make commissions for one purpose to
advise Congress what to do, we cannot discriminate and
must grant them whenever there seems to be an earnest
demand for them. It amounts purely to delegating the
power of Congress to investigate and formulate legislation
to that class of our citizens who desire the legislation.
And while that might work well in case of a monetary
commission, it will work very badly in the end, in my
judgment, if that is understood to be the policy of Congress.
. . . If we begin with commissions we shall very soon
farm out legislation into the hands practically of men who
want to secure it. Saying this, I do not conclusively say
that I cannot favor a monetary commission, but such action
is against all previously formed convictions.

He was then a member of the Finance Committee, and

was in constant touch with Mr. Aldrich in the consideration of all measures affecting the currency. During
the summer of 1899, preceding the meeting of the
Fifty-sixth Congress, there were conferences of members
of the Finance Committee at Narragansett Pier and
Manhattan Beach. President McKinley in his annual
message impressed upon Congress the necessity of
enacting a law to insure the maintenance of the gold
standard. The Act of March 14, 1900, embodying
explicit recognition of the gold standard, was the result
of the endeavors of the Senate and House to come
together. It was a long step in advance of previous
legislation, but it was not by any means the ideal scheme
which currency reformers had in mind; nor did it fully
satisfy any of the men who were entrusted with the
task of framing the law. Mr. Platt, as a member of
the subcommittee of the Finance Committee, had a
great deal to do with getting the bill into shape. He
joined in the debate with the free-silver senators who
opposed it and was engaged with Mr. Aldrich and Mr.
Allison in bringing about an agreement in conference.
He did not speak at length but in the course of the
discussion he made it clear that he believed the United
States could take no step more likely to advance the
cause of international bimetallism than to let it be
understood to the world that until we could secure the
concurrence of other nations we were going to maintain
the gold standard.

No sooner was the Law of 1900 enacted than advocates of reform began to pelt the men responsible
for it with demands for legislation still further advanced. Mr. Hanna representing the monetary conference had two purposes: the interchangeability of
all forms of currency and bank circulation based on

assets. As a member of the Finance Committee Mr. Platt received numerous letters urging his co-operation in these projects. But he was not inclined to hurry. He thought the Law of 1900 a much better measure than its critics would make out; "not that it is perfect, but it is easier to lament imperfections than it is to overcome them." To one correspondent he replied with a suggestion of mild reproof:

I wish people would believe that those who are responsible for legislation are as anxious to get things right as they are, but perhaps see more of the difficulties to be overcome.

The venerable Timothy Dwight of New Haven wrote him expressing the earnest hope that the Finance Committee would finally settle the currency question during the session so that there should be no further possibility of question or danger as to the permanent establishment of the gold standard. He also inquired whether the time was not ripe to adopt the measures which the Indianapolis Committee was urging. For Dr. Dwight's opinion Mr. Platt, a friend of many years, had a profound respect, and in reply he was at considerable pains to make clear his own position:

I assure you that I wish to do everything that may be necessary in order to prevent the possibility of the gold standard from being interfered with. The suggested legislation, however, presents many other serious questions that need the most careful consideration. I have not time for a long discussion of the subject, but right in the beginning of it are two matters to which I will allude.

The present law provides for the redemption in gold of about $430,000,000 of Government paper, greenbacks, treasury notes, etc. For this redemption we thought it necessary to provide for the establishment and maintenance at all times of a reserve fund of $150,000,000 in gold. That is a large sum to lock up in the Treasury department. If a law is to be passed that makes all our money redeemable in gold, it will add to the volume of money to be redeemed enough of silver to bring it up to more than a thousand millions. If $150,000,000 was necessary to provide a safe redemption fund for $430,000,-000 of paper, I cannot see why $300,000,000 would not be necessary as a fund to redeem a larger amount, and to shut that amount up in the Treasury, never to be used except for redemption purposes, would involve:

First, I think the necessity of selling more bonds to provide for it; and

Second, a withdrawal of an amount from circulation which might make serious trouble. I know it is said that it would be necessary to increase the redemption fund; that when it was once provided by law that redemption of the silver currency would be made in gold, nobody would want to redeem; but that argument is very much along the line of the greenbackers, that it is the Government fiat which gives value to currency.

The second matter to which I allude is the claim that the Government should provide that all public and private debts should be payable in gold. In other words, that it should declare primarily that our bonds, which on the face of them are payable in coin, should be payable in gold only, and that all obligations of the Government, and of private individuals should be thus payable. The House bill which came over to the Senate contained this provision, and it also contained the provision that the present legal-tender quality of the silver dollar should continue. I do not see how it is practicable to provide that all obligations of the Government should be payable in gold, and still keep the legal-tender quality of the silver dollar, and there is certainly an inconsistency in saying that silver shall be a legal tender to pay obligations to the Government, while the Government shall pay all its obligations in gold.

I only allude to these two matters to show that it is much easier to say that there should be further legislation for the security of the gold standard, than to determine just what form that legislation should take. There are a great many other matters connected with our system and its practical operation which furnish difficulties to be thought of when further legislation is proposed. Our currency is pretty safe now in the hands of officers who wish to maintain the gold standard. No law that could be passed would make it safe if there should be a political change which put the Government in the hands of those who desire to destroy the gold standard. I cannot think that with all the delicate and difficult problems to be solved by further legislation, it is wise to be in haste about it.

In other letters he went into greater detail. It seemed to him that the declaring of our different kinds of currency to be exchangeable would hardly do away with the necessity for a gold reserve. Simply calling silver money gold, or as good as gold, would not make it so. Our money other than gold would be greenbacks, treasury notes, silver dollars, and silver certificates, and they would have the value of gold simply because what is gold in the treasury could be exchanged for them. It was true that the people did not want their money if they were sure that they could get it, but it was this very fact which made it necessary to provide what Tilden used to call "a central reservoir of gold":

There is not and there will not be as long as present conditions endure, any practical difficulty. The country can carry this paper because it provides a sufficient fund for the redemption of all but the silver currency; and, as to the silver currency, it takes it in payment of debts due to it, and the volume is so limited that it is thus practically exchangeable for gold. . . . We have more gold in this country now than any other country in the world, and more in our Treasury than any other nation has in its treasury. It will be a question before long what we are going to do with it, and I hope that, as the situation begins to emphasize itself to the apprehension of the people, a disposition to retire all our paper currency will make headway; I mean all paper that is not issued upon the deposit of an equal amount of gold; in other words, gold certificates. I think the whole idea of paper currency issued by the Government upon any other basis is vicious, and must eventually make trouble. And yet, the popular business sentiment is now entirely against the retirement of our paper currency. As a practical measure, the greenbacks cannot be retired without either substituting something else for them or contracting our currency to the extent of their retirement. A radical contraction of currency would plunge us into all sorts of financial trouble; that is the objection to taking in greenbacks and keeping them except when someone wants them in exchange for gold. One of the things that has made business good and keeps it good is the fact that there was a little bit of expansion of the currency in our last financial bill, not to the extent of real inflation, but an expansion which kept pace with the demand of business. I do not think that people have generally thought of that. A simple declaration of the gold standard, without providing this means for an expanded currency mostly through the national banks, would scarcely have kept things as satisfactory as they have been kept. This is a pretty wide question, and it is like other great questions in that every one can agree on the purpose to be accomplished, while they cannot agree on the details. It is easy to say of the shipping bill that it is a measure calculated to restore our merchant marine and, from that standpoint, every one wants it; but when you come to the question of how it is to be done, the best of people are in doubt. It is just so with the money question. Every one agrees that we should do everything in our power to maintain the gold standard, but when you come to consider the special steps by which this is to be accomplished, people may well be puzzled.

In spite of the pressure from business interests nothing tangible was done for over two years. President Roosevelt in his message of December, 1902, suggested the desirability of additional measures

with the view of encouraging the use of such instrumentalities as will automatically supply every legitimate demand of productive industries and of commerce, not only in the amount, but in the character, of circulation, and of making all kinds of money interchangeable and, at the will of the holder, convertible into the established gold standard.

After waiting sufficiently long upon the initiative of the House, Mr. Aldrich, early in February, 1903, less than a month before the adjournment of Congress, introduced and reported from the Finance Committee a bill which if enacted would have relieved the situation to some extent. It authorized the Secretary of the Treasury to deposit in the national banks public money received from all sources, including customs, and to accept as security certain state and municipal bonds as well as United States bonds, the banks to pay not less than one and one-half per cent. interest on government deposits. It also gave to Panama bonds all rights and privileges of two per cent. consols deposited as security for circulation, and authorized the Secretary of the Treasury to retain in the general fund national bank-notes received in the ordinary course of business and pay them out in current expenditures of the Government.

Consideration of this bill was prevented by wanton

obstruction, but it served as a text for subsequent
discussion and contained the substance of future legislation. After the adjournment of the Fifty-seventh
Congress in the spring of 1903, the Senate leaders felt
that the time had arrived for an understanding if
possible in regard to a measure to be enacted during
the approaching long session of the Fifty-eighth Congress. A conference of Republican members of the
Finance Committee was called to meet at Hot Springs,
Virginia, in May. Mr. Platt was ill with an attack of
acute indigestion and could not attend. Another
meeting was held at Senator Aldrich's home at Warwick,
Rhode Island, in the first week in August. Those
invited to attend it were Senators Allison, Spooner, and
Platt. Mr. Platt felt that the outlook for intelligent
legislation was anything but clear. Personally he
believed in the establishment of a Central National
Bank as a sound financial programme, but he feared that
the time was not ripe for proposing such a measure to
the country. Writing to John H. Flagg, of New York,
on July 29, 1903, he said:

On the 6th of August I go down to Aldrich's as one of
a subcommittee to consider financial matters. Sometimes
I think it is almost a farce that I should be taking part in
proposed legislation affecting our financial system, and at
other times I think perhaps I know fully as much about
it as those who are better financiers. This present condition seems to be one of deciding where doctors disagree.
I find the people who think themselves financial experts
have many different schemes, and each thinks his own
scheme is the only way possible out of what I think is
universally admitted to be a defective governmental
system. I doubt if any of them point the way out. I
agree that, if there were some way of making a more elastic

currency without running the risk of depreciating its security, it would be a good thing to do, but I doubt very much whether issuing an emergency circulation, secured only by the assets of a bank and taxation, would be a real remedy for the defects which exist, or indeed, would serve to make a more elastic currency, while on the other hand, it is possible that it would be the first step towards what, in old times, was called "wild cat banking," a situation which was met by requiring that when banks issued circulation, there should be undoubted security behind it. I do not know. I am all at sea about the matter, and my only consolation in that respect is that I think others are as much afloat as I am, though they do not seem to know it.

A greater trouble to my mind than the want of an elastic currency is that, so long as our receipts exceed our expenditures, actual money must be locked up in the vaults of the sub-treasury. If we, in this country, could have a national bank, or a governmental connection with a strong bank, as in England, France, Germany, and other commercial countries, and thus do away with the sub-treasury, I think we would be better off, but that is impossible, in view of public sentiment. It is strange how ideas developed by a particular situation which occurred years, and even a century ago, dominate public sentiment now. The national bank idea was sound finance, but its experience made every one opposed to a national bank, and you have only to mention one now to stir up the whole community to hostility. It is just another instance of ideas which fitted one set of circumstances controlling another and entirely different set in after-times, like the Alien and Sedition laws, which became so unpopular as the result of political party contention, that now any attempt to punish even the utterances of anarchy is howled down by a shout about returning to the old Alien and Sedition laws. Any attempt to have a decent army is met by the old cry, first raised in the time of our Revolution, as the result of hatred of the British, that a standing army is a menace to our liberties. But, however all this may be, it is manifest that we cannot revive the idea of a national bank. The reduction of taxation, even to the extent of making it necessary to use some of our surplus, is, in my judgment, the real remedy for money stringency, but that is difficult of accomplishment, and when we do reduce taxation to what we suppose is the level of expenditure, it turns out that we have still a surplus of moneys that we cannot use, which must go either into the sub-treasury or be deposited in banks.

If we are to have bad times our receipts will fall off, and there will be no trouble about the locking up of money, but the banks which have received deposits of government money seem to think that the Government must not call on them for repayment, and so we are in danger of the deposit in banks becoming permanent. I confess I do not know what to do. I should like to do something to relieve the situation. If this Wall Street experience is the beginning of bad times in business, no one knows what the result of the next Presidential election will be. You see it is a serious problem.

The conference at Warwick went into the subject of currency legislation with great thoroughness, but, in view of the conflicting opinions of the advocates of a reformed system, there was little expectation of affirmative action by Congress. It was understood that Congress was to meet in extraordinary session to take up the question of Cuban reciprocity, and this ought to give time for consideration of financial problems, but Mr. Platt did not feel much encouraged regarding legislation. Writing to Mr. Flagg on September 14, 1903, he said:

It looks to me as if the House would not pass any bill whatever. Fowler, at the head of the Banking and Currency Committee, has evolved a scheme, consisting of three propositions: (1) Retirement of the greenbacks; (2) payment by banks of two per cent. interest on government deposits; (3) asset currency. I do not believe that the Republicans of the House will adopt his ideas. I do not think his plan has many advocates in banking or financial circles. I need not go into lengthy argument to show why I do not think it a wise or safe scheme. I merely say that I shall be surprised if it meets with favor in the House. The Secretary of the Treasury has a cure-all, in a plan to allow national banks to issue emergency currency up to fifty per cent. of their circulation, secured by a six per cent. tax and a lien on assets. I think that would be a dead failure. I do not believe banks would take out that currency. It has many and fatal defects, in my judgment, even if they would. We shall probably propose the Aldrich bill with modifications. . . . Probably we could pass such a bill in the Senate after the Democrats are through trying to formulate an issue for the Presidential campaign, but the necessity for an additional supply of money to move the crops will have gone by long before we could get it to a vote. The Democratic Presidential campaign is of course to be conducted upon the theory that the Republicans favor the great moneyed interests of the country at the expense of those who are poor or have only moderate capital, and any effort which is intended to relieve the monetary condition will be said by them to be a part of our general plan to build up the millionaires and impoverish every one else, so that, though we may pass such a bill as we shall probably propose, it will come too late to be of service this fall, and then, if, as I surmise, the House passes nothing, that will be the end of it. If the House should pass some kind of a bill, we might, in conference, get some items of minor importance, which we could agree upon. If we could get the main features of the Aldrich bill passed by Congress quickly, I am sure that it would obviate any money stringency this fall, but this I do not look for. The Fowler plan and all others which involve asset currency, taxable or untaxable, look to the complete change of our currency system, and it seems to me that it would be folly to attempt such a change by legislation in this Congress, on the eve of a presidential election. We have a safe currency now. It is also an abundant currency for the ordinary conditions of business. If we had the two additional features, permitting deposit of all receipts in banks, without interest, and the right of the Secretary of the Treasury, in his discretion, during times of stringency, to waive redemption by national banks of their notes, using them in the current business of the Treasury, the same as greenbacks are used, while the emergency lasted, we would have no trouble, but you can see as well as I the difficulty in reaching any such conclusion as this. I should not be surprised to see the session go by without any definite legislation. I hope that something may be evolved along the lines I have suggested, but my hope is not very strong.

Mr. Platt's doubts were justified. The President recommended the passage of a bill authorizing the deposit of customs receipts in national banks—a mild measure enough—but the Congress went by without action of any kind, owing to the impractical attitude of the members of the Banking and Currency Committee in the House, and the Senator never had another opportunity to participate in financial legislation.

CHAPTER XVII

A STAUNCH PROTECTIONIST

The Cleveland Message of 1887—Attack upon the Administration Policy—A Comprehensive Plea for Protection—Defender of American Industries—Opposition to the Mills Bill—Contrast between Labor and Industry North and South—The Duty on Tin Plate—The Tariff not Responsible for the Trusts.

PROTECTION to American industries was one of the cardinal tenets of Mr. Platt's political creed, and this must constantly be borne in mind when considering his course in legislation. No measure which even remotely threatened to weaken the protective system received his support unless on careful consideration he concluded that some greater end could be advanced by its enactment. His career in the Senate embraced a period during which four measures were formulated there involving a general revision of the tariff, and several abortive attempts at tariff legislation were made in the House.

The tariff of 1883 claimed his attention because he was the representative of a great manufacturing State, and because for that reason, if for no other, he would have been expected to see that manufacturing interests did not suffer at the hands of Congress. But he was comparatively young in the service then, and it does not appear from the records that he took any conspicuous part in the deliberations of the Senate. He had no patience with the theories of tariff reform which about

that time agitated American politics, but there was no
occasion for exploiting himself in debate and he confined his activities to looking after the interest of the
industries upon which his State so greatly depended.

The revision of 1883 was preliminary to a general
agitation of the whole tariff question to which the
campaign of 1884 contributed, and which was stimulated
by William R. Morrison and the " Horizontal " bill with
which for a time he beguiled the Democratic House of
Representatives.   But the discussion might have continued for years to have little except academic interest
had it not been for President Cleveland who in the
middle of his first term precipitated the issue in his
annual message of December, 1887.   The question then
became in a flash the most vital issue before the American people, and it remained so until the enactment of
the Dingley law in 1887 brought industrial contentment
after a long period of political and economic unrest.

The message of 1887 seemed to Mr. Platt what it
seemed to many others,—a wanton attack upon a
hitherto accepted American policy, entered upon with
no reason then apparent, except the plain political
reason of furnishing an issue upon which the party
then in power could go to the country in the hope of
continuing its predominance.

During the winter of 1887–8, it served as a text for a
general tariff debate, introducing a controversy which
kept the industries of the United States in a turmoil for
years.   Mr. Platt by this time had become one of the
recognized authorities in the Senate on industrial and
economic questions, and this was a subject upon which
he had deep rooted convictions.   The lines were form-
ing for the contest which was to come in 1888 and which
he hoped would bring Connecticut back to the Repub-

lican ranks. He could hardly have kept silence if he
had wished to, and he contributed to the debate a
speech which occupied in delivery a part of two days,
February 6th and 7th. It was the most comprehensive
argument on the tariff question which he ever undertook, for although in later years he came to have a
commanding influence in the shaping of tariff legislation he left to others the discussion of principles involved. It was an orthodox plea for protection which
exhibited familiarity with the discussion preceding it
and with the general literature of the subject, as well
as with the statistics of the industries likely to be
affected by a revision of the tariff. It attracted the
attention of the country and served as a text for count-
less other arguments.

With the straightforwardness which was characteristic of all his political utterances he put the question
bluntly: "Is the President of the United States a free
trader?" And letting his argument develop from that
inquiry, he carried it on to a far-reaching defence of
the doctrine of protection:

I do not propose to be deterred from asking, and if I can,
from answering this question, because the President suggests that "to dwell upon the theories of protection and
free trade savors too much of bandying epithets." I am a
protectionist and I consider it no epithet when I am called
so. If the President of the United States is a free trader
he ought to be willing to be called so and not consider it
an epithet if that word is used to define his position.

The immediate timeliness of the speech did not
exclude many truths which were of permanent application, as applicable to the discussion to-day as they
were twenty years ago:

Are the manufacturers of this country realizing "immense profits"? Are they the millionaires of the land? You can count upon your fingers and thumbs and without counting them many times over, all the manufacturers of this country who in manufacturing have accumulated a fortune equal to a million dollars, and in nine cases out of ten either these men or their fathers have struggled from the bottom, where poverty pinched the hardest and where privation was the greatest, up to their success. They have been workmen at the bench, at the loom, in the factory, in the shop, in the mill, and what they have they have obtained in a manner which the common judgment of mankind says is honest and fair. There is not a laboring man in this country who when he comes to think of it levels his claim that men are obtaining the rewards of investment without the rendition of a fair equivalent therefor against the manufacturer. No—they are not the millionaires. Who ever heard a manufacturer called a "king"? We hear of "cattle kings," and "wheat kings," and "iron kings"—but you never hear that word applied to a manufacturer.

He warned the men who were seeking to destroy the protective tariff that they must not delude themselves with the idea that they were aiming their blows against New England:

The New England manufacturer is the man who has least interest of all classes of men in the preservation of the protective system. He is interested in it, indeed, but others, and all others are interested more. If I were to name the order in which the different classes are interested in the maintenance of a protective tariff, I would say first the laborers everywhere, in whatever field they wipe the sweat from their brows; more than any manufacturers are the wage-receiving men of this country interested in its preservation. The blow hits them first and it may as well be understood, and they are coming to understand it all over the land. First, the men who work in manufactories, the artisans, are hit; next, agriculturists and the men who work on farms; next, manufacturers in other sections of the country where they are not as well established, and where the industries may indeed be said even now to be infant industries; next, those engaged in transportation; next, those engaged in merchandise; and last, and least, if you please—the manufacturers of New England.

If the policy of free trade is to prevail, if our progress is to be arrested and our development hindered, and if the inevitable results of it are to follow and we are to have disaster and ruin, the first men who will emerge from the ruin will be the manufacturers of New England, the first who will adjust themselves to the new order of things and go on once more as they have in the past, endeavoring to build up and develop and make a strong, powerful, glorious nation. The interest of the New England manufacturer is more that he may have a market in which he can sell his goods than anything else. That is what he wants. That is where free trade hits him hardest—the surrender of our market to the foreigner.

Then he took up the argument for free raw materials which at that time was just beginning to appeal to the manufacturers of the East:

But perhaps as favorite a method of attack upon the tariff by the free trader as any is the claim that raw materials should be free, and why? Because the free trader knows that the protection of raw materials is the keystone to the protective arch; that when you have once ceased to protect the production of what are called raw materials in the country, there is no logical ground upon which any article can be protected here. If that kind of production which employs the greatest percentage of labor in this country cannot receive protection, then nothing should receive protection; and it is, therefore, that the assault upon protection is made upon what are called raw materials.

It is more than that; it is an appeal to the supposed selfishness of manufacturers. The manufacturers are told —told by the President in his message—that they can cheapen the cost of production if they can have free raw materials. Sir, the manufacturer who seeks to obtain raw materials free and demands a tariff upon his product is a selfish man, and selfish almost to the point of criminality; and the manufacturers of New England, as a class, spurn that bribe. When in the preparation of the bill advised by the leading free traders out of Congress in this country, the proposition is made to purchase the support of New England manufacturers by free wool, by free iron, by free coal, I tell you that they mistake the manufacturers of Connecticut and the rest of New England. They know that this is a system or it is nothing. They know that every industry must be protected to thrive and they know that protection alone can make us generally prosperous as a nation. They are not to be diverted from this issue.

The only raw materials are those which grow out of the earth or those which repose beneath its surface. The moment you dig out the iron, and the coal, and the copper, and the marble, and the salt, and the clay, that moment human labor is added to the natural product, and from that moment it is no longer raw material. When you cut down the tree and begin to saw it into timber or into boards it is no longer raw material.

When the farmer raises or buys his flock of sheep and produces his wool by means of his labor, that is no longer raw material. Human labor, the great energizing, civilizing force of the world and of humanity, has entered into that product. I would not put it too strongly if I were to say the soul of man has entered into and transformed that natural product. It is no longer raw material. Go into any one of the manufacturing establishments of this country; look at one that I have in my mind in my own State. In that factory they take copper in the ingot as it comes from the mine into the front door. When it goes out again it goes in the shape of copper wire of four one-thousandths of an inch in diameter. Into that crude copper ingot has passed the highest thought of man; his brain is in the wire—his soul is there.

In the course of his speech, Mr. Platt came to the question of the surplus which had ostensibly moved President Cleveland to his sensational and radical recommendation. To the thrifty Connecticut statesman the existence of a surplus did not seem to be an unmixed evil and, indeed, for those who have become familiar with the Treasury statistics of the last ten years since the Dingley law went into effect, it is difficult to conceive of the consternation into which the comparatively meagre accumulations of 1887 threw those who were entrusted with the administration of the Government. He pointed out that the actual accumulation in the Treasury on February 1, 1888, was only about $35,000,000. He asked why this accumulation had been permitted if it were such an evil:

Why has taxation not been reduced—the taxation which created from year to year this accumulation? Why has the Democratic party in power in that section of Congress which originates measures of this character not sent to this body some bill looking to the reduction of taxation? It stood pledged by its platform, by the professions of its leaders on every stump and at every hustings in the United States, immediately upon its accession to power to take steps for the reduction of the surplus. They misrepresented the amount of the surplus in their presidential convention of 1884, as I will show; but if there was any one thing which they stood pledged to do it was immediately and without delay to adopt measures for the reduction of this surplus accumulation in the Treasury. . . .

What reason can be given for this delay in the past,

what reason can be given for this delay to-day, if it be not that the accumulation of money in the Treasury and our annual surplus income are being used and deliberately used, to force Congress into a destruction of the protective system of the country?

He reminded the Senate that in less than three years we had a debt falling due of $230,000,000, and asked why the administration did not try to anticipate the payment of that debt:

What would be good financiering for a business man if he had money on hand which he had no use for, and had a debt falling due at a distant date? Would it not be to go to this creditor and say: "I have money on hand which I have no use for; you have a note against me falling due in future; I wish to make some arrangement with you whereby I can take up that note now." Why has not the Government done so? It would have made money by the transaction. It will make money if it will adopt that policy now instead of the policy of allowing the money to accumulate in the Treasury and in national banks until the debt falls due. . . . Why should the Government insist upon this money lying idle in the Treasury rather than attempt to anticipate the debt of the Government? If one quarter as much time had been spent in attempting to devise some fair plan by which an arrangement with the creditors of the Government could be made for the anticipation of the debt which should be satisfactory to them and profitable to the Government as has been spent in conferences to try to devise some scheme for striking down the industries of this country, that arrangement could long ago have been perfected.

My experience in life has taught me—and somewhat painfully taught me—that it is not a pleasant condition to be in, and that it is not good business for a man to be in a situation where he has no money in his pocket except

that which he must pay out for his daily expenses. That
man is not very well off financially. What is true of the
man is true of the United States. The idea of reducing
so that there shall be no money in the Treasury, depleted
entirely, run from day to day and hand to mouth, using
its daily receipts to meet daily expenditures, is a policy
which is entirely unwarranted by any sound financial
theory. . . . I would expend more. I would have a
little patriotism instead of so much penuriousness. I would
have some coast defences. I would not be longer at the
mercy of foreign powers, at the mercy of England, whose
system it is sought to engraft upon our republican institutions. I would have a navy built as if we intended to
have a navy, and not in the pottering way in which it has
been going on under this administration, and I would have
reasonable appropriations for internal improvements.

I would have, even if I do not think very much of our
foreign representation, our diplomats, our ministers, our
consuls, enabled to represent this country abroad in a respectable manner, to say the least, and I would pay them
enough so that they could do so. . . . I would have an
American policy, and whatever was reasonably calculated
to extend and develop and foster that American policy
and give us a foothold amongst the nations and respecta-
bility everywhere befitting the condition of a free Republic,
I would spend money for.

He agreed to the necessity of some reduction, but he
did not believe in the reduction of taxation on the
President's plan, which in his opinion would result in
the destruction of the protective system. He would
have made the reduction elsewhere than on manufactured articles:

Why not reduce by repealing internal-revenue taxation?
Because the protective system would be left in force in
this country. War taxes! There is one tax that is abso-

lutely a war tax, and that is the internal-revenue tax. The
tariff tax, if it were a tax, existed to some extent before
the war. . . . The war tax of the country is the internal-
revenue tax. Why not repeal that or as much of it as is
necessary to get the required reduction?

It is a tax upon our productions, be they tobacco or
corn. It is a tax that operates unequally and yet the President of the United States says directly that no one objects
to that; and this great accumulation, this surplus of money,
must pile up in the Treasury rather than touch the internal-
revenue tax! How is it that this war tax, about which
we have heard so much, has all at once become so sacred?

He asked how manufacturers were to be compensated
for the loss which the President proposed to inflict on
them:

They can get cheap raw materials and then he says they
can compete with other nations in the markets of the
world. The poor, pitiful privilege that they are to have to
save them from ruin is to go away from their own country
to seek markets in other countries. Foreign trade is de-
sirable, but it is not worth obtaining at the sacrifice of the
trade of this country. The trade of this country is the
marvel of God's own civilization, and to give up any portion
of it in the hope that we may in some way compensate
ourselves by getting the markets of the world, as they are
called, is the height of folly and absurdity.

Where are the "markets of the world"? Not in England,
not in Germany, not in France, not in Belgium or Holland.
We are not going to sell our goods in England or the other
countries I have named in competition with the foreign
manufacturers. Freight and factorage are against us.
We are not going to sell in lands which England holds by
the strong power of her army. We are shut up to South
America; and if we could get all the trade of South America,
it would not be 6 per cent. of our home market. I wish
we had it; but the idea of opening our ports, taking off

our tariff duties, letting the foreigner flood our market
with his goods, and then telling American manufacturers
and American laboring men that we can compensate ourselves by going into the markets of the world if we can only
have reduced duties, it seems to me is idle, and, of all free-
trade sophistries, is the shallowest.

His concluding words were:

Sir, it is too late in the century to belittle the system of
protection by asserting, as the President and all other free
traders assert, that it lays a tax upon the consumer paid
to the manufacturer. It is too late in the century to seek
to destroy that system by appealing to the disquiet of
laborers in the hope of arraying them against it because it
protects alone or primarily the manufacturers and brings
"immense profits" to their pockets.

Protection is for the whole of United America; its benefits
are as extensive as our boundaries; its "immense profits"
are as widely diffused as our citizenship—it blesses and
beautifies every home, it helps and strengthens every
citizen, the importer of foreign wares alone excepted. It
is the policy of United America in its competition with all
the world. Under the fostering influence of that system
America has gained its rightful place in front of the grand
procession of the nations. And unless we blindly permit
a Democratic President and a so-called Democratic party
to destroy this, our sure safe-guard of national success,
United America will continue to lead the world in the
grand struggle for human advancement.

In due season after many hearings, Roger Q. Mills presented to the House from the Committee on Ways and
Means the tariff bill which bore his name. The bill
occupied the attention of the House for several months.
It gave William McKinley the opportunity for recognition as the apostle of protection which ultimately
made him President, and it gave Thomas B. Reed the

chance for leadership which made him Speaker of the
House. When it reached the Senate an enervating
summer had already laid its hand upon the capital.
The great national conventions were impending, and
the country was on the threshold of a campaign for the
Presidency which it was seen must turn in large measure
upon the issues presented by the Mills bill and the
Cleveland message.

The Senate Committee on Finance, which was domi-
nated by a Republican majority, consisting of Morrill,
Sherman, Jones of Nevada, Allison, Aldrich, and Hiscock,
had framed a bill of its own, along protection lines, and
this was reported to the Senate as a substitute for the
measure passed by the House. It was known of course
that no bill could become a law, and the debate which
followed was purely for effect upon the approaching
election. The discussion continued until within three
weeks of the election day.

There was little for any member of the Senate to do
except to remain in his place to contribute to a quorum,
to vote on motions which required a record, and
occasionally to speak.

Mr. Platt contented himself with following the Committee on Finance, interposing an occasional question
during the debate, and voting with due regularity. He
made only one speech of greater length than a few
sentences. This was near the close of the session, on
October 11, 1888. Then he discussed the issue of
protection from the interesting view-point of the
development of labor and industry North and South:

Two systems of labor were established contemporaneously
in this country. About a year before the *Mayflower* touched
the Massachusetts shore, a ship landed at Jamestown,
Virginia, loaded with slaves. From that time these two

labor systems have been antagonistic forces in the country, and all our woes and troubles and conflicts have been occasioned by the "irrepressible conflict" between these two labor systems. One system involved the idea that labor should be unpaid and ignorant. At first it involved the idea that capital should own the laborer, but always to this day the idea that labor shall be poorly paid and ignorant. The other system involved the idea that labor should be well paid and should be intelligent.

The Southern system, if I may so call it without disrespect, was based upon the idea that the laborer should have no status in society, that he should have no political rights, no civil rights, no "inalienable rights." The other was based upon the idea that the laborer should have an equal status in society with every other man; that he should have political rights and civil rights; that he should be one of the citizens of the Government, responsible for its administration and responsible for its progress; that he should be in the broadest sense a freeman. The Southern system where the laborer was unpaid, where he was kept ignorant, where it was a criminal offence to teach him to read even the Scriptures, was adapted only to the rudest cultivation of the soil. The Northern system, where the laborer was well paid and intelligent and free to engage in the "pursuit of happiness," inevitably tended to the diversification of industries.

These two labor systems determined where manufactories should first be planted in the United States. It was not the enterprise of capitalists; it was solely and purely the character of labor which spread over these different sections of the United States which determined where manufacturing should spring up and flourish. The New England States, where this labor system was first planted, could but attempt to engage in manufacturing. The Southern States, where the ignorant and unpaid systems of labor prevailed, could only engage in the raising of cotton, sugar, tobacco, and like agricultural products. Skill, education, and aspiration in the laborer not only make agriculture profitable, but are absolutely essential to even the rudimentary development of mechanical industries.

To have supposed that manufacturing could at that day have found a foothold in the Southern section of this country was to suppose that you could reverse a universal law of political economy.

In the second session of the Fiftieth Congress, after the defeat of Cleveland by Harrison, the Senate continued to debate the tariff bill which was still on the calendar; and to this useless debate Mr. Platt contributed occasional remarks. One brief speech which he made on the proposal to impose a duty on tin-plate is interesting by reason of the success which finally resulted from the imposition of the tin-plate duty:

I want to vote for every duty which will establish a new industry in this country—that is to say, an industry which under any circumstances it can be supposed can be profitably carried on in this country. If employment can be found for 70,000 additional workmen in this country in the manufacture of the whole or a large portion of these 283,000 tons of tin-plate which we now pay our money to England for, I want that opportunity for the employment of labor to be satisfied; and I do not believe that this duty is going to result in any great increase of the price of tin-plate; I think it very doubtful whether it results in any, if the usual course pursued by foreign manufacturers is adopted by them. When they see there is a probability that tin-plate factories will be established in this country, they will put down the price quite equal to the amount that is added to the duty; and even if the price is temporarily raised, all the experience of this country shows that it will immediately fall to or below its present price.

On another occasion he considered briefly the relation of the tariff to the trusts:

As it appears to me, the question of trusts has nothing whatever to do with the question of duties. It seems to me that the righteous indignation which exists at a great many trusts in this country (against all trusts that have the features which make them obnoxious) is made use of to attack the tariff.

Trusts are not indigenous to the United States. The worst trusts are to be found abroad, and many of them in England, where there is no tariff. There is not a worse trust for the United States than the copper trust which exists in France. There is no trust which is bearing upon our people more unfavorably, more injuriously, and the tariff has nothing to do with that; the rate of duty has nothing to do with that.

I merely rose to say that while I join in the indignation against those combinations which put up the price of necessaries of life, which put up the price of articles that enter into general use, I do protest against this continued reiteration in the Senate that they are the result in some way of protective duties.

CHAPTER XVIII

THE FATEFUL FIFTY-FIRST CONGRESS

McKinley Tariff and the Lodge Elections Bill—Democratic Obstruction in the Senate—An Unswerving Supporter of the Party Programme—Argues for Enactment of Both Bills—The Quay Resolution—Enactment of the Tariff Bill—The Election Bill Postponed—Lukewarm towards Blaine's Reciprocity Proposal—Unchanged by Republican Defeat.

ON the assembling of the Fifty-first Congress in December, 1889, the Republican party, controlling both legislative and executive branches of the Government, for the first time in years found itself in a position to undertake constructive legislation. First among the measures to which the party had pledged itself was a revision of the tariff along the lines of protection, next the enactment of a law to insure the integrity and purity of Federal elections. In order to fulfil either of these promises or to do other essential things it was necessary first to revise the rules of the House so as to give the majority a chance to do business, as the Democratic minority, lacking only a few votes of control, made no concealment of its purpose to prevent, by obstructive parliamentary tactics, the enactment of all measures which they did not like. Speaker Reed by heroic measures early in the session effected the change of rules which won for him the title of "Czar" and thus placed the House in a position to carry out its part of the political programme. The McKinley Tariff bill and the Lodge Elections bill, taking their names from the chairmen of the committees which reported them, were promptly passed and sent to the Senate. There the two measures, possessing nothing in common except the stamp of party regularity, were to run along for months, impeding one another's progress and each threatening the other's chances.

On April 24, 1890, Senator Hoar from the Committee on Privileges and Elections reported the Elections bill to the Senate. Senator Pugh of Alabama for the Democratic minority made a report in which he declared with emphasis that the passage of the bill would be resisted by every method known to parliamentary law and to the Constitution. On June 18th, Senator Morrill from the Finance Committee reported the Tariff bill with amendments, which was in effect a substitute, founded on the measure reported as a substitute for the Mills bill in 1888. The Finance Committee had the same Republican membership as in the preceding Congress. Mr. Platt was not a member, though by long service and demonstrated usefulness he was close in the councils of Allison and Aldrich, who had most to do with the initial steps of shaping tariff legislation

In the face of threatened Democratic obstruction, the Republican majority was concerned chiefly in bringing the bill to a vote so that it might go into operation well in advance of the November elections, and all unnecessary speaking in defence of the measure was to be discouraged. This was especially agreeable to Mr. Platt who, following his usual practice, took no part in the debate except at times when he believed he could be of immediate service, and the *Congressional Record* contains no report of any speech from him which would occupy more than fifteen minutes in delivery. He did no

talking for his constituents; and was interested solely in
seeing that the bill should be evolved as speedily and in
as favorable a form as possible.   But he was solicitous
that the two great political measures of the session
should become laws,—as much concerned about one as
about the other,—and for a long time it looked as though
the Senate would be able to come to a vote on neither.
After the farce of unlimited debate had been going on
for several weeks, the country began to call upon the
Senate to get to work.   The press, instead of condemn-
ing the minority, which was responsible for the delay,
turned its batteries upon the majority, which was doing
its very best to bring about a vote, and, coupled with
this criticism, illogically enough, was a wholesale
denunciation of the very bills upon which action was
demanded.   Mr. Platt was kept busy explaining to
people at home just what the trouble was, and he did
not mince words in upholding the policy of his party.
To one correspondent who had written him a com-
plaining letter he replied:

I do not suppose the people who are talking in opposition
to the "McKinley bill" as it is called have any very definite
idea of the bill as a whole.

We carried the Presidential election on two issues: The
one, that we would enact a protective tariff law; and the
other, that we would endeavor to have honest elections.
. . . Now what are we going to do—abandon the idea
of protection to American industries?   And are we going
to abandon our opportunity to secure fair elections?   If
so we need never again talk of protection and honest elections.   For it will be said that having the three branches
of the administration and the opportunity to pass laws,
we deliberately refused to do so. . . .   I am a protectionist
whether in public or in private life; and I can not abandon

my lifelong views on this subject whatever the result may be personally or politically.

, I am sorry to see you speak of the "election bill" as a "force bill." There is not an element of force in it from the beginning to the end of it. If the Republican party, having the opportunity to enact a law, the sole purpose of which is to allow people to vote in Congressional elections and which contains no element of force, deliberately declines to do it, how can it ever again complain that the nation is governed by a party which exists only by a fraudulent suppression of votes? And what is the Republican party to contend for if it abandons these two issues?

With equal frankness he wrote to William C. Miner of Madison, Connecticut:

I don't see how or where you got your idea about "reimbursing interested parties for money advanced to the campaign fund of '88 by an increase of taxes." I should not suppose that such a fiction was seriously believed anywhere. . . . I fear that you have been giving too much heed to the misrepresentations persistently and continuously reiterated in certain newspapers that seem to think the country would be better off if its industries were crippled here and transferred to other countries. . . . Financially, socially, morally, and politically, I believe that protection is the best thing for Connecticut, for the United States, and for all the people of the United States; and so believing I am bound to support it. I believe too in allowing people to vote everywhere; and when it is a question of the election of members of Congress, where a suppression of the vote in any State is a direct and absolute wrong to my own State, I believe it is the duty of Congress to provide for honest elections everywhere. I don't speak of any particular election law. We have a law now, under which marshals were appointed at the last Congressional election in Meriden, as well as in New Haven, Hartford, Waterbury, Bridgeport, and the other large towns. They

were appointed by Democrats; they did n't hurt me and
they did n't hurt any one. And I know of no reason why
such a law should not be extended so that the officers
appointed in Connecticut to have an oversight of Congressional elections can be appointed in the States where the
great wrong on Connecticut is, I believe, perpetrated. As
to the details of the bill, that is another question. They
ought to be of uniform application, and so guarded that
no injustice shall be done. But if we are going to have a
republican form of government, we must have honest
elections.

The leaders of the Senate plodded painfully along
while the critics were snarling at their heels, until signs
of restlessness began to show among some of those who
must be depended on if the party programme was to
be carried through. A little group of Republicans, most
of them from far Western States, were hostile to the
Elections bill, believing it to be a bad political move,
while others representing great industrial States were
ready to sacrifice the Elections bill or any other measure
in order to insure the enactment of a protective tariff
law. One of these was Quay of Pennsylvania who,
after the Tariff bill had been two months before the
Senate, undertook to open a way for its passage by
offering a resolution fixing the order of business. The
resolution provided that during the rest of the session
the Senate would take up for consideration no legislative
business other than the pending Tariff bill, conference
reports, appropriation bills, and certain other measures
among which the Elections bill was conspicuous by its
absence; the consideration of all bills other than those
mentioned, to be postponed to the following session and
a vote on the tariff to be had on August 30th. While
the resolution was never acted on, its mere introduc-

tion, suggesting an arrangement between the Democrats
and a few Republicans, was a sufficient indication of
what was bound to happen.   Mr. Platt, who had been
urging a change in the rules to fix a limit to debate, took
this turn of affairs to heart: "The situation here in
the Senate is exasperating beyond measure," he wrote
to A. H. Kellam of New Haven, on August 18th, the
day on which Quay's resolution was introduced:

It has been perfectly evident that the Democrats have
been consuming time in debate in every possible way that
they could devise, short of laying themselves open to the
charge of wilful obstruction, their object being so to pro-
long the consideration of measures that the Elections bill
might not be reached at this session.   Since we came to
the consideration of the Tariff bill I think they have laid
themselves open in its discussion to the charge of wilful
obstruction.   With no rule in the Senate by which we can
limit debate, they can discuss the Tariff bill till the first
day of the next session, and they intend to do it unless we
will bargain with them not to take up the Elections bill.
This is the dilemma: How can we avoid it?

The newspapers say, "Change the rules so as to cut off
debate."   Then the question arises, "Can we change our
rules?"   In answering this it must be understood that
we have ten majority in the Senate, that a working quorum
is forty-three, that we have one Senator (Stanford) in
Europe, two Senators at home sick, and so sick that it is
questionable whether they could come here, and some
Senators—variously reckoned at from three to six—who
are openly opposed to the passage of any elections law and
who consequently would not consent to a change of rules
when every one knows that the object of such change is the
passage of an elections law.   Again, we have some Senators
who don't believe there ought to be any limitation of debate in the Senate, who at the same time are heartily in
favor of an elections bill; and others who on a final vote

would vote for the Elections bill, but doubt its expediency so much that they would join with its opponents in opposing a change of rules.

But suppose this difficulty obviated. The question then is, can we change the rules? The Democrats would then insist on discussing this resolution as they do now the Tariff bill, and they can discuss it just as long as the Tariff bill unless the presiding officer of the Senate, when the discussion had proceeded as long as the Republicans thought it ought, should refuse to recognize any one and put the question. This would be a direct violation of our present rules. It would not be the situation that it was in the House on the adoption of rules, for the House had no rules. Our rules permit debate; and to put the question when any one desires to speak would be an open violation of them; and the presiding officer could not do it successfully unless he had a majority of the Senate at his back to sustain him. He would then be exercising his arbitrary power in the interest of a minority and not of a majority. Can he do that and be sustained by even the Republican sentiment of the country?

If then it be conceded that the rules cannot be changed any easier than the Tariff bill can be passed (I don't concede it, but I think most of the Republican Senators do as a practical question), nothing would be gained by dropping the Tariff bill and going into a heated contest for a change of rules. What then is to be done? Two courses are open, —first, keep at the Tariff bill, fight it out on that line if it takes till the 4th of March, and throw the responsibility of obstruction and delay and possible failure to pass it, on the Democrats. This is what I think we ought to do. But you will observe that no Republican newspaper criticises the Democrats or would be likely to. They criticise the Republican Senators with a sweeping and undiscriminating criticism.

The practical situation leads some Republican Senators who honestly favor an election law as well as those who are opposed to one to try to bargain for the passage of the Tariff bill, by agreeing to postpone consideration of the Elections bill—and that is the secret of the Quay resolution. They think that the delay and failure to pass a Tariff bill, in working great injury to the business interests of the country, creates dissatisfaction and disaffection among business men, and that it is better to assume that we can't get both and secure the passage of the Tariff bill at any sacrifice—even by an agreement with Democrats which virtually means the abandonment of the Elections bill. I cannot go with them and I will not. I believe if we had spunk and persistence we could pass the Tariff bill; then we could, if we had votes enough, take up the Elections bill and honestly try to pass it. If we failed the responsibility would not be on the Republicans. My plan would involve staying here continuously and honestly trying to do those things which the Republican party in the last election decided should be done. To purchase the passage of the Tariff bill by a bargain with the Democrats which involves the abandonment of the Elections bill, I regard as a weak and cowardly surrender.

If the Republicans of Connecticut and the Republican newspapers of the State would back up those Republican Senators who are trying to carry out the wishes of the Republican party, and attack the Democrats, putting the responsibility of delay and possible failure on them, the situation would not be as embarrassing as it now is. But I ask you if you have seen one word of vigorous criticism in a Connecticut newspaper on the course of the Democrats?

Quay's resolution which indicates the bargain will probably come up on Tuesday, and I presume has Republican votes enough behind it, added to the Democrats, to pass it. But I wash my hands clean of it. It will probably give us a Tariff bill—but acquired at what a sacrifice!

The programme of the Quay Republicans prevailed. The Elections bill went over, the Tariff bill passed the

Senate on September 20th, and on October 1st became a law. The bill as a whole Mr. Platt regarded as a well constructed measure, and he struck powerful blows later in its defence, but he had no great fancy for the reciprocity provision adopted in response to the sentiment aroused by Mr. Blaine in his letter to Senator Frye, flung into the controversy after the bill had passed the House. His opinions in later years were somewhat modified, and, after all, the reciprocity proposed by Mr. Blaine, and limited to the countries of South and Central America in its practical working, was quite a different thing from the reciprocity of the Dingley bill which embraced the commercial nations of the world or the reciprocity which ten years later President McKinley hailed as the handmaid of Protection. It had nothing in common with the arrangement with Cuba which as a matter of national policy and square dealing Senator Platt during the Roosevelt administration was instrumental in bringing about.

Though he did not oppose reciprocity in the Senate he was free in his comments on the newly projected issue.[1]

[1] To A. H. Kellam, of New Haven, he wrote on July 19, 1890, what he called a few "crude and tentative suggestions" on the question which was then just beginning to loom on the political horizon:

"I notice in the Hartford *Post* edited by Porter, a nephew of William Walter Phelps, a little article to the effect that the announcement of Blaine's views on reciprocity and the tariff is taken as an indication that he is a candidate for the Presidency in 1892, and if so would be put there by a phenomenal majority, and all that sort of thing.

"So far as I can learn the Blaine pronunciamento seems to have excited more interest in Connecticut than anywhere else. All this question of reciprocity trades with South America, Cuba, and Canada is by no means a new thing   Mr. Blaine has no patent on it any more than he has on the Pan-American Congress which

To Lynde Harrison, of New Haven, for instance, he
wrote on August 23d:

I don't know what will be done in the Senate about
anything looking to what is called "reciprocity"—a very
taking and very indefinite word.   And I am a little afraid

was strongly recommended by Cleveland, and earlier than that by
Mr. Frye.   If anything is done looking to trades with other countries on sugar, it won't take the line of keeping the present duty on
sugar; and it seems a very queer position for protectionists or free
traders to take, that they would keep up the high duty on sugar in
the hope that some time or other we might make a trade with some
country that produces a little, when the sugar duty is one that is
not required upon any principle of protection and when, taking
it off is a direct benefit to the people of the United States of fifty
millions of dollars.

"To my mind the only way to reach such a reciprocity, or rather
trade with a sugar-producing country, would be to take the duty off
sugar, and then provide that at a certain time, say July, 1891, or
January, 1892, it should be restored as against all sugar-producing
countries that have not in the meantime signified their willingness
and agreement to take certain things from us free.   Then the people
would get the benefit of free sugar, and we would hold out an induce-
ment to sugar-producing countries to take some goods free from us.
In other words, we have the game in our own hands, when if we
keep the duty on sugar in the hope that we may trade with them,
they will have the game in their hands.

"The whole question of trades of this sort is more complicated
than it appears.   In the first place, if a sugar-producing country—
Brazil or Cuba—has a treaty with foreign countries containing a
'most favored nations' clause, any agreement they might make
with us would have to be made with all other countries with whom
they have such treaties.   In the second place there is no telling
if we should enter upon such a policy, where it would end.   The
parties who want to make sugar trades say that there is no principle involved in it—it is merely a business arrangement.   But
if we begin, for instance, with Brazil on sugar, the demand will
immediately be made that we shall extend it to wool with the
countries that produce coarser wools.   That you see hits the wool
producers of the United States, with the probable effect of turning
them against the protective policy of the country.

"Again, if we make such trades with reference to sugar and wool,
why not with reference to tea?   The whole western coast that can

of it because every Democrat and Free Trader in the country is shouting for it and for Blaine. But the real difficulty is, first,—to apply it to sugar and not to wool and hides; secondly,—to agree on what articles we shall trade for it. When the Mexican and Spanish treaties were made it turned out that Connecticut got nothing; that is, nothing

---

trade with China, perhaps on better terms than any foreign nation, would insist that we should put a duty on tea, if China did not agree to take certain American products.

"Again, what products shall we insist shall be taken free by countries from which we want to get goods free? Shall they be confined purely to agricultural products? Or shall we go beyond that in our demands and include—say, agricultural implements? If we include agricultural implements, why not other manufactured products—cotton cloth; and if cotton cloth, why not woollen cloths and machinery? And if machinery, why not carriages? Where is it to end? Would not the producer of articles not included in the trade be greatly dissatisfied? And is not any general policy of extending our trade by stipulations with certain countries, that we will take certain products of theirs free, if they will take certain products of ours free, the beginning of breaking down the protective policy of this country?

"Now I have said enough to outline some of the difficulties which underlie this whole question of reciprocity trades. I mention only a few of them. It is a serious question, and one but little understood. It has a certain fascination about it in the idea that through it we may enlarge our trade with foreign countries. I suppose that the entire purchases of the Central and South American States and Cuba combined, amount to perhaps five hundred millions of dollars. We could not expect to get it all; but if we could, it would probably equal in round numbers seven per cent. of our home trade. If we could get these reciprocity trades with the western nations lying south of us it might add to our trade an amount equal to two or three per cent. of our home market.

"The question then comes to this—whether it will be worth what it will cost. I have never been quite satisfied on this point. But I am clearly satisfied that Blaine's idea of keeping up the duty on sugar, in the hope that we may be able to make a trade some time, is not sound. If anything is to be done, it is to take off the duty and then provide for a restoration of it as against those countries which in a specified time do not allow us reciprocal advantages such as we may require.

manufactured in Connecticut was included in the list of
what those countries would take in consideration of our
taking some of their products free; third,—it would give
a great boom to the idea of Canadian reciprocity, which
is all against New England interests, especially our agricultural interests along the border. And yet I think the
drift is toward a provision that if by a certain time the
countries raising sugar do not accept free from us certain
things that the President shall ask that the duties shall be
restored. We got nothing when we made coffee and tea
free. I am afraid of it—afraid it will be the beginning of
the end of the protective system. It is very fascinating
as I have said, but we never made a reciprocity treaty yet
by which we did not lose.

Reciprocity and all, the McKinley bill had a rough
time when it came to be passed on by the people.
While the bill was on its passage through Congress the
Democratic opposition was busily engaged in fanning
into flame the discontent which is an invariable accom-
paniment of every revision of the tariff. The cry went
up that the new rates of duty were prohibitive; that the
bill was framed in the interest of the rich as against the
poor; that the workingman's dinner pail was heavily
taxed; that the burden pressed cruelly upon the family
of moderate means. Merchants all over the United
States in every city and village arbitrarily raised the
price on every kind of commodity, feeling that they
could safely charge the increased cost to the increased
rates of the McKinley bill. In numerous instances the
bill was held responsible for the increase in retail price
of articles which were in no way affected by it. The
women of the country, influenced in their shopping by
the outcry against the McKinley rates, joined in it,
to the consternation of political leaders. The Repub-

lican party was charged with reimbursing campaign
contributions out of the pockets of the people; and to
swell the cry, the Democrats South and North bayed
lustily against the proposed Federal Elections law,
which, borrowing a political epithet of the Grant administration, they had dubbed the "Force bill." The
McKinley bill was so late in becoming a law that in the
few weeks preceding election its real character could not
be made known and the long session of Congress kept
Senators and Representatives in Washington, where
they could not explain it to their constituents. The
result might have been foreseen. The Republican majority in the House was overturned and for the last
half of Mr. Harrison's administration a Democratic
majority of almost unprecedented size helped to thwart
his plans.

Mr. Platt was not politically blind, and he recognized,
as did others, the tendency of the time, but he sturdily
refused to be swept off his feet by popular clamor and
up to the very end he contended stoutly that the
McKinley bill carried a message of promise to American
industries.

Republican defeat in the November elections did not
discourage him. It was in the winter of 1890–91 that
his own re-election was pending, but fortunately there
was no Republican opposition to his return and he was
free to go his own way politically.

To a Connecticut member of the House who had
asked his advice about a speech he had in contempla-
tion the following winter after the defeat in the November election, Mr. Platt wrote on December 3, 1890:

Of course I don't want to influence you against what
you think is right and proper ground to take at the board

of trade meeting. I don't believe free lumber and free
coal would help us a particle. As you say, taking half
of the duty off of pine lumber has raised the price of it. I
don't think the taking off of the whole duty would decrease
the price at all, either on pine or spruce. It would simply
add so much to Canadian stumpage and to transportation.

We should not buy Nova Scotia coal as against American
coal, if it were free. We might possibly get American coal
a trifle cheaper, but I doubt that. What I fear is the giving
aid and comfort to the Democrats. I do not want them to
be encouraged just at present. They will twist anything
you say, if it is in the slightest degree favorable to taking
the duty off from any raw material into a condemnation
of the whole protective policy, just as they did what Blaine
said about reciprocity. The first step in the Democratic
free trade programme is free trade on what they call raw
materials, and, if they can get any one to advocate that,
even as to any one item, they immediately claim a convert
to their doctrine. We have trouble enough on hand, and
my idea is that we had better not show any weakening
anywhere along the line whatever we might think it best
to do in the future.

To the end of his career he never wavered in his
faith.

CHAPTER XIX

THE WILSON-GORMAN BILL

An Aid to the Finance Committee—Mr. North's Experience—
Active in Debate—Keen Analysis of the Democratic Position
—"Incidental Protection" Ridiculed—A Deadly Blow at
Farmers—Opposed to Free Raw Materials.

THE McKinley tariff was doomed to a life altogether
too brief to demonstrate its effectiveness as a
protective and revenue-raising measure, and its existence was confined to a period of political uncertainty
which placed it continually at a disadvantage, so that
its real merit as a piece of constructive legislation will
never be known. The Democratic party, which got its
foot into the stirrup in the elections of 1890, vaulted
into the saddle two years later, and, having made its
campaign on the issue of the tariff, felt compelled at
least to attempt a fulfilment of its promise.

In the abortive tariff legislation of the Fifty-third
Congress, in 1894, resulting as it did in the hybrid
Wilson–Gorman act which President Cleveland stigmatized as a work of "perfidy and dishonor," Mr.
Platt, as one of the minority in the Senate, was obliged
to participate. He was not a member of the Finance
Committee, although he probably would have been, had
there been a Republican majority, as Mr. Hiscock's
retirement from the Senate had left a vacancy among
the Eastern members of the Committee to which

Connecticut might reasonably have laid claim.   But
although not a member he was taken freely into the
councils of the minority members, and certain schedules
of the proposed bill were turned over to him for consideration.   An interesting light is thrown on his methods
of work by S. N. D. North, afterwards director of the
census, who came closely in contact with him at this
time:

I shall never forget the occasion of my first meeting
with Senator Platt. I was assisting Senator Aldrich as a
tariff expert. Senator Platt sent for me. He said:

"I want to know all about the woollen schedule. At
present I know very little about it. I wish you would help
me out."

We sat down in his room at the Arlington, and he began
asking me questions. I never went through so searching
a cross examination in my life. There was not a detail
of the schedule that he did not want to know all about.
Finally I was compelled to cry for mercy. I discovered
that the thorough information which he had in mind to
get was something which I was not in a position to give
without further preparation, so I begged for time to look
into the question a little more at my leisure, and then I
went back to him. He resumed his cross examination and
I did the best I could. What particularly impressed me
was his evident determination to get at the truth; the real
reason for every item of the woollen schedule, and the
clearness of his mental powers. He had a marvellous
memory. When the bill came up for discussion every
question he asked showed that the knowledge I had helped
him to obtain stood in his mind.

It was like him to debate more freely the Wilson–
Gorman bill to which he was opposed than any one of
the measures which he favored, and in the framing
of some of which he had an important part.   He was

satisfied that the various paragraphs of the McKinley
and Dingley bill should be put on their passage without
controversial contribution from him, but there was so
much in the Wilson–Gorman schedules to which he
took exception that he threw himself into the combat,
delivering effective blows where they would do most
good.   It was an opportunity for exposing the fallacies
of the Democratic position which few others were so
well qualified to take advantage of as he.   His familiarity with industries and schedules and his forceful
unadorned manner of speech rarely came into more
effective play.   Of his work it was said at the time
by a Connecticut newspaper:

Never before has Senator Platt so revealed his strength
of mind, his capacity for labor, his equipment for debate,
his sound moral basis, his warm heart, his true regard for
the common people and his lofty patriotism. . . .   Sound
judgment, common sense, ready wit, pat and luminous
illustrations have abounded in his speeches and made them
wise, interesting, and forcible. . . .   He has especially
pleaded for the people of New England, and in doing it
he has shown much of the sturdy, strongly moral, deeply
thoughtful, shrewd humorous qualities that mark the New
England character.   In our opinion no man in the Senate
has done so much work in this debate or done it so well.

In advocating a duty of sixty cents a ton on coal
instead of forty as recommended by the committee, he
said:

I wish the Democratic Free Trader could get the one idea
into his mind as to what a benefit it is to the country to
have all our work done here, what a benefit it is to have our
wool grown here, and our ore dug here, and our coal mined
here, rather than to have it done somewhere else.   I should
suppose that the underlying patriotism of American

Senators would get the better of their party predilections
and party pride, so that they would not put into the bill anything which would strike down industries in this country.

I stand for the system of protection because I will not
desert the American laborer. I have no special right to
call myself his champion, and I believe that the continuance of all these industries in the United States by American
labor is the salvation of our civilization, and it is for that
reason that I am a protectionist. No supposed sentiment
that we could get coal a little cheaper in New England will
for a moment turn me from the plain, straight path of
protection, which a man who acts from principle and not
from selfish aims ought to pursue.

The Wilson bill as it came from the House had at
least the virtue of consistency. It was a genuine
tariff-for-revenue measure. Protective duties had been
ruthlessly slaughtered. By the time it had come from
under its treatment at the hands of the Senate Committee it had lost even this merit. Higher duties had
been restored here and there at the demand of Democratic Senators interested in certain industries until the
original measure was hardly recognizable. But the
remodelling had not been in accordance with any
economic plan. Mr. Platt declared the difference
between the two bills to be like the difference between
electrocution and death by slow poison:

The one is sudden and painless as the death of industries
would have been under the Wilson bill; the other is tor-
turing and lingering as the death of industries will be
under the bill which we are now considering, should it
become a law. . . .

This is not a protective bill. It is not in any sense a
recognition of the doctrine of protection high or low. It
is not a bill for revenue with incidental protection. It is

a bill (and the truth may as well be told in the Senate of the United States) which proceeds upon free-trade principles except as to such articles as it has been necessary to levy protective duties upon to get the votes of Democratic Senators to pass the bill. I insist that never before in the history of this country has such a spectacle been presented in either branch of the National Legislature, and I pray to God it may never occur again.

The bill as it came from the House of Representatives was mainly free from such a charge, but reaching here it was discovered that there was not a majority upon the Democratic side of the chamber to pass it. There was a body of Conservatives, as they were called, estimated at from five to fifteen, who were charged all over the country in Democratic newspapers with being traitors to the Democratic party, and in great head-lines Democratic newspapers called upon the Democrats in the Senate who stood by the Chicago platform and proposed to pass a tariff bill, which should not be objectionable to the charge that it was robbery, to read the Conservatives out of the party. It was more of a task than the majority of the Democratic Senators desired to undertake. Consequently they surrendered to these conservatives, and the price of their votes appears in the protective duties which the bill contains; and there are no other protective duties in it. . . .

It is strange, passing strange, that Senators who say they do not believe in protection, that Senators who say that the McKinley bill was the most infamous measure that was ever passed, should be found voting for duties equivalent to the McKinley rates upon some of those matters which most closely touch and affect the interests of the people of the United States. No such marvel has ever been seen under the sun as all the Democratic Senators, with the possible exception of the Senator from Texas (Mr. Mills), giving way to this demand of the sugar trust. How this chamber has rung with denunciations of the sugar trust! How the ears of waiting and listening multitudes in

Democratic political meetings have been vexed with reiterated denunciations of this sugar trust! And here every
Democratic Senator, with one exception, is ready to vote
for a prohibitive duty upon refined sugar!

He ridiculed the idea of "incidental protection"
which Democrats looking for an excuse to impose
duties on their own pet products made much of. He
declared that there was no such principle:

If by incidental protection you mean that the metal
working industries of Connecticut and the other Eastern
States are to be absolutely slaughtered and destroyed by
the bill and that the sugar trust is to have a prohibitive
duty upon refined sugar, you will find plenty of it in the bill;
but I had not supposed that was the doctrine of the Democratic party. If you would make duties all along the bill
protective, there would be no "incidental" protection in
it; it would be "deliberate" protection. If you reduce the
duties all along the bill below the protective point, there
will be no "incidental" protection. You cannot so construct a bill; it is impossible. You might as well attempt
to have two and two make five as to construct a bill upon
the principle that you will impose duties for revenue,
which, while they do not protect, carry incidental protection with them.

He turned against the majority their own argument
that the American consumer pays the protective tariff
tax. It was estimated that the bill carried a reduction
of thirty-one per cent. in duties. Then, from the standpoint of a tariff reformer, he pointed out the value of all
goods on hand at the time the bill was to take effect
would be reduced thirty-one per cent.—practically one
third. It might be all very well to punish the manufacturers but why punish the merchants? In the denunciation of protection he had never heard anything

about the "robber merchant." It had always been the "robber manufacturer" upon whose head the vials of wrath had been poured.

The proposed legislation he declared to be a crime. On the eighth day of November, 1892, every man in the United States who was willing to work could find employment at remunerative wages. The "army of peace" was better fed, better clothed, better housed than the workingmen of any other nation or of any previous time:

Now, the very threat of the passage of this bill has changed all. The men who are coming to the capital of the United States to present petitions—if they are as represented to be, peaceful and peaceable citizens, not tramps or vagrants, "Coxey's Army"—are men who on the eighth day of November, 1892, were at work at good wages, and the very threat of the passage of this bill, among other dire results, has reduced them to the condition of the unemployed. I say that to adopt a policy which throws the citizens of the Republic into necessary idleness is a crime; and no greater crime can be devised against the Republic than that. . . .

I would not indulge in class legislation. I do not believe under our Constitution and under our system that we can provide work directly by the Government for the citizen who is unemployed; but I do believe that when two systems of finance are presented to the country, and one of them will give employment at remunerative wages to all our people, and the other will deprive our people of work and force them into the great army of the unemployed, it is not only folly, but criminality, which adopts that system which must fill the streets of our cities and the highways of our agricultural community with idle men who have no means of support. . . .

We managed from 1890 to 1893 to keep all our people

employed; we furnished work even for those who came from foreign countries to these shores to better their condition; but when we adopt a bill, the purpose of which and the avowed object of which is to buy goods in foreign countries, because, as is supposed, they can be bought cheaper there than here, then we displace so much labor in this country. It is no longer a question of whether wages are to be kept at their present standard or to be reduced; it is a question what is to be done with the men who want to perform the work which others are performing in other countries when they find no demand for their labor in this country.

When he came to the discussion of the wool schedule he suggested another line of thought. He declared that the tactics of the free trader from the beginning had been, first, to bribe the manufacturer of woollen goods with the idea of free wool and protected manufacture of woollen goods, and then, when that had been accomplished, to excite the hostility of the wool grower and the farmer against the manufacturer. The first proposition of that plan involved the idea that the manufacturer of woollen goods could be bribed.

He pointed out that the pending bill seemed to strike its deadliest blow at the farmers all around. It was not wool alone which was slaughtered; but there was to be free wheat, free corn, free rye, free oats, a reduction of one half of the duty on hay, the largest crop in the United States, and innumerable reductions below the protective point upon the products of the farm:

Why is it? Is the farmer the "robber"? Is the farmer the "robber baron"? Is he the "greedy monopolist"? Is he the man who is plundering the people? There is but one reason for it; there is but one explanation of the policy of the bill, and that I have already given. It is, strike the farmer first, then arouse his hostility against the protected industries in the country.

I said that the woollen manufacturer of New England was not to be purchased by that bribe, and was not to be caught by that bait. I have too much faith in the agriculturist of the country to believe that he will fall into the trap which has been set by the free traders. There is no reason why this should be done. No excuse can be given for it. If a revenue tariff is the doctrine of the Democratic party, there is no article upon which a revenue duty could be more properly imposed than upon wool. If a revenue duty with incidental protection be the doctrine of the Democratic party, there is no article upon which an incidentally protective duty could be more properly levied than upon wool. This proposition is without excuse, wicked and monstrous, throwing away the revenue which is derived from this article, and which ought to be derived from it, upon a pretended benefit to the consumer of woollen goods.

After the Senate by a vote of 46 to 4 had defeated Senator Peffer's motion to put iron on the free list,— only one Democrat, Hill of New York, voting in the affirmative,—Mr. Platt moved to increase the rate from 40 cents to 60 cents a ton. He made his amendment the text for a short sermon on the attitude of New England:

I move this amendment because I am a protectionist, and because I wish to vote for protective duties for all industries. As a New England man, since there has been so much said in this discussion about our desiring in New England to secure protective duties for ourselves with alleged indifference to the other industries of the country, I do not wish to let that suggestion pass without notice. We mine no iron ore to speak of in New England. There is a little mined in one county in my State, a little in Berkshire County, Massachusetts, and a very little in Maine, but the production of iron ore in New England is so small that it cuts no figure in the great production of iron ore in this country.

We have been told that New England is for free coal, free iron ore, and free wool. If I know the sentiment of New England and the New England manufacturers, the New England workingman and the New England merchants do not desire or ask for free raw materials, as they are called in this respect. We do not want free iron ore; we do not want free coal, and we do not want free wool, for the reason that we are protectionists, and we desire that there shall be extended to every industry in the United States, whether it be mining, farming, or manufacturing, the same protection which we believe to be good for our own industries in New England.

We believe in protection as a system; we believe that every industry in the United States carried on by American labor needs such protection as will enable it to fairly compete with the industries carried on by the laborers of other countries, and we propose to stand by it no matter what its immediate effect may be upon the particular industries in our section.

Impotent though the Fifty-third Congress was, it contrived to send the Tariff bill to the White House through the abject surrender of the majority in the House of Representatives in accepting the Senate schedules without amendment. President Cleveland allowed the bill to become a law without his signature, but the Wilson-Gorman act was branded at its birth. Even before its passage, it was recognized that the party which framed it and forced it upon a reluctant Executive was doomed; that the House of Representatives to be chosen in the following November would have a Republican majority, and that in all probability the President and Congress to be chosen two years later would be Republican, thus insuring a speedy substitution for the Wilson-Gorman act of a consistent protective tariff.

CHAPTER XX

THE DINGLEY TARIFF

A Member of the Finance Committee—A Controlling Factor in Tariff Legislation—Attitude toward the Reciprocity Clauses— A Strong Advocate of Administration Policies.

AS a sequence to the extraordinary exhibition of legislative imbecility afforded by the Fifty-third Congress, the House of Representatives in the Fifty-fourth Congress, elected in 1894, was Republican by a majority which nobody had ventured to predict. Two years later William McKinley, the "Advance Agent of Prosperity," was nominated for President by a great majority, mainly because he stood in the popular mind emphatically as the representative of those issues which were the antithesis of the issues which for four years had spelled financial upheaval and distress, free soup-houses, and idle mills. He was elected by a majority equally striking, because in spite of Mr. Bryan and the free-silver diversion the Republican party, under his leadership, was known to stand for protection and prosperity.

The first task set for the new administration was to place on the statute-books a tariff act which should embody the protective principle, and a special session of Congress was called for that purpose to meet immediately after the inauguration. In anticipation of the special session, the Ways and Means Committee of the House, of which Mr. Dingley of Maine was Chairman, spent the entire winter of 1896–7 in framing a bill to be laid before Congress as speedily as possible after its assembling. In due season this bill went over to the other end of the Capitol there to meet the remodelling which is the fate of every revenue measure. Mr. Platt had been placed upon the Finance Committee at the beginning of the Fifty-fourth Congress as soon as the Republicans secured control of the Senate, and at the beginning of the Fifty-fifth Congress he was the fourth member of the Committee in seniority, outranked only by the venerable Chairman, Morrill of Vermont, Allison, and Aldrich. Other Republican members were Wolcott of Colorado, Burrows of Michigan, Jones of Nevada. It was the understanding that Aldrich, Allison, and Platt were to pull the laboring oars. Their duty was to understand the proposed bill, schedule by schedule, to defend it on the floor of the Senate, and to act as managers for the Senate in the conference between the two Houses. Mr. Platt went at this work with his accustomed thoroughness. Even while the bill was under consideration by the House, he and his associates on the Committee were conducting their own inquiries and tentatively framing their own schedules. Russell of Connecticut was a member of the Ways and Means Committee, as useful at one end of the Capitol as Platt was at the other. The two men were the closest of friends and they worked together in effective harmony.

Whenever a Connecticut manufacturer applied to either Senator or Representative for help he was likely to be cross-questioned in a way to convince him of the advisability of knowing his own business, as when a New Milford man received the following:

In talking with Mr. Russell I find that he would be glad to be more fully informed as to the nature and extent of your business. One who has a proposition to make in regard to a duty upon any article needs to be fully informed. Will you therefore kindly state the uses to which this material is put when manufactured, and the proportions of its use—that is, what proportion of it may be used for a porcelain, for pottery, and for other things? Do the three words "quartz," "silica," and "flint" mean the same thing, or are they different materials? How are they used when ground? Are they mixed with clay and earths and kaolin? What foreign article comes in competition with them? It is not easy for one not familiar with the business to see how black pebbles come in competition with white quartz. What should a duty be placed upon? What language should be used in order to cover all the materials or products that come in competition with this?

I think you will appreciate how fully and particularly one has to know these things in order to frame language which will be suitable for the purpose intended, or to know in what class of articles of the bill as hitherto read the new articles subject to duty should be placed; and then how much is invested in the business in this country approximately? What is the value of the product here? How much have importations been? What is the value of the raw material and of the finished product? Where is the raw material produced—anywhere except in the western part of our State, and where do the things which come in competition with it come from—what countries? These are some of the questions which it is necessary for any one considering the matter to be quite thoroughly informed about. Have you any suggestions to make as to the particular language which ought to be employed in a bill to effect the object you desire? All these and other questions which will readily suggest themselves to you I hope you may be able to answer.

He was continually in correspondence with many
men from many States, was occupied practically every
waking hour for many weeks in committee or in conference, was in his seat in the Senate constantly while
the Tariff bill was under consideration, was as potential
as any other man in shaping the Dingley bill, and yet
in the whole course of the debate he did not make a
single speech of even moderate length. He answered
questions, gave information in regard to the most
complicated of the schedules, was watchful, helpful,
industrious, invaluable, but although he was on his
feet scores of times, he did not indulge in a flight of
oratory for home consumption. The nearest approach
to it was when a Democratic Senator asked him if the
foreigner paid the tax, and tempted him to reply:

I must ask to be excused from entering into a discussion
of the principles upon which the protective system is based.
Unfortunately the Senators who would like to explain it
fully and at great length, and answer the very remarkable
and wonderful statements which have been made on the
other side for the last three or four weeks, are compelled
to sit still in order to secure the passage of the pending
bill within any time that will satisfy the country.

Business interests everywhere were pressing Congress
to get the new law into operation, not only because the
discussion of any tariff bill leaves commerce in a state
of uncertainty, but because the country was for having
the Wilson-Gorman act wiped off the statute-books
with the least possible delay. Mr. Platt sympathized
with this feeling, and yet he appreciated the importance
of making haste slowly with legislation which was so
vitally to affect the welfare of the country. He was
ready to devote many weeks to the consideration of

the bill. This feeling he expressed in writing to Charles Hopkins Clark, while the bill was still in the House:

I saw a long editorial in the Hartford *Courant* with reference to the duty on books. I think that was one of the items which probably received very little consideration, owing to the haste which was supposed to be necessary by the Committee in completing its consideration of the Tariff bill so as to get it before the new Congress at its opening, and that a mistake was made in that as in many other matters, by reason of the supposed necessity of immediate action. I think there is no doubt that it will be corrected, by the House probably, if not, then by the Senate. I presume that the same pressure for the passage of the bill quickly will be brought to bear upon the Senate, and I simply want to excuse, in advance, any seeming delay which may occur there by saying that the demand for the passage of "a" bill is all well enough, but we cannot afford to pass an ill-considered bill. If we did, the country in six months' time would be blaming us a good deal more than it will if we take time for careful investigation. In the House nothing is considered, but is put through arbitrarily. In the Senate, some one must be ready to give a reason for every rate of duty, for every classification, and to explain the scope and effect of every use of language.

To that task he devoted himself. The Dingley bill remained in the Senate from April 1st, to July 7th, a period of over three months, and he was on duty with Mr. Aldrich and Mr. Allison all that time, laboring often far into the night. The end crowned the work; for a measure was finally enacted under which the industries of the country were to thrive to a degree beyond the dreams of those who framed it, and which is now acknowledged, after twelve years of practical test, to have been the most scientific tariff bill ever constructed.

He not only supported the reciprocity clauses of the

Dingley law, but, after the law had gone into effect and Mr. Kasson by direction of President McKinley and Secretary Hay had negotiated treaties accordingly with various countries, he sustained the administration in its attempt to secure ratification of the treaties in the Senate. It was not an easy thing for him to do, and he seems to have given the matter considerable thought before making up his mind. In writing in December, 1899, about the French treaty he said:

I am inclined to think that the sentiment of the Senate with regard to reciprocity treaties is still in an unsettled condition. Of course every Senator is being urged, by some one who thinks that his business is going to be more or less injured, to oppose the treaty on that ground, but I do not think that it is going to be looked at from such a narrow standpoint as that. The broader view is the one which ought to be taken, and that is whether the reciprocity treaties, on the whole, will be beneficial to the United States or otherwise, and I think that there has been more prospective opposition to the French treaty created by the publications which have come from Paris than in any other way. The French Government, to overcome the opposition to the treaty there, seems to have allowed a statement to go out that the French negotiators won a great advantage for France over the United States by the treaty, and people who do not understand the matter very well, whether they are Senators or business men, are likely to say that if that is so we do not want the treaty: I do not know how many things Kasson gave away at the last in order to get the treaty signed, but I know he gave a good many, and some of them hurt. Still a man who is himself a fractional element, even though it be a small fractional element, of the treaty-making power, ought to look at such agreements without prejudice and not be governed by minor considerations.

I really do not feel quite settled myself about this matter. It all turns, in my mind, upon the question of whether we have obtained fair equivalents for the concessions we are making. From the standpoint of a man who is making a bargain, we might, however, afford to give away something if we were sure of bringing about pleasant, mutual, and satisfactory relations between ourselves and France. In other words, good-will would be worth paying something for, if you could rely upon a Frenchman's good-will, but, as I say, I have not yet any decided convictions or opinions in regard to this French treaty. I have been waiting rather to understand it more fully than I do. It went to the Committee on Foreign Relations, and I suppose, although I do not know that I am right, that when they have heard Mr. Kasson's explanation of the treaty they are likely in some way to ask information and advice of the Finance Committee, and I suppose that when that time comes I could get a little more intelligent idea of the situation here. I have been holding my mind in a receptive state. I do not think that there has been much talk about it among Senators. I do not think that any political feeling has developed, and I imagine that a good many of the Senators are in my state of mind about it—that is, that they want to ratify it unless we have so decidedly the worst of it in the treaty that we ought not to do it. I do not think that the doctrine of protection is very much involved in it, though I am and have been a protectionist, because I believed in the doctrine. But protection and reciprocity have not been thought to be incompatible, and I am quite sure that there are a good many articles on which we have allowed reductions that were somewhat over-protected in the Dingley bill.

The duty on fruits was forced upon us, but later, like a good many other articles, parties engaged in producing them could stand a reasonable reduction of the duty without practical loss. In some instances, either from intention or because our commissioner had to agree in order to get any treaty at all, there have been reductions which will be somewhat harmful.

I do not know where I may finally bring up on it. My opinion is that I shall be for the treaty, although Connecticut people suppose that they are hit all along the line.

CHAPTER XXI

FREE CUBA

Opposed to Recognition of Belligerency—Tries to Prevent War—
Pleads for Moderation—A Pillar of Conservatism—A Strong
Aid to the Administration—Growth of the War Sentiment—
Destruction of the *Maine*—The President's Message—Adop-
tion of Resolutions for Intervention—In a Small Minority—
Hostilities Precipitated.

IN the spring of 1895 a situation developed in Cuba
which was to exert a far-reaching influence upon
the future of the United States, and which called into
play, before its course was run, the highest powers of
American public men. The insurrection which was
precipitated by the landing of José Marti in February,
1895, rapidly assumed proportions setting it apart from
the many uprisings with which the "ever faithful Isle"
had been infested at intervals for seventy years. In
six months the insurgents had taken possession of
Santiago and of all the rural districts as far west as
Havana—more than had been accomplished in the
entire course of the "ten years' war" which had ended
twenty years before. Sympathy in the United States,
aroused by constantly increasing newspaper exploita-
tion of the gallant struggle for liberty going on so near
our shores, became acute as the session of Congress of
1895–6 approached. There was an insistent demand
that the sentiment of the American people should find
voice at Washington. President Cleveland and Secre-

tary Olney were opposed to any action; and the attention of the Cuban sympathizers was turned to Congress. Many resolutions were introduced—some declaring for the immediate recognition of independence, some embodying a recognition of belligerency, others declaring for intervention, still others for neutrality. Senator Platt felt that Congress for the time at least should keep hands off. He regarded the recognition of belligerency as a matter primarily for the Executive branch of the Government. The position which he assumed was far from popular. The trend of sentiment everywhere was unmistakably toward the recognition of the insurgents. Yellow journals were inflaming the public mind and Connecticut was no less Cuban-mad than other States. Mr. Platt's re-election to the Senate was pending. Ambitious rivals were watching their opportunity. But he did not care what effect his attitude might have on his personal fortunes. He did not shrink from the issue. On January 16, 1896, he said in the Senate:

Recognition of the insurgents as belligerents is not a matter which is due to them; but it is a question which pertains solely to the interests of the United States. If a proclamation of neutrality were issued . . . it would be considered, and justly considered under international law, as an unfriendly act to the parent Government. . . . We in this country sympathize naturally with every people that is seeking to establish a republican form of government; but I think that we ought not to rush hastily into a matter of according belligerent rights to such a people. We ought to observe the rules which have been laid down by international comity with reference to such matters. I should be very sorry to see any resolution passed here which in any way would indicate that the President of the United States and the State Department were not doing all that

that branch of the Government ought to do with reference
to the conflict now pending in a neighboring foreign country.

He felt that Congress could not with propriety go
beyond a declaration of sympathy unless it intended
frankly to declare war. Resolutions were adopted
by House and by Senate, one declaring that the United
States ought to be neutral, the other that the United
States ought to intervene. The Senate managers of the
Conference Committee recommended that the Senate
abandon its own resolutions and adopt those passed by
the House. Senator Platt urged that the report of the
Conference Committee be disagreed to, and on March
23, 1896, as expressing the real sentiment of the Senate,
he submitted the following:

Resolved, That the Senate (the House of Representatives
concurring) hereby expresses its earnest desire and hope
that Cuba may soon become a free, independent, and republican government, and that the friendly offices of the United
States should be offered by the President to the Spanish
Government to secure such result.

That he thought deeply on this subject is shown by
his correspondence. Writing on March 7, 1896, to
Gen. E. S. Greeley of New Haven, he said:

I have a very decided feeling that we are letting our
sympathy run away with our judgment, and yet it is
undeniable, I think, that Spain has treated its colony of
Cuba with more harshness than has ever been shown by a
parent country to such a colony; has taxed them heavily
without representation, and has been severe and almost
brutal in its treatment. Then General Weyler's published
orders seem to indicate a barbarous and cruel spirit in the
matter of conducting the war against rebels, or patriots,
whichever they may be. Under such circumstances it is

almost impossible not to sympathize with the people of Cuba if they are in good faith and earnestly striving to throw off Spanish authority and establish free government. To what extent this condition of things exists it is almost impossible to ascertain. Reports are very conflicting and, as I believe, so exaggerated on both sides that we don't know the truth of the situation. I have not believed that there was a case outside of the ground of sympathy for the recognition of the insurgents as belligerents, and yet I am inclined to think that I would vote a resolution of sympathy.

A few days later, on March 12th, he wrote to A. D. Osborne of New Haven:

I do not propose to vote for the Cuban resolutions in their present form, and if I get the opportunity shall state my reasons therefor.

On March 14th, he wrote to Rev. E. P. Parker of Hartford:

It has been understood here, at least since January, that I did not believe in the foolishness which prevails with regard to Cuba. I send you from the *Record* of the sixteenth of January a few words that I said; I don't suppose they had much influence, but they indicate what I thought of the subject at that time. A strange thing in all this discussion is that the Committee on Foreign Relations does not seem to have examined the law or the facts with regard to Cuba, at least they have not referred to the law and have been quite chary as to the facts. Probably we cannot stop the passage of these resolutions, but we will get enough votes against them as they now stand to show quite a conservative element, and I intend, some time before the debate closes, to make my position known.

On March 16th, he wrote to H. Wales Lines:

If I get a chance at Cuba, I am going to say that it is quite proper for Congress to express its desire that Cuba should become a government, republican in form and spirit, but at that Congress ought to stop; that we ought not to recognize belligerency, because there is no warrant for it in the conditions existing in Cuba considered with reference to the rules of international law for a hundred years, and our own position frequently and vigorously stated; and that above all it is entirely wrong to talk about intervention on account of the proximity of Cuba or the loss which people of the United States may be sustaining in the way of trade. If what I say shall be unpopular, I cannot help it. I shall at least try to make my position clear and then must take the verdict of the people upon it.

To Franklin Farrell of Ansonia, he wrote on March 30th:

I should be very glad to see free government established in Cuba, but I don't think that the United States ought to go to war with Spain to secure that end, or depart from its established policy in dealing with foreign nations.

The resolutions finally adopted after much debate and conference declared that a state of war existed in Cuba, that the United States would observe strict neutrality, and that the President should offer the good offices of the United States with the Spanish Government to secure the recognition of the independence of the island.

As might have been expected, this declaration had no effect. The insurrection continued, likewise the agitation in the United States. It was the year of the Presidential election. Both great political parties at their national conventions passed resolutions of sympathy with Cuba.

A Republican President and House of Representatives were elected by great majorities, and in the winter preceding the inauguration of President McKinley the

Cuban question became still more acute. The Committee on Foreign Relations, through Senator Cameron of Pennsylvania, on December 21, 1896, reported a brief resolution recognizing the republic of Cuba. It was accompanied by a voluminous report. The business community was agitated. Stocks went tumbling. Secretary Olney came out in an interview in which he declared that President Cleveland would pay no attention to the joint resolution, even if it passed Congress over the veto; because the right of recognition pertained solely to the Executive, and the resolution would be only the expression of opinion of "certain eminent gentlemen." In the closing hours of the administration it was not thought well to force such an issue and so the resolution slumbered on the calendar.

Senator Platt was greatly exercised by this agitation in Congress and among the people. It seemed to him that the United States was being thoughtlessly forced into a position where war with Spain would be inevitable. On December 18, 1895, we find him writing to Isaac H. Bromley of the New York *Tribune* as follows:

Your articles in the *Tribune* about Cuba are in accord with my judgment. But if the sober, thoughtful business interests of the country don't want a resolution passed through Congress recognizing "the independence of the republic of Cuba" they must speak out and speak quickly and loudly. This false devotion to the cause of liberty, the uneasiness which prevails, and the desire for patriotic notoriety is acting and reacting on members of the Senate and House who are usually level-headed, and things are being worked up to a frenzy that is sweeping such men off their feet. It seems to be pretty much understood that our Senate Committee on Foreign Relations is going to report such a resolution, and if it does, the great probability now is that it would pass the Senate. It is hard to stem the water when the dam breaks away. There is no republic of Cuba, and the people there who claim there is have not established their independence any more than the Armenians have theirs in Turkey. The newspaper rot about what is going on there, though published one day and contradicted the next, seems to stir up all the aggressive spirit in the minds of the people, and the Cuban junta or legation, or whatever it is called, is active and pestiferous in circulating its views of the situation. It is a case of Naboth's vineyard. Men whose love of humanity was not fluttered when in Texas about a year ago a negro was covered with kerosene oil and burned to death on a public platform in the presence of 7000 yelling people, are shedding tears over the sad fate of Maceo. So I repeat what I said in the first place, that if those who do not want a war with Spain (because if we recognize an independence which does not exist, we ought to go and establish it and should probably be forced into a war anyway) had better bestir themselves. It is another case like the sound-money sentiment of the country sitting still and allowing silver to be howled in every schoolhouse of the United States without making a reply.

On the following day he wrote to Charles Hopkins Clark, editor of the Hartford *Courant*:

The Foreign Relations Committee is going to report on Monday a resolution recognizing "the independence of the republic of Cuba," and unless people are ready to sit still and see that done without protest, they ought to give expression to their opinions at once.

To Hon. John Birge he wrote:

To pass such a resolution would be mockery and ludicrous if we did not intend by armed force to help the insurgents to achieve the independence which we recognize, though in fact it does not exist. If we pass such a resolution we ought to send the army and navy there to make independence and a republican government an accomplished fact. And I cannot look upon a question so grave and serious as this from the mere standpoint of sentiment.

The legal and constitutional question involved—as to whether the right of recognition of belligerency did not rest exclusively with the Executive—was one which disturbed even some of those who were favorable to the adoption of unequivocal resolutions, although, as in all such cases where Congress has set its mind on the accomplishment of a certain end, the doubtful constitutionality of the action would not have been permitted to block the path of its legislative purpose. Mr. Platt was one of those who believed the President alone was empowered to recognize belligerency, but there were lawyers, equally distinguished, who held to the contrary opinion.

On December 21st, the day the resolution was reported, he indicated his perplexity in a letter to former Senator George F. Edmunds:

My own view is that, under the Constitution, the matter of dealing with foreign powers and recognizing their sovereignty or the recognition of belligerent rights is committed to the Executive branch, that Congress has never yet attempted to pass any resolutions which did not recognize either in terms, or tacitly, this doctrine, and that all our diplomatic history confirms the understanding of lawyers and statesmen that the power rests alone with the President.

Of course, I have not investigated it as closely on authorities and precedents as a Senator should in order to talk about it, but the claim that the President cannot effectively recognize a foreign power without the aid of Congress is rather embarrassing. He cannot send a minister without

an appropriation for his salary by Congress, so that, as in
most of the cases where power is committed to one branch,
the concurrence of the other is necessary to make it effective.
It is plain to my mind that Congress should not attempt to
pass a resolution which assumes to recognize the independence of a revolutionary people, but I am a little troubled
about the effect of such action by joint resolution passed
over the Presidential veto. It would be an embarrassing
situation to say the least, and yet I cannot think that it
would operate as such a recognition of the new Government
as that the courts in the cases which might arise would hold
it to be an accomplished fact.

With the incoming of the new administration there
was a lull for a while and then fire broke out afresh with
increasing fury. Weyler's system of reconcentration
was achieving its cruel ends. Outrages on American
citizens—most of them naturalized Cubans—called for
redress. President McKinley, more alert than his
predecessor, demanded release and redress in the case
of every American prisoner, and by the end of April
all were released. On May 20, 1897, the Senate without division passed a joint resolution recognizing Cuban
belligerency. It went to sleep in the House under
Speaker Reed's careful nursing. But just then President McKinley, informed by consular reports that, under
the reconcentration system, American citizens as well
as natives were being starved to death, sent a special
message to Congress asking for $50,000 with which to
send supplies to those Americans who were suffering at
the hands of Spain. Congress acted immediately. The
act was approved May 24, 1897; and, with the consent
of Spain, American interference was at last a fact,
through the feeding of starving Americans and others
in the devastated island. The next six months was a

period of negotiations, of demands and propositions on
the part of the United States—of broken promises
and procrastinating assurances on the part of Spain.
At last the administration determined to send a battleship to Havana for the protection of Americans there.
The *Maine* arrived in Havana on January 24, 1898.
On February 9, 1898, there appeared the letter of
the Spanish Minister in Washington, Señor Dupuy de
Lome, written on December 25, 1897, containing coarse
and insulting references to President McKinley. Seven
days later, on February 16th, while public feeling was
still high, came the destruction of the *Maine* in Havana
harbor. The smouldering embers of war broke into
flame.

Senator Platt, watching with apprehension the
growth of national passion, maintained his poise. He
was in thorough sympathy with President McKinley
in the endeavor to compose all differences without
resort to arms, or, if that failed, then to postpone the
conflict. He was not for "peace at any price." He was
not governed by the protests of "business" and Wall
Street against agitation which might unsettle values.
He deplored war for its own sake, and looked with dread
upon the prospect that the United States would plunge
into it and bring all its horror upon the American
people. Through these trying times he was an avenue
of communication between the Capitol and the White
House. His counsel was sought constantly by President McKinley; and his pleas for moderation were
listened to respectfully even by the most ardent of
those who cried for war. There was a long, tense
period of waiting while the Sampson board of inquiry
was completing its work, and preparing its report on
the cause of the destruction of the *Maine*. After

that report was sent to Congress on March 28th, it was plain to almost everybody that the resources of diplomacy had failed; but up to that time Senatoi Platt and those who acted with him continued to use their powers of persuasion in what they felt to be an almost hopeless cause. On March 23d, writing to Rev. William B. Carey of North Stonington, Connecticut, he said:

I can understand, I think, how intensely people get wrought up by the anticipation of war. For myself I believe that any relations existing between Spain and the United States are quite susceptible of amicable adjustment and if, as I believe, peace can be brought about in Cuba by peaceful methods by the United States, it would be a great crime to attempt to drive us to bring it about by fighting. It is very well to talk about destroying the Spanish navy. God alone knows whether it would be destroyed, whether it would not destroy us in case of war. Regiments of black soldiers would undoubtedly be good soldiers in Cuba when they were recruited, and organized, and disciplined, but, before that could occur, any emergency for their use would doubtless have passed. No one knows that we would ever get to Cuba if we undertook to send soldiers there, or, if we did get there, having destroyed the Spanish navy, that the necessity for any great number of soldiers would be obviated. I do not see how people contemplate war without horror or talk about it without shuddering, and unless it should appear that the *Maine* was destroyed by Spanish agency, I should not be able to formulate the rules which would justify the passage of a resolution declaring war. The consequences of war cannot be computed in dollars and cents; only in lives, and, if we succeed, what shall we get by it all? It is quite the time now for people to have cool heads. Hot talk should give way to calm judgment and dispassionate utterances. I only say this because I feel that some one must be level-headed now or our nation will be put in a wrong light in the eyes of the world and in the final judgment of our own conscience.

On March 25th, writing to H. Wales Lines, he said:

The situation here may be described as serious and critical. There is a fear that the radicals in Congress might be able to override the President and pass resolutions which would lead to immediate hostilities, but I think that danger is now past. Certainly I think the Senate will keep still until the President shall say to Congress that he has exhausted all means in his power to provide for closing the contest in Cuba. If he fails to bring about some action on the part of Spain which will look to the early settlement of the difficulties in Cuba, and communicates to Congress the fact that he has failed, I think there will be no possibility of preventing then the passage of a resolution for forcible intervention. Those who have been clamoring for liberty and freedom and war, have worked up a spirit in the country that something must be done and done quickly to stop the condition of things in Cuba, and I think Congress believes that sentiment to be stronger and more general than it really is. I think the President himself believes that the people of the United States will not tolerate much longer the war in Cuba and that, if he cannot end it by negotiations, the people will insist that he shall do so by force. In the meantime, he will do all in his power for peaceful adjustment; but the difficulty is with Spain. Spain does not want war, but will not and apparently can not agree to independence, and it seems to have come down to about this. Will the people sustain the President in accepting from Spain any proposed settlement which does not include absolute independence for Cuba? Spain might be induced to make more truly liberal propositions for autonomy as it is called, or in the direction of self-government for Cuba than she has yet made. The question is, if she did, and the President believed that the proposition ought to be accepted by the insurgents, will the country sustain him in saying so if they feel sure of Cuban independence? This sets forth the gravity of the situation. There has not been openly manifested yet a sentiment which indicates that the people do not want the United States to fight Spain to liberate Cuba if its independence cannot be brought about by peaceable methods. The report of the naval board of inquiry is likely to excite them still more, but I think the conservative people of the United States and Congress will be able to prevent action over the President's head. If the President cannot get a settlement with Spain and the insurgents, which is equivalent to independence, I fear nothing can restrain Congress from declaring for intervention, which is the same thing as declaring war.

On the same date in a letter to Governor Cooke, he said:

A few of us have determined that there ought to be no war if it can be avoided and yet we know that the situation is serious and critical and a little thing may plunge us into a conflict. It is very difficult to resist what is supposed to be the war spirit of the country. Representations are made here all the time that the country is ready for war, and members of Congress urge the President to bring matters to an immediate issue; that unless Spain immediately surrenders control of Cuba and gives independence to the insurgents, he should recommend Congress to pass resolutions directing intervention, which, of course, is equivalent to declaring war. What we who are classed as conservatives are trying to do is to prevent Congress overriding the President and gain time for negotiations which we hope will result in some satisfactory adjustment of the conditions in Cuba, or in propositions on the part of Spain which ought to be satisfactory in the nature of things, so that we can have presented to Congress and to the people the alternative of accepting a settlement of affairs in Cuba which ought to be satisfactory to clear and reasoning people, or of going to war. I believe that if that alternative can be presented the sober second thought of the American people will keep us out of war. As I say the situation is critical. Members of Congress are frightened to do so lest they should be defeated in case absolute independence is not secured either by negotiation or by hostilities. The President has been very doubtful whether he could hold Congress in check but I think has now come to the conclusion that the conservative element in Congress will stand by him. The pressure, however, for immediate action and intervention is very strong.

Now, I have told you all that any one can know. It may come to war before the week is out. I think it will drift along for some time to come, and I hope that Spain may be induced to make propositions which under the circumstances ought to be satisfactory. I think I see the embarrassment you feel. If you should call a special session of the Legislature to put the National Guard in a state of efficiency, it would, of course, add at once to the general alarm. The tension is so great that anything done looking even remotely to hostilities tends to inflame public sentiment. I suppose that letters have been written to you as to the governors of New York and Massachusetts asking what could be relied upon from the State in case of necessity. The condition as it seems to me is serious enough, so that it would be well for you to come down and talk it over with the President and Secretary of War.

A third letter, addressed to John H. Flagg, contains this paragraph:

I suppose that the President for two or three weeks has been trying by such indirect methods as he may employ to get Spain to consent to a liberal government in Cuba; Canada and Australia being suggested as models. I think that if Spain would give that degree of freedom to Cuba, it would get the moral support at least of the United

States. Speaking without information, I suppose that
Spain has shown some inclination in this direction. It
has been understood here by those who have the President's
confidence, that there would be no objection on the part
of Spain to our sending supplies to the sufferers, and there
is evidently something, I do not know how much, in this
idea of an armistice, probably not a technical armistice,
but some cessation of hostilities while our negotiations are
pending. To this extent there is probably foundation for
the rumors in New York,· but I do not think the situation
clears up any. I think, as I telegraphed you, that the
sentiment that there must be immediate action to the end
that the conflict in Cuba shall cease, is growing, and is every
day becoming more difficult to hold in check, and it has
been a question all the while whether if Spain should propose
anything short of absolute independence, no matter how
liberal and just it might be, Congress would support the
President in the acceptance of it or insist upon going to
war. I have felt that the Congress would stand by the
President, but I am getting a little shaky about it to-day.
We had last week the Democrats pretty solidly agreeing to
stand by the President and now they show a disposition to
make their support conditioned on knowing what he is
going to do to put an end to conditions in Cuba. I cannot
give you any more complete statement of the situation. I
understand that speeches advocating intervention are to be
kept up in the Senate. Foraker and Billy Mason are going
to speak, and it is rumored that Frye is. What the Foreign
Relations Committee, which meets on Wednesday, will do no
one knows. It has been thought that they might report
an intervention resolution, and then again we have thought
that they would not do it until the President was ready for
intervention, and that if they did do it, we could beat it in
the Senate; but everything seems unsettled to-day.

About the same time he gave to the press the following brief interview:

I think there is altogether too much war talk. War is only to be contemplated with horror and should not be flippantly talked about. The United States must never engage in war except as a necessity, the necessity of defending its possessions or its honor. We must have no war unless we have a cause which shall justify it in the eyes of the world and to our own conscience. I do not think the sober second thought of the American people is for war, and I believe that our relations with Spain are susceptible of an amicable adjustment.

The report of the naval board placing the responsibility for the destruction of the *Maine* upon Spanish agencies brought negotiations up with a sharp turn. It then became a question of days as to when the President should send a message to Congress which should serve as the foundation of resolutions providing for intervention by the United States. In the tenseness of feeling all over the United States every delay of twenty-four hours seemed an eternity; and the more earnest of the war party in Congress were suspicious of every postponement as an endeavor on the part of the administration to secure some kind of adjustment which would involve peace at the price of honor.

Finally it was given out that the message would be sent in on Monday, April 4th. Then word came that it would surely go to Congress on Wednesday, April 6th. On that day the Capitol was crowded with an expectant throng; but no message came. Instead, the leaders of House and Senate were summoned to the White House where the President showed them a dispatch from Consul-General Lee saying that if the message went in that day, he could not answer for the lives of Americans in Havana and asking until Saturday to get them out of Cuba.

For this memorable time Senator Platt's letters to his friend Flagg almost constitute a diary. Writing on April 2d, he says:

There is not a great deal to be said to-day. If the President has made up his mind as to the particular points of his message to present to Congress he has not communicated the same in detail even to the members of his Cabinet yet. He has been much in consultation with Judge Day, and with the Attorney-General. He still wants, if possible, to avoid any immediate declaration of war by Congress, has still some hope that further negotiations may result more favorably. The difficulty is to get at it. Spain's answer seems to have closed the door to everything except an ultimatum. He has not yet said even what he thinks it would be wise for Congress to do; he has taken to-day and to-morrow to put his message in shape. Very much depends upon his message. Congress, as indicated last night, is considerably sobered by the situation, but I think in each House they are anxious that action be inaugurated looking to hostilities. The situation is very awkward. Spain, by reason of the rescinding of the reconcentration order and the application of $600,000 to care for the suffering, has taken the humanitarian motive quite out of the question, and men who have been for war at all events, but have been putting it on the ground of humanity, now find that they must seek other grounds. They have been declaring that they did not propose to go to war on account of the destruction of the *Maine*, and now that seems to be the real ground on which they must proceed, if they can bring this at all within any international rules. It is impossible to say to-day what will take place Monday, and the President may not get his message ready so as to send it in Monday, perhaps Tuesday. I think I know pretty nearly as well as any one the President's mind, but I do not know precisely what he is going to say or do. I think he is still deliberating. There is not any very logical ground for a declaration of war, and those who have been most eager for it are casting about for reasons to give for it.

On April 6th, again writing Mr. Flagg, Senator Platt said:

As I telegraphed you this morning, I think the hope of a peaceful solution is pretty much gone. The Foreign Relations Committee seems to have made up its mind in advance of the message and at the present moment is writing perhaps a resolution which will recognize the independence of Cuba, and, counting on the destruction of the *Maine*, which, it says, was either a criminal act or negligence equally criminal on the part of Spain, the barbarous and inhuman warfare, and its inability to maintain a government on the island, demands the withdrawal of its troops, and authorizes the President to use the military and naval forces of the United States including the militia to that end. A good many of us believe the recognition of independence is entirely unnecessary and would like something in the way of a resolution which will give Spain an opportunity to back down before actual hostilities are begun on our part. But the war party is evidently in the majority and will push its views thinking that no one dare stand up against it. While I say this it must be added that the Foreign Relations Committee is not unanimous in insisting on the recognition of independence and it is possible that by to-morrow that feature may be dropped. It is said that the message is not likely to go to the Senate before three or four o'clock to-morrow afternoon. It will be referred to the Committee I think without debate and no report will be made by the Committee until Thursday. The reason for this delay until late in the afternoon is that our consuls may have time to get away from Havana and the island. The *Fern* has been ordered to bring them away. There seems to be a question whether, if this resolution should pass in the form which the Foreign Relations Committee now contemplate, it would be equivalent to a declaration of war or whether it would be the duty of the President first to communicate the demands contained in the resolution to Spain and get an answer from Spain before the commencement of actual hostilities.

I have given you in a few words I think the situation. There will I hope be a conference to-night between the Committee on Foreign Relations and the President in the hope that the resolution to be reported may be in accordance with his views, but Foraker has seemed to dominate the Committee and any change will have to be over his head.

On April 7th, he further wrote Mr. Flagg, as follows:

There is really no change in the situation to-day; unless Spain between now and Monday gives assurances that she will give up Cuba, Congress will take some action insisting upon that as the only condition of peace. The precise character of the resolution is understood. The President and those who sustain him do not want a recognition of independence, do not want any haste, but a simple resolution directing the President to take at once such steps as may be necessary to terminate hostilities in Cuba, to form a stable government there, and to this end to employ the land and naval forces of the United States. Jingoes want independence and intervention. The contest between the President and his opposers will go along this line. Yesterday we could have passed such a resolution as we desired in the Senate, but the startling dispatch of Lee upset everyone. To-day we are looking up again—to-morrow we may be demoralized. It is comparatively quiet here.

The message came in on April 11th. Resolutions were promptly reported in Senate and House. Those reported in the House followed the moderate lines of the President's message. They directed the President to intervene at once to stop the war in Cuba:

To the end and with the purpose of securing permanent peace and order there, and establishing by the free action

of the people thereof a stable and independent government
of their own in the island of Cuba,

and authorized the President to use the land and
naval forces to execute the purpose of the resolution.
This phraseology did not meet the requirements of
those who insisted that Congress should demand, without equivocation, the expulsion of Spain from Cuba.
The resolutions reported as a substitute by the Senate
Committee on Foreign Relations were longer and had
a fighting edge:

WHEREAS the abhorrent conditions which have existed
for more than three years in the island of Cuba, so near
our own borders, have shocked the moral sense of the people
of the United States, have been a disgrace to Christian
civilization, culminating, as they have, in the destruction
of a United States battleship, with 226 of its officers and
crew, while on a friendly visit in the harbor of Havana, and
can not longer be endured, as has been set forth by the
President of the United States in his message to Congress
of April 11, 1898, upon which the action of Congress was
invited; Therefore,

Resolved, by the Senate and House of Representatives
of the United States of America in Congress assembled,

First: That the people of the island of Cuba are, and of
right ought to be, free and independent.

Second: That it is the duty of the United States to demand
and the Government of the United States does hereby
demand, that the Government of Spain at once relinquish
its authority and government in the island of Cuba, and
withdraw its land and naval forces from Cuba and Cuban
waters.

Third: That the President of the United States be, and
he hereby is, directed and empowered to use the entire
land and naval forces of the United States, and to call into
the actual service of the United States the militia of the

several States, to such extent as may be necessary to carry these resolutions into effect.

A minority of the Committee, consisting of three Democrats and Senator Foraker, proposed to amend the first paragraph by inserting after the word "independent" the following:

And that the Government of the United States hereby recognize the republic of Cuba as the true and lawful goverment of that island.

There at once arose a spirited debate wherein bitter attacks were made upon the motives of the administration. A little band of ten Republicans, headed by Chandler and Foraker, stood out with the Democrats and Populists for the minority amendment, and that amendment was adopted by a vote of 51 to 37. The entire debate turned on this question. The real question of peace and war, contained in the second paragraph, was quite lost sight of—even to the point where the House concurred in the Senate resolutions with an amendment striking out the words, "are and" in the first paragraph and the entire clause embodying the recognition of the insurgent government. Senator Platt entered earnestly into the debate. On April 16th, he delivered one of the strongest and most impressive speeches of his entire career in opposition to the proposed amendment.

In beginning the speech he said:

The time for oratory and impassioned utterance has passed. The time has never been for hot words, for epithets, for intemperate speech. Oratory will not bombard Morro Castle. Stinging words, ungracious and unjust epithets may reach and wound the President of the United States but they will not pierce the armor of Spanish battleships.

His concluding words were:

We ought to pass resolutions here which we can justify. We ought not to give our consent to resolutions unjustifiable in their character, for the reason that we desire to accomplish the great purpose in view. When Abraham Lincoln put his name to that immortal document which struck the shackles from the limbs of 4,000,000 people, after having suffered abuse, vituperation, vilification which the abuse heaped upon President McKinley does not parallel, he wrote these magnificent words:

"And upon this act, sincerely believed to be an act of justice warranted by the Constitution upon military necessity, I invoke the deliberate judgment of mankind and the gracious favor of Almighty God."

Mr. President, I implore, I adjure the Senate to pass no resolutions upon which it may not write in spirit, if not in fact, the words:

"And upon this act we invoke the deliberate judgment of mankind, and the gracious favor of Almighty God."

The resolutions as amended were adopted by the Senate by vote of 67 to 21, Mr. Platt helping to form the minority which consisted of 19 Republicans and 2 Democrats, and after a day and night of intense dramatic interest, the House, in the early morning of April 19th, accepted the Senate resolutions word for word. They were signed by the President on April 21st, and war was on.

After the passage of the resolutions Senator Platt dictated—exactly for what purpose does not appear— the following statement which may be taken as an epitome of his position:

These resolutions mean too little or too much. If they do not mean that there is now in the island of Cuba a free and independent government, then to whom is Spain to

relinquish its authority and government? And when it
has been compelled to withdraw its land and naval forces,
what then? The President has asked that he be empowered
to take measures after the securing of the full and final termination of hostilities, to secure the establishment of a stable
government, etc. These resolutions refuse to grant him
that authority. Under these resolutions it will be the duty
of the President to withdraw the forces simultaneously with
the forces of Spain. If there is no government recognized
by these resolutions, except the government of Spain, we
should certainly see that one is established before our troops
are withdrawn. If there is one, certainly nothing else can
be meant by the resolutions than that it is recognized as a
government. I believe the legal and practical effect of the
first resolution is to recognize the sovereignty of the pretended self-government of the insurgents. What else can
the resolutions mean? The people are free and independent. Do they use these words only in the sense that they
would apply to mankind in general? Every one knows that
that phrase is used to designate a free government. So
we see clearly the purpose of these resolutions. First,—
to do affirmatively what the President recommends us not
to do. Second,—to refuse to do what he asks us to do—a
most impotent conclusion as ever was.

First I wish to state my conviction and position and to
state it so clearly that I will not be misconstrued or misunderstood. The time has come when Spanish rule in
Cuba must cease—it has been too long a record of misrule
only. I will not pause to frame the indictment. The
reasons why it must cease are known to all Americans and
are set forth clearly, forcibly, and patriotically in the
message of the President of the United States. It has
imperilled our peace, it has inflicted injuries upon us, it is
inconsistent with our commercial and national interests,
it outrages every sentiment of mankind, it makes against
all civilization. It must end. With this conviction and
this unassailable purpose I have hoped and, until recently,

believed that it might be ended without war, without the burdens and horrors and the losses of war. I believe to-day that what I, together with all America's citizens, desired might have been accomplished peaceably had it not been for the intemperate and inflammatory statements and misstatements of those who from the first have desired to plunge this country into war. I have not been among those who desired war. I would if possible have averted it, never for a moment losing sight of the purpose to be accomplished. And I have only unstinted praise to bestow upon, and the heartiest thanks to give to the President of the United States, in the execution of the great responsibility that has desired the attainment of the end in view through peace rather than through war. To longer hope that the Spanish misrule in Cuba can be ended peaceably seems to be against hope. From the position taken by the President of the United States upon the failure of diplomatic negotiations to secure the emancipation of Cuba, the United States cannot recede, ought not to recede.

In the language of the Executive: "The war in Cuba must stop, and in that island there must be established a stable government, capable of maintaining order," etc.

If this, our determination, results in war, it must come. We should be false to ourselves and to humanity, to the world, and recreant to duty and cowardly, if we hesitated or faltered now.

CHAPTER XXII

EXPANSION AND IMPERIALISM

For Unrelenting Prosecution of the War—Results of the War
Accepted—Annexation of Hawaii—Urges Retention of Philip-
pines—Letter to President McKinley—Letter to Professor
Fisher—Strongly Advocates Ratification of Treaty of Peace—
Speech of December 19, 1899—The Constitutional Right of
the U. S. to Acquire and Govern Territory.

ADMIRAL SAMPSON'S fleet set sail for Cuba on
April 21st, and with that act of war there came
an end to divergent policies in Washington. Hence-
forward there was only one party and that party was
bent on prosecuting the war to a successful issue. For
the next four months while the American forces were
pressing the enemy by land and by sea we find Senator
Platt lending his encouragement by voice and vote.
He accepted heartily all the results of the war. When
the news came on the second of May that Dewey had
sailed with flaming guns into Manila Bay, he was not
one of those who tempered praise of American valor
with censure of a sailor's rashness and sent up prayers
that our ships should be recalled. Having set out in the
path he would follow it to the end. The depths of his
nature were stirred. The opening up of the Philippines to American civilization appealed to him as a
religious opportunity which it would be a national crime
to neglect. Even while the war was still on, and before
Sampson's fleet had destroyed Cervera's ships off San-

tiago, the question of expansion came to the front
in resolutions providing for the annexation of the
Hawaiian Islands. This was a question which had been
inherited by the McKinley administration. From the
time in February, 1892, when President Harrison had
sent the treaty of the annexation to the Senate down
through the unfortunate experiences of the Cleveland
administration with "Paramount" Blount, and his
great and good friend, Liliuokalani, the Hawaiian
question had developed into one of party policy, although a few eminent and powerful Republicans had
ranged themselves strongly against the idea of acquiring
insular territory. Senator Platt had little patience
with the position assumed by the reactionaries who
chirped assent to Speaker Reed's motto—"Empire
can wait." In the second session of the Fifty-third
Congress resolutions had been presented in the Senate
looking to the pacification of the Sandwich Islands.
One of the paragraphs of the resolutions declared "that
it is unwise and inexpedient under existing conditions
to consider at this time any project of annexation of
the Hawaiian territory to the United States." Senator
Platt favored the general import of the resolutions as
did many other Republican Senators but to this declaration he refused to subscribe. He made his position
clear in a brief speech on January 24, 1894. He said:

I do not believe that the annexation of the Hawaiian
Islands to the United States would violate either the proclaimed or the traditional policy of the United States.
I believe on the other hand it would be consonant with and
in accord with both the proclaimed and the traditional
policy of the United States. I believe it would be in direct
line with all that has been said by Presidents and Secretaries
of State in reference to this subject for the last fifty years. I

believe it would be in direct line with all the movements for annexation which have taken place heretofore in our history. I believe when we have come to be sixty-five—yes, seventy million people, nearly, we can no longer shut ourselves within narrow limits; and while I have no disposition to acquire territory for the sake of territory, for the sake of aggrandizement or glory or power, I firmly believe that when any territory outside of the present limits of the United States becomes necessary for our defence or essential for our commercial development, we ought to lose no time in acquiring it, if it can be done without injustice to other nations and other people.

From this position he never swerved. When the resolutions of annexation came before the Senate in the summer of 1898 he voted for them and aided in the debate against those who argued for purposes of delay that the business should be undertaken by treaty instead of legislative action; and when a little later the far more momentous question of acquiring the Philippine Islands during the negotiations of the treaty of peace with Spain became absorbing, Senator Platt was one who insisted most stoutly that for the United States to abandon the Philippines would be a colossal error, to be regretted forever.

The protocol looking to the treaty which brought the war to an end was approved at Madrid on August 11, 1898. The air was full of rumors that in drafting a treaty of peace the administration would agree to withdraw American forces from the Philippines and leave them again in the hands of Spain. That it was the inclination of the President at that time to accept just as few responsibilities as possible in the far East was well understood. In theory that may have been the wisest position for an administration to assume. But it was not in harmony with the feeling of the people of the United States. The most clear-headed and far-seeing leaders of Congress perceived that the fact was already in effect accomplished—that responsibilities already assumed could not be evaded. Senator Platt's reputation for conservatism and strength proved of vast importance at this crisis. Others clustered about him as about an oak. He did not waver from the beginning in his conviction that the United States should retain control of the entire Philippine group. The arguments of the anti-imperialists seemed to him preposterous— almost lacking in patriotism. At the time of the signing of the protocol, Congress was in recess and he was at his home in Connecticut, close in touch there with the heart of his own people. It was a time, he thought, for communicating to President McKinley his judgment of what should be done and he acted unhesitatingly. Under date of August 15, 1898, from his home in Washington, Connecticut, he wrote as follows:

DEAR MR. PRESIDENT:

I feel that I ought to say that during the past week I have been well over the State of Connecticut and I am satisfied that nine tenths of the people of the State have an intense feeling that we should insist upon the cession of all the Philippine Islands. Those who believe in Providence, see, or think they see, that God has placed upon this Government the solemn duty of providing for the people of these islands a government based upon the principle of liberty no matter how many difficulties the problem may present. They feel that it is our duty to attempt its solution. Among Christian, thoughtful people the sentiment is akin to that which has maintained the missionary work of the last century in foreign lands. I assure you that it is difficult to overestimate the strength and intensity of this sentiment.

If in the negotiations for peace Spain is permitted to retain any portion of the Philippines it will be regarded as a failure on the part of this nation to discharge the greatest moral obligation which could be conceived.

I have spoken of the Christian sentiment but the feeling that we should not allow Spain to retain possession of the Philippines pervades all classes of our people. If I am to be guided by the views of the best people in this State and the large majority of all the people, I shall be compelled to vote against any treaty which allows Spain to continue to exercise sovereignty over any of the inhabitants of those islands.

Very respectfully,

O. H. PLATT.

In this brief letter to the President was condensed the entire argument for retaining the Philippines. It was the expression of a statesman of deep religious feeling, firmly confident that he was reading rightly the pulse of the people and reassured to know that their settled judgment coincided with his own. In all the months and years of debate that followed the signing of the treaty of peace, no really convincing argument was advanced, the germ of which was not contained in those few pregnant sentences. Senator Platt himself subsequently elaborated his position both in personal letters and congressional debate, but never more effectively.

He seems to have been stimulated by the anti-expansion sentiment which found grateful nurseries under the elms of New Haven and in the college yard of Cambridge. The Yale College band of anti-expansionists was especially dogmatic and self-assertive. Mr. Platt's personal relations with the leading members of the Yale faculty had always been close and friendly, and therefore he was peculiarly the object of their missionary zeal. From one of the most eminent of them, George P. Fisher, Professor of Ecclesiastical History in the Theological Department, he received, only three days prior to his communication with President McKinley, an argumentative letter against the retention of the Philippines. The immediate response to this was the luminous note to McKinley; and a few days later he disturbed his well earned summer's rest to write a long and comprehensive letter to Professor Fisher, which, as a contemporary document throwing light on the forces at work to determine the issue of an historic time, may profitably be reproduced here:

I have yours of the twelfth instant, and I think so much of your opinion that I want, if I can, to outline briefly the reasons which induce me to think we ought to insist on American control of the Philippines.

First,—There is no sovereignty there to-day but ours. Spain in surrendering Manila has lost her sovereignty and cannot regain it unless we give it to her. We did not covet or seek possession of the islands; that has come to us in the course of events we did not foresee and which we were powerless to control. When as a necessary step in the war with Spain orders were sent to destroy the Spanish ships, there was never a thought of acquisition; Providence foreshaped the events which forced upon us the question, what should be done with those islands? If we had withdrawn our fleet after the Spanish ships were destroyed, the insurgents with whom wisely or unwisely we were acting in concert, would have been abandoned to the mercy of the Spanish. In a certain sense they were our allies. We had espoused their contest for liberty such as it was. If from a humanitarian standpoint we were impelled to assist Cuban insurgents, we could not in decency abandon the Philippine insurgents. If this was a war for humanity, Spain's inhumanity in the Philippines was as flagrant as in Cuba. If you say Cuba was nearer, the answer is plain—the duty of succoring the oppressed is not limited by distance—only by present ability to afford it, and we were there and able to discharge that duty. If it had been in our power to succor Armenia, we should not have withheld aid because of the distance. We, did not withdraw—we accepted the consequences of our first step, we are there, in control, in real occupation and authority and charged with all the responsibility and obligation that comes with that occupation and authority. What then shall we do?

Second,—There are several things we may do. We might have relinquished all we had gained, given up all claim to authority, ignored all demands of duty and all sense of obligation; left Spain and the insurgents to fight it out. But is there any one in the world who thinks we ought to have done that? The mere suggestion brings a blush of shame to the cheek of every American. But we cannot do that. The procotol provides that we are to keep the bay and port of Manila. That is settled. From that we cannot recede. We have already stipulated for and secured more than a coaling or naval station. We have acquired that much territory and we must hold and govern it.

Shall we then let Spain repossess a portion of the island of Luzon and all other islands and sit by indifferently while the conflict between Spain and her revolted people goes on, careless spectators of results, assenting to her cruelty, injustice, and oppression if Spain succeeds, assenting to universal loot and plunder perhaps, if the insurgents succeed, powerless to interfere? I cannot but believe that to allow Spain to retain any portion of those islands would be to invite endless complication, trouble, and conflict. Remember that Spanish authority and Spanish sovereignty are of the past. Shall we invite other powers, England, Germany, Russia, or France, any or all of them, to take our possessions off our hands because we are in doubt how best to deal with them? Think of the friction which that would surely create. Manila now is the port of commerce of all the islands, it flows into and out of that port naturally. Any other nation possessing the rest of the islands would seek to divert the commerce to a port of its own. We should seek to retain it and bad blood would at once be stirred up. But as I have before said, we are in control now. By conquest all the Philippines are ours unless we relinquish them. Are we not then under the most imperative moral obligation to protect that people and establish there such a government as is best adapted to their need and condition? If they are entitled by Divine endowment to "life, liberty, and the pursuit of happiness" are we not bound to protect them in their enjoyment so far as it may be done? Who can do it better than we? Who can do it so well? Shall we deliberately shirk the duty because we fear that its performance may be attended with difficulty?

Third,—We of this country have always asserted our firm belief in an overruling Providence. We have professed to recognize the hand of God in history. Does not Providence, does not the finger of God unmistakably point to the civilization and uplifting of the Orient, to the development of its people, to the spread of liberty, education, social order, and Christianity there through the agency of American influence? Can any man, even the least thoughtful, fail to see that the next great world wave of civilization is to overspread China, and how much that means? What kind of civilization is it to be, Russian, German, French? Or shall it be the civilization of the English-speaking people, led indeed by the United States?

Fourth,—So far as to duty, in this case duty and interest coincide. American civilization and institutions will go only where our trade goes—"Trade follows the flag"— civilization goes along with trade. The missionary may be the pioneer of civilization but he works at a terrible disadvantage amid the institutions of heathenism. Commerce clothes the missionary with power.

We must stand with England or England stand with us for "the open door" in China. Neither can keep the door open alone. Combined, the rest of the world is powerless to shut it. Can you fail to see that in the Providence of God the time has come when the institutions of the English-speaking people are in final conflict with the institutions of despotism and irreligion, and that China is the battle ground? The nations that control the commerce of China will impress their institutions upon that people. Have we no call to that conflict? Again we can only be truly great as we reach out beyond ourselves. Selfishness is poverty and misery both. To lose a man's life is to save it, and this is as true of a nation as of a man. The national policy of isolation is no longer for our best interest. To pursue it with all that is claimed for it by its advocates is national selfishness. When we were weak in numbers and in resources it was a good policy, but a nation of seventy-five millions of people, greater in resources and power than any other nation, can no longer, in justice to itself or humanity, insist on isolation. We are first in the family of nations; the head of the family has no right to disclaim an interest in the welfare of the other members. If we are to let our light shine as you say, must we not carry it where it can be seen? Is it quite enough to have a statue of liberty enlightening the world at the entrance of New York harbor?

Speaking in a selfish and materialistic sense, no nation can be great in the truest sense until it takes its full share of the commerce of the world, till it is as strong on the sea as on the land. With commerce come riches and power and true greatness as well as the opportunity to benefit the world.

Shall we reach out beyond ourselves, shall we go forward or stand still? If we would maintain ourselves in the front rank we must go forward. We must claim and secure our fair share of the opening trade of the East. With the Philippines we are in a position to demand it, without them we have no advantage of position, and can be easily ignored. With Hawaii, Guam, and the Philippines we have three

almost equidistant stations on the shortest route which
any nation has to China with its trade now marvellously
to expand.

Fifth,—But why can we not Americanize the Philippines?
Is American enterprise and influence limited in these days
of steam and electricity by the distance between us and
them? Have we not Americanized the Sandwich Islands
where we had no government control, and were they not
weeks farther away from us when our missionaries first
went there than the Philippines now are? Are we not
nearer to the Philippines now than we were to London in the
days of the Revolution? Nearer than we were to California
in 1840? Are the Filipinos more barbarous, savage, and
untamable than were the Sandwich Islanders? Have they
not at least shown a longing for liberty as they understand
it, when they have thus maintained this warfare against
Spanish misrule and injustice? Nor can I understand why
it is supposed to be necessary to incorporate them into our
political community in any dangerous sense.

Has England incorporated South Africa into its political
community? In a certain sense it has, but only in the
sense that it exercises control and provides for the people
that come under its sway a better government than they
ever enjoyed otherwise, and the government best calculated
for their happiness, freedom, and development. The
Philippines would belong to us rather than become part of
us. We should govern them or see that they were governed,
and if we discharge our duty to them in that respect as
we should, it will be to their incalculable benefit. The
idea that we cannot under our system acquire or possess
any country, territory, or even island of the sea unless we
intend to admit our acquisition to the full privilege of
statehood has, in my mind, no foundation to rest upon. If
our own defence, our necessary development, or real interest requires us to take other territory, we should take it
and then proceed to govern it in the best possible way.
Canada and Australia are instances of what such communi-

ties might in the lapse of years become without any detriment to our system. I would not acquire for the sake of mere acquisition or aggrandizement, nor would I on the other hand refuse to do what duty or national interest may require.

"New occasions teach new duties" and I cannot help the conviction that the United States is called by Providence to a great work for mankind—that each ship in Manila Bay was a new *Mayflower* steering boldly through the winter sea, the harbinger and agent of a new civilization for lands where its beneficent influences have been unfelt and unknown.

Pardon my enthusiasm. I am so full of the idea that I cannot write or look upon the situation tamely.

The unerring logic of Senator Platt's contention was fully justified by the event. When the peace envoys came to consider, on the ground and face to face with real conditions, what should be done with the Philippines it was found, as the wiser statesmen of that day had foreseen, that there could be no sure way of a lasting peace except through an agreement that the United States should continue to hold the islands where Spain's sovereignty had been dethroned.

It was not in the books, however, that the conclusions of the peace commission should be accepted by the Senate without question. The anti-imperialists kept on smiting the air with a fury which was in inverse ratio to their number and influence. The ablest of their number in the Senate, the one whose utterances commanded the most respect, was George F. Hoar of Massachusetts. Speaker Reed in the House also contributed the influence of his great position and prestige, with a biting wit which in another cause might have been compelling. It was a source of grief to Senator

Platt that on this question which he regarded as vital
he should be obliged to take issue with Senator Hoar,
long esteemed by him as a personal friend as well as
one of the ablest and purest men in public life. But
having set his hand to the plough he could not turn back
—considerations of friendship must yield to demands
of public duty. Various resolutions were introduced
by Senators who believed that the United States should
not retain control of the Philippines. The passage of
any one of them would have resulted in placing the
United States Government in a false position in the
event of the ratification of the treaty and might even
have evidenced a feeling in the Senate which would
have caused the treaty's defeat. The mere discussion
of them watered the seed of insurrection in Luzon. For
a time at the beginning of the session the "Antis"
seemed to be having things their own way. Senator
Vest of Missouri on December 6th introduced the following resolution, which opened up an opportunity for
debate:

Resolved, by the Senate and House of Representatives
of the United States of America in Congress assembled,
That under the Constitution of the United States no power
is given to the Federal Government to acquire territory to
be held and governed permanently as colonies.

The colonial system of European nations cannot be
established under our present Constitution, but all territory
acquired by the Government, except such small amount
as may be necessary for coaling stations, correction of
boundaries, and similar governmental purposes, must be
acquired and governed with the purpose of ultimately
organizing such territory into States suitable for admission
into the Union.

Upon this declaration the anti-imperialists took their

stand. Vest, Hoar, and others delivered speeches which
were undeniably able and plausible. It remained for
Platt to voice the opinion of the administration, the
majority of the Senate, and of the overwhelming majority of the American people. On December 19th,
he took the floor to present an argument in opposition
to the Vest resolution which was to serve as a text-book
for all who came after him. He said in the beginning:

I do not propose to discuss the so-called policy of expansion nor the features of a government which we may
authorize or establish in any territory which we may acquire. I will simply remark, in passing, that expansion has
been the law of our national growth; more than that, it has
been the great law of our racial development, and the United
States has shown a capacity for government in all trying
times and under all trying conditions, and has shown that
it is equal to any circumstances which may arise. . . . I
propose to maintain that the United States is a nation; that
as a nation it possesses every sovereign power not reserved
in its Constitution to the States or the people; that the
right to acquire territory was not reserved and is therefore an inherent sovereign right; that it is a right upon
which there is no limitation and in regard to which there
is no qualification; that in certain instances the right
may be inferred from specific clauses in the Constitution,
but that it exists independent of these clauses; that in
the right to acquire territory is found the right to govern
it, and as the right to govern is a sovereign right, not limited
in the Constitution; and that these propositions are in accordance with the views of the framers of the Constitution,
the decisions of the Supreme Court, and the legislation of
Congress.

It is to be regretted that the limitations of this work
forbid the reproduction here of this speech in its en-

tirety. It was profound, and comprehensive, packed
with citations from the debates on the Constitution,
from decisions of the Supreme Court, and from the actual experience of the United States in the acquisition
and control of territory.   Some of his most fruitful sentences were in the form of replies to questions put by
Senators on the opposing side.   In response to Allen
of Nebraska he declared:

I do not think there is any limitation upon our power to
acquire territory.

And again:

I do not believe there is any obligation on this government to give to people who may inhabit territory which we
may acquire the right to self-government until such time
as we think they are fit to exercise it; and that is the doctrine
we have always maintained in dealing with the territory
acquired.

He expressed his agreement with Daniel Webster
that Congress:

may establish any such government and any such laws
in the territories as in its discretion it may see fit.   It is
subject of course to the rules of justice and propriety but
it is under no constitutional restraints.

But the sentence by which this speech will be longest
remembered—a sentence that filled the souls of the
" Antis " with rage and for a time concentrated upon its
author the venom of their attacks—was in reply to a
question put by Mr. Hoar.   Consumed as he thought
with the fire of patriotism, Hoar had listened with
ill-concealed impatience through the greater part of
Platt's speech and then he arose.   This colloquy
followed:

MR. HOAR: May I ask the Senator from Connecticut one question at this point?

MR. PLATT: Certainly.

MR. HOAR: It is whether, in his opinion, governments derive their just powers from the consent of the governed?

The trembling voice with which the aged Massachusetts Senator put this question betrayed the tenseness of his feeling. It was the conclusive, damning appeal to the Declaration of Independence which was so conspicuous a feature of the anti-imperialist propaganda, and when Senator Platt replied with quiet emphasis, " From the consent of *some* of the governed," there was a gasp of dismay. Then Senator Platt went on to explain: " The State of Massachusetts governs people who cannot read and write, and it governs them pretty effectually too. If they commit any crime, it punishes them, but it does not allow them to vote." He did not deny the principles of the Declaration of Independence but pointed out that all sorts of qualifications for voting had been adopted in the United States:

There are 250,000 American citizens within five miles of the spot where I stand. They are governed by Congress. Not one of them can vote. His consent is not asked. The government in the District of Columbia certainly does not depend upon the consent of the governed. Does the Senator from Massachusetts hold that this provision for governing the District of Columbia, exercised under that clause of the Constitution which says that Congress shall have exclusive jurisdiction of ten miles square in the District of Columbia, is a violation of the doctrine of the Declaration of Independence, that all governments derive their just powers from the consent of the governed? Does he hold that that is a violation of the principle for which we contended when we revolted and severed our connection with Great Britain, because there was taxation without representation? Oh, no, Mr. President. In his fear and doubt the Senator from Massachusetts sees lions in the path that are not there; if we go straight forward, though it may be the Hill of Difficulty, we shall find that the lions at least are chained, and we shall arrive at the House Beautiful.

In conclusion, I cannot understand either the sentiment or the motive of those who are unwilling to concede that our Government is a nation, and who fear to see it clothed with every element of sovereignty which a nation should possess and does possess.

Why should any man, why, especially, should any Senator, wish to detract from, to diminish or belittle the power of his government? Why strive by subtle, metaphysical, and logic-chopping arguments to hamper its operations and circumscribe its province? Rather should we in our national love rejoice to see it invested with strength. Rather should we bid it Godspeed in its mission to relieve the oppressed, to right every wrong, and to extend the institutions of free government. For this is the people's government; the government of a great people, a liberty-loving people, a people that can be trusted to do right and to guarantee to all men who shall come under its beneficent sway and be subject to its jurisdiction the largest measure of liberty consistent with good order and their general well-being.

Rather let us have faith in the Government, faith in its future. Stilled be the voice of timidity and distrust, stilled be the utterance of captious and carping criticism. Let us have faith that the powers of Government will never be unrighteously exercised. Like Lincoln, when he met the contention that the Government had no power adequate to its self-preservation, let us turn from disputatious subtleties and "have faith that right makes might, and in that faith dare to do our duty as we understand it." In that faith the mountains of doubt will be removed and the way of duty become straight and plain.

Little more than a century has passed since from the tower of Independence Hall in Philadelphia, when we severed our connection with Great Britain, the Liberty Bell rang out the message, "Proclaim liberty throughout the land and to all the inhabitants thereof." We were small and weak then. Timid doubters said there was a lion in the path, but the spirit of the Constitution was in that message. With that Constitution came nationality and sovereignty. Under that Constitution, in the name and by the power of the nation, liberty has been proclaimed to regions never dreamed of by the fathers. Is it for us now, when we have become great and strong, though timid doubters still say there are lions in the path, to declare that neither in the spirit of the Constitution nor by the exercise of national sovereignty can we proclaim liberty a rood or a foot beyond our present territorial limits? Oh! for the faith and the courage of the fathers!

From that day less and less was heard in the long drawn out discussion about the Declaration of Independence and "the consent of the governed." Senator Platt had effectually punctured the bubble of that particular argument against the acquisition of the Philippines.[1]

[1] On October 11, 1899, Mr. Platt delivered an address on "Expansion" before the Union League Club of Brooklyn, from which the following excerpts are taken:

"Very strange as it seems to me, there are some persons who think we ought to abandon or surrender our new possessions, but there is nothing in the history of our development to justify the expectation that when the United States has once acquired territory, it will ever give it away, barter, or sell it, or surrender it to armed force. There can be no distinction drawn between Porto Rico, the Philippines, or the smaller islands in this respect. Rather does our whole history show that with every acquisition of territory we have fully recognized our obligation to provide good government therein, government by which the rights of the people are respected and their best interests promoted. We have never plundered or misgoverned new territory and we never shall. We have never oppressed the people in new territory, nor shall we do so now. To allege that we intend to misgovern or oppress in our new possessions is to slander our Government, and I can think of no more atrocious slander than that. All this newly acquired territory belongs to the United States, and we are going to keep it, provide for it with the best possible government, and immeasurably benefit its people. It has been acquired by conquest and treaty. The treaty which confirmed the conquest is the supreme law of the land, and the performance of every obligation specified or involved in that treaty is as truly a national duty as the execution of any law upon our statute books. . . . I really have not discovered the anti-imperialist who urges constitutional objections respecting the acquisition of Porto Rico or feels that the Declaration of Independence was violated when Spain ceded it to us and we accepted it as the result of the war. Democratic platform makers would, like the ancient Augurs, be laughing in each others' faces if a plank in their platform should denounce the acquisition of Porto Rico alone. Not a soul of them would listen to a proposition to give away, sell, barter, or surrender that island. So I say that I find great difficulty in speaking of the Philippines as disconnected from Porto Rico. Our right is the same to each, our title as perfect to one as the other, the difficulties of administration as great in one case as the other, and the fact that our people as a whole are satisfied with the acquisition of Porto Rico shows that no one really believes there is anything in the Declaration of Independence or the Constitution of the United States, or the principles upon which our Government is founded, which made our acquisition of the Philippines improper or forbids our retention of them. All of this talk about the consent of the governed, Filipino independence, the wickedness of sub-jugation, and the denial of constitutional rights to the people there, is simply a false issue. The thing which really troubles the few anti-imperialists is that they fear the United States has made a bad bargain. . . . All the consequences of war must be accepted by the nation that engages in war, and the unavoidable conse-quence of our triumph in Manila Bay was that we should assume control of the Philippine Islands; that a duty arose when the Spanish ships went down. Neither man nor nation can avoid duty and achieve just success. It is the glory of our nation that it has always met and performed national duty. If the war with Spain was, as we believed and avowed, a war for humanity, our obligation to Spanish subjects in the Philippines was just as great as to Spanish subjects in Cuba. If we were liberators in Cuba, we were equally so in the Philippines. The assumption of control in the Philippine Islands was a duty which we owed to the nations of the world, to ourselves, to the inhabitants of those islands, and to mankind. It would have been criminal neglect to have abandoned the Filipinos either to Spain or a Malay dictator. We emerged from our war with honor. We should have been dishonored if we had shirked the obligations which that war imposed upon us. . . .

"Expansion has marked every step of our national growth and progress. Every expansion of our territory has been in accordance with the irresistible law of growth. We could no more resist the successive expansions by which we have grown to be the strongest nation on earth, than a tree can resist its natural growth. The history of territorial expansion is the history of our nation's progress and glory. It is a matter to be proud of, not to lament. We should rejoice that Providence has given us the opportunity to extend our influence, our institutions, and our civilization into regions hitherto closed to us rather than contrive how we can thwart its designs. When Admiral Dewey was asked how he accounted for the fact that so little damage was done by the Spanish guns at Manila he is said to have replied: 'If I were a religious man, and I hope I am, I should say that the hand of God was in it.' Your own Dr. Dix said the other day in his pulpit that he felt 'that some unseen and mysterious power had been, and is, at work conducting and compelling a certain end, to be accomplished by peaceful methods if possible, but if not peacefully then by the whole force of the powers of the State.' I believe with Admiral Dewey and Dr. Dix, that the United States has found in its Philippine problem the greatest opportunity for the extension of freedom and beneficent government which it has ever enjoyed."

CHAPTER XXIII

NATIONAL DUTY

Debate with Senator Hoar, February 11, 1902—The Destiny of the Republic—Favors a Colonial System.

ONCE more Platt and Hoar came together on this question of the Philippines. It was during the long continued debate on the Philippine tariff in the session of 1901–2, when the entire question of the retention of the archipelago was lugged into the discussion. Aguinaldo was in captivity, and the guerilla bands who had been resisting American authority in the islands were rapidly disappearing so that American military forces, no longer needed to preserve order, were gradually withdrawing and the islands were approaching a condition of permanent peace. But the anti-imperialist propaganda in the United States was still busy, and it had its chief encouragement from the little band of irreconcilables in the Senate at Washington. On February 11th, Senator Teller had occupied almost the entire day in a violent assault upon the Government's Philippine policy. Toward the close of the afternoon he rested and Mr. Platt took the floor to reply to certain criticisms of the character of our officials, lauding the work of the Philippine Commission, and dwelling upon the rapid progress of the pacification of the islands:

I think [he said] if we take facts and not fancies, if we take things as they really are, and not as they are conjured up by the party of protest and disapproval, we shall see that we are getting along very well in the Philippine Islands, and are progressing very rapidly toward a condition there, in which the Filipinos themselves will have a very large share of participation, which will be entirely satisfactory to them and which they will welcome as a blessing to themselves and the archipelago.

This incident would have ended there had not Senator Hoar undertaken to reply, disputing Platt's assertions, questioning the genuineness of the elections which had been held in the provinces, and belittling the quality of the free schools established by American authority. " I hope," he concluded, " the rosy view of my friend, the Senator from Connecticut, will turn out to be all right, but I confess I am afraid he will have to try again."

The manner of the attack stirred Platt to a response which the newspapers of the day describe as a " revival of the best traditions of the Senate." He regretted the sneers at the efforts to educate the children of the Philippine Islands, and then he took up the question of treason against the United States. He read from the statutes of Connecticut the law which relates to treason and misprision of treason and proceeded to apply it:

As I understand that statute, Mr. President, there are certain persons living in the State of the Senator from Massachusetts who, if they had come into the State of Connecticut and commenced to carry on intercourse with the Filipinos with intent to aid them or to defeat or embarrass the measures of the Government of the State or of the United States, would have subjected themselves to the penalty of this statute; and yet the people of Con-

necticut have not been chafing under it. The people of
Connecticut think that is right, and that a man who, when
there is a rebellion against the State or the United States,
enters into communication with the enemy for the purpose of
embarrassing the operations of the State or United States,
commits a crime, and subjects himself to punishment.

If we are a Government worthy of the name, worthy of
living, worthy of a place in the present or the future [he
exclaimed with fervor], wherever men take arms against
the Government of the United States in any country,
district, or territory where the sovereignty of the United
States prevails, we will put down that rebellion. . . .
No perversion of the doctrine of independence and no
perversion of the glory of liberty is going to convince
this American people that it is not only its right but its
duty to itself to put down armed resistance against the
Government wherever it may rear its hateful head.

He compared the situation in the Philippines with the
attitude of the South at the close of the Civil War:

I do not want to say anything to revive the memories of
the saddest war of recent times, but I cannot refrain from
alluding to the fact that for four long years we resisted this
doctrine that government in its strict and literal sense depended upon the consent of the governed, and that eleven
States and the people of those States, claiming that they
could not be coerced, claiming that they were struggling for
liberty and establishing an independence of their own, for
four long years fought that question out with us, and we
prevailed.

And now, if I understand, we have done the same thing
in the Philippines. Some people over there, a few only
compared with the great mass of people, followed the fortunes of one Aguinaldo. Did he have any consent of the
governed upon which to rely? If the doctrine of the consent
of the governed must be strictly enforced here, I inquire
what consent of the governed this vaunted and eulogized

Aguinaldo had in the Philippine Islands? What right had he, any more than we, to demand the right to govern those islands?

In all the range of his public speech there is no finer bit of exalted eloquence than the words with which he brought this unpremeditated utterance to a close:

Talk about commercialism! Is this matter to be weighed by bookkeeping to see where the balance of advantage is in dollars and cents? I think the United States of America has a high call to duty, to a moral duty, to duty to advance the cause of free government in the world by something more than example. It is not enough to say to a country over which we have acquired an undisputed and indisputable sovereignty: "Go your own gait; look at our example. In the entrance of the harbor of New York, our principal port, there is the statue of Liberty Enlightening the World. Look at that, and follow our example."
No, Mr. President. When the Anglo-Saxon race crossed the Atlantic and stood on the shores of Massachusetts Bay and on Plymouth Rock that movement meant something more than the establishment of religious and civil liberty within a narrow, confined, and limited compass. It had in it the force of the Almighty; and from that day to this it has been spreading, widening, and extending until, like the stone seen by Daniel in his vision cut out of the mountain without hands, it has filled all our borders, and ever westward across the Pacific that influence which found its home in the *Mayflower* and its development on Plymouth Rock has been extending and is extending its sway and its beneficence.

I believe, Mr. President, that the time is coming, as surely coming as the time when the world shall be Christianized, when the world shall be converted to the cause of free government, and I believe the United States is a providentially appointed agent for that purpose. The day may be

long in coming and it may be in the far future, but he who
has studied the history of this western world from the twenty-
second day of December, 1620, to the present hour must be
blind indeed if he cannot see that the cause of free government in the world is still progressing and that what the
United States is doing in the Philippine Islands is in the
extension of that beneficent purpose.

He had inflicted wounds which were never to be
healed. As he took his seat after delivering his fervid
peroration, Senator Hoar came over and sat beside him.
"Mr. Platt," he said in a broken voice, "I fully expected that somebody would say all this; but I did n't
think that you would be the one." From that hour
the personal relations between the two great Senators
were never quite as they had been before, although
toward the end there was a restoration of kindly feeling, and Platt's tribute to Hoar on the occasion of the
eulogies of the latter in the Senate a few years later was
one of the most beautiful and appropriate then spoken.

Believing as he did in the constitutional power of
this Government to acquire territory when and where
it might see fit, Mr. Platt at the same time held clearly
defined opinions as to the manner in which such
territory should be governed. He was unalterably
opposed to any proposition looking to the annexation
of non-contiguous territory with any understanding
that it was ever to become an integral part of the
United States, entitled to the privilege of statehood.
This question first arose acutely in his mind with
reference to Hawaii, after the passage of the resolution
of annexation in the summer of 1898. We were in the
midst of the war with Spain when our future course
with regard to conquered territory was still unsettled,
and he felt that in Hawaii we should proceed with

caution as establishing a possible precedent for more serious questions later to arise.

He was in consultation with President McKinley on this subject and on July 9th, after a call' at the White House, he wrote to the President, as follows:

Since seeing you this morning I have thought much of the work of the commission to prepare a code of laws for Hawaii. I trust that in preparing this code of laws nothing will be done or agreed upon which will in any way commit the United States to the project of their making a state of the Hawaiian Islands, or incorporating them with an existing State. It seems to me that we must now mark out our policy for all our future as to territory which we may conquer or be obliged to take, and that it should be understood that statehood is out of the question.

We have Alaska now, we have Hawaii, we may have possessions that we conquer from Spain. We may be obliged either for self-defence or for our own development, to acquire territory elsewhere, as for instance along the route of the Nicaragua Canal if we ever build it. We shall need coaling stations, and there are various emergencies in which a nation like ours may be compelled to acquire territory. In saying this I am far from being what is called an "expansionist," but I recognize the fact that we can no longer shut ourselves up within our present limits.

Our history and tradition have begotten the idea in the public mind that we cannot have colonies or dependencies except we incorporate them into our system as states. This will never do, and we must educate our people to understand when we acquire possessions outside of our integral territory that we have the right and the power, and that it is our duty to see that the best possible government is provided for such possessions, but that they have no claim to become states. Contrary to the general belief, such was the view of the wisest men who framed the Constitution. I merely

speak of this now from an indefinite fear that our commission
to prepare a code of laws may in some way encourage the
idea that the Hawaiian Islands may in some remote future
become a state or a part of a state, in our Government.

I think they ought to be very careful in this respect,
and I hope that in talking with them you will impress this
view upon them. President Dole and Chief-Justice Judd
are very astute men. I have a little fear that Senator
Morgan may think that they have the right to territorial
government which we have always said was a pledge of
statehood. I think we may well follow the policy of
England, adapting the government of her colonies or
dependencies to the capacity of the people. England has
every kind of a government for her colonies from what is
called the "Crown" government to the liberal governments
of Canada and Australia, which are practically republics
with a nominal subjection to the mother country.

Our duty and our only duty is to see that the best government for which the people have capacity is provided for
Hawaii and any other dependencies which may become
ours. In other words, the United States should see to it
that they have good government and should stop there. If
we for a moment tolerate the idea of present or future
statehood, we shall have infinite trouble.

Will you pardon this brief expression of my views?
I think the question of what kind of a government shall be
provided for Hawaii may be left to the future. It is not
necessary to determine it fully now. The laws of Hawaii
are to remain in force until Congress adopts new ones, and
there need be no haste about planning and putting into
operation a specific form of government there. We ought
not to even use the word "territory" in connection with the
Hawaiian Islands.

A similar question arose five years later when the
proposal was made to organize the Territory of Alaska.
In the course of a letter which he wrote on June 11, 1903,

to Senator Dillingham of Vermont, Mr. Platt declared his position again, without equivocation:

I am very decidedly of the opinion that our policy should be, and should be declared to be, that we do not propose to admit states from outside of what may be called our home territory. I felt it when we adopted a form of government for the Sandwich Islands, Porto Rico, and the Philippines, but I thought the time was not ripe then to say just what I thought about it. My idea is that as to those outside possessions, we should retain over them the complete right of government as might appear to be for our own and their best interests, without any promise or intimation of future statehood. It makes no difference by what name such a government is to be called, whether colonial or independent or despotic. I do not believe we can afford to let in states from outside our older territory— in other words, I believe that the United States should be bounded on the east by the Atlantic Ocean, on the north by the British possessions, on the west by the Pacific Ocean, and on the south by the Gulf and by Mexico; that whatever territory comes in outside of that should be governed by us, and not by the people therein in the capacity of states admitted upon equal footing with the present States.

I told Senator Beveridge that if he brought in a bill for the organization of the Territory of Alaska, and the appointment of a delegate, I should have to oppose it, or at least propose an amendment, which should declare the policy of the United States to be against its future admission as a state.